COMMEDIA DELL'ARTE
An Actor's Handbook

John Rudlin

ROUTLEDGE
Taylor & Francis Group

London and New York

First published 1994
by Routledge
2 Park Square, Milton Park, Abingdon, Oxon, OX14 4RN

Simultaneously published in the USA and Canada
by Routledge
711 Third Avenue, New York, NY 10017

Reprinted 1994, 1995, 1997, 1998, 1999, 2000, 2002

Routledge is an imprint of the Taylor & Francis Group

© 1994 John Rudlin

Typeset in Palatino by
Florencetype Ltd, Stoodleigh, Devon
Printed and bound in Great Britain by
Biddles Ltd, Guildford and King's Lynn

British Library Cataloguing in Publication Data
A catalogue record for this book is available from the British Library

Library of Congress Cataloguing in Publication Data
A catalogue record for this book is available from the Library of Congress

ISBN 0-415-04769-2 (hbk)
ISBN 0-415-04770-6 (pbk)

per Dina e Marcellina

Contents

Illustrations

Introduction

> The actor may get bored with perfecting his craft in order to
> perform in outdated plays; soon he will want not only to act but
> to compose for himself as well. Then at last we shall see the
> rebirth of the theatre of improvisation.[1]
>
> MEYERHOLD

The purpose of this book is to help give *commedia dell'arte* back to the actor
in the hope that it may again provide one of the base languages of a
theatrical lingua franca. It is also founded on a personal conviction that if
there is to be a regeneration of the theatrical medium in the next century,
it must come via the re-empowering of the performer rather than the continued hegemony of playwright and director. In saying that, I am minded
that the etymology of the word Esperanto, designed in 1887, derives from
the Latin verb for to hope. Commedia, however, is an actual language,
dispersed and fallen into disrepair, rather than an artificial one with a
majority purpose and a minority uptake.

Throughout the twentieth century the question has been (and still
remains despite the efforts of Craig, Meyerhold, Copeau, Reinhardt and
later directors) how to retrieve information from scholarship in such a
way that actors' efforts at self-authored Commedia improvisation are not
merely illustrative of what the original form may have been like. Craig was
first to the heart of the problem:

> History, to creative minds, is often a dry dead thing. It is the story
> of the past. Creators are concerned with the Present and the
> Future. It concerns our old friends Harlequin, Pantaloon,
> Pulcinella or Punch and their companions . . . the Doctor,
> Brighella, Scaramuccia, Coviello and the Captain. What fun, you
> think. Yes, what fun . . . but what genius also, for the inventors of
> these figures were men of genius. Whether the inventors were

1

peasants or actors or both is immaterial. The point has not yet been decided: but it has been very clearly decided and recorded that the inventors were not *play-writers*.[2]

Towards the end of the century his point has still not been decided and furthermore it never can be, at least not by scholarship alone as Kenneth Richards and Laura Richards, in their recent translation of key source documents, allow:

> For all that we possess a wealth of documentation, literary and pictorial, from its beginnings through to its apparent decline, the *commedia dell'arte* remains elusive. What were its origins? Can it appositely be called a species of 'popular' theatre? Was it characterised primarily by improvised performance, and if so, how was the improvisation executed. . . ?[3]

The fact is that scholars, directors, teachers and actors alike are dealing with an oral tradition, not a literary one: a phenomenon of the folk which became part of their lore before being patronised by the mighty, an organic growth from popular origins which only latterly became a set of cultivated conventions that could be adopted by 'play-writers'. The culture of the people was illiterate, but only in the sense that, say, many an Irish jig violinist cannot read music. Those who can notate find such improvisations almost impossible to score. As with folk music, there is a literacy of performance of Commedia which was originally developed without a conscious sense of culture as a common social denominator between performer and spectator.

In Augusto Boal's view, what separates the human community from that of other primates with species-specific vocal and bodily sign systems is theatre. As in monkey language,

> originally, actor and spectator coexisted in the same person; when they separated, when some became specialised into actors and others into spectators, then theatrical forms, as we know them today, were formed. 'Theatres' were also born, destined to sanctify this division, this specialisation. The profession of the 'actor' was born.[4]

During the sixteenth century in Italy, actors took pre-existing folk forms, improvised masking, music and dance and developed them into a theatrical medium. Over the next two centuries the performance techniques they developed were passed on highly selectively to their siblings and other younger members of their troupes as, virtually, professional secrets. There is a marked similarity with Japanese Noh theatre in this respect: the symbol or *kana* for Noh means 'accomplishment' or 'professional ability'; the word *arte* (which will be discussed further in the chapter on 'Origins'), should properly be translated as a combination of 'tradesmanship' and 'artistic know-how'. Within the family-based *Ryu* of the Noh the treatises of Zeami, its first great actor, were passed from generation to generation in secret veneration, remaining unpublished until 1909, when the need for spectators as specialised in understanding as actors in performing had become essential to the survival of the form. No such treatise exists for Commedia, however: the works of Perucci, Riccoboni, Gherardi, etc. were written in hindsight during the mature inflorescence of Commedia and do not reveal much that is of use to a more than general reader. Barry Grantham, as 'Harlequin in Residence', wrote in the programme of the 1985 Brighton Festival (which was devoted to Commedia):

> Unfortunately for present day performers these skills were regarded as professional secrets and they produced no handy manual for our use. The evidence has to be sought, not only in Commedia sources, but in those related contemporary performing arts. Our understanding can also be considerably enlarged by attempting to set up 'laboratory conditions' duplicating the circumstances in which the comedians worked. We then compare the experience gained with the material, particularly iconographic, that we do have against that of more easily recoverable recent traditions like pantomime, Music Hall, and a particularly rich source, the silent movie.[5]

It is a function of training to conduct such a quest, of active research through practice, rather than archaeological reconstruction. In doing so, the benefits of the *arte*, paradoxically, may not be just for the practising or intending professional actor, but also for developing a literacy of performance in the non-specialist. Throughout the twentieth century there have been schools attempting the former, notably Copeau's at the Vieux Colombier in Paris and Burgundy, Dullin's at the Atelier in Paris, Saint-Denis's in London, New York and Canada and Lecoq's in Milan and again in Paris. At the present time, American schools such as the Dell Arte, our own courses in the Exeter University Drama Department, the *stages* led by Carlo Boso and Patrick Pezin and above all, in my experience, Antonio Fava's International School of the Comic Actor in Reggio Emilia, continue to make investigations. Craig's question and affirmation remain with us: 'Is it possible? Can a Drama which holds the stage for two centuries be created without the assistance of the literary man? It can. Then if it can be created once it can be created twice? It can.'[6]

The present volume is dedicated to that possibility and, as well as collating otherwise diverse information under a single cover, seeks to offer the English reader more demystification of professional secrets than available elsewhere and, perhaps, just enough 'do-it-yourself' possibilities to suggest that *commedia dell'arte* can point the way forward as well as back, in the search for a common international language of live performance.

First, though, a short trace on when, why and how Commedia 'died' (or rather went into suspended animation) may help to set the scene. No theatre form fully dies until the culture which generated it disappears. Even then fragments remain for scholars to pore over, shards from which to make guesswork reconstructions as, for example, has been the case with Greek tragedy. *Commedia dell'arte*, too, was thought to have perished as a living theatre form as long ago as the late eighteenth century. Originally a folk form, as the first chapter of this book attempts to chronicle (popular history being often so sparsely documented), Commedia had progressively been monopolised by well-to-do 'society', painted and engraved by artists such as Callot, Watteau and Domenico Tiepolo, written up by playwrights such as Goldoni, Molière, Beaumarchais and Marivaux, and, eventually, like any other fashion, condemned as outmoded; a seemingly exhausted seam of amusement which it was no longer rewarding to work.

> The old *commedia dell'arte* had sunk into decrepitude. It was not merely that the type itself was exhausted, though subsequent circumstances proved this to be the case. What was more important is, that the popular taste veered round against it. Under the prevailing dominance of French fashions, a style of drama, hitherto unknown to the Italians, came into vogue. The so-called *comédie larmoyante*, or pathetic comedy (of which Nivelle de la Chaussée, a now forgotten archimage of middle-class sentimentalities and sensibilities, is the reputed inventor), caught the ear of Europe.[7]

Like so many of the vital rites of yesteryear, Commedia was relegated to the nursery where its imagery, in bowdlerised form, continued to animate the minds of the young through toys and picture books. The outward shell was returned to the people for whom, in the fairground booth and the puppet show, it lived on as popular as gondolas and gallopers – and arguably as culturally significant. We now know that it also survived as theatre, not only in the bizarre afterpiece of the English pantomime, the harlequinade, but also in modest touring companies in Italy, the country of its origin, where – like most commonplaces – no one bothered to record it. The sole example of such a troupe surviving to the present day is that of the Carrara family, whose work is described in Part II of this book.

By the mid-nineteenth century, however, a consciousness of something special being lost, of a unique species endangered almost to extinction, was already stirring. One dull evening in the winter of 1846 at Nohant in France, near La Châtre in Berry, a group of genteel literati composed of the novelist George Sand, her family and a circle of close acquaintances including her current partner, the ailing Chopin, decided over dinner to pass the rest of the evening playing charades. 'It was Chopin who invented the theatre at Nohant. In the beginning it was he who improvised at the piano while the young people acted scenes or danced comic ballets.'[8]

The scenario of their first playlet, a curious piece entitled *The Indelicate Druid*, was devised during the main course, read out during the dessert and performed an hour later. This extempore method formed the accidental basis of their later discoveries, as from the outset they instinctively eschewed written texts for their scenes. Gradually these *divertissements* became more and more complex, as did their subsequent analysis of them:

> We naturally began to discuss the origins of theatre; none of us
> had studied them, some were still children with no notions,
> however vague, of the history of this art form. We asked ourselves
> what theatre really was, and if the convention of written dialogue
> had not destroyed rather than enhanced it.[9]

After exploring and discussing in their amateur academy all the phases of Greek, Roman and medieval popular forms, they finally came to one which seemed to them to be the most extraordinary and fascinating, the Italian *commedia dell'arte*:

> We looked through two volumes of comic operas . . . but found
> nothing that would serve our purpose, but we took well-known
> names, each creating a type that whose character and costume was
> to their liking: Scaramouche, Pierrot, Cassandre, Léandre,
> Colombine. We mixed them up with all sorts of situations set in
> different eras.[10]

Obviously, from the names used, the Masks they played with initially were the Franco-Italian transplants of the seventeenth and eighteenth centuries, not the original sixteenth century forms of the Italian piazzas, or their reference would have been rather to Scaramuccia, Pedrolino, Pantalone, Leandro and Colombina. But, as we will see, *commedia dell'arte* had spread itself all over Europe as companies found they could profit more from exile than from the strictures of the Council of Trent. Dissemination went as far as Russia, Czechoslovakia and Denmark, and wherever Commedia found itself, without compromising in essentials, it adjusted to local circumstances and such national variations contributed to, rather than detracted from, its universality. Developments made in France in the seventeenth century were even reimported to Italy by the itinerant companies.

In Nohant, two centuries later, the game of reconstruction now became a fixation which lasted until January 1848, resulting in the creation of a small theatre with a wardrobe and scenery, then a marionette theatre, before finally recording its research in a book written by one of George Sand's two sons, Maurice. Their work, and that book, have remained a crucial resource throughout the twentieth century. It is possible, even, that Maurice Sand's illustrations for his own book have had too much influence, fixing the fixed characters in his image of them. (See Plate 20.)

The still living resource for the amateur researcher/performers of Nohant was the *théâtre de la foire* where the Italian Commedia performers had retreated after the closure of the Parisian Théâtre Italien in 1697. They had not been allowed back on the legitimate stage until 1716, by which time many had permanently returned to the ways of the piazza:

> The Italian players in France went back to an earlier day, reverting to the portable trestle stage and lustier repertoire of their ancestors, travelling through the country at a discreet distance from the capital, and experiencing hardship of a kind they had never imagined.[11]

Dialogue was not permitted in the fairs by law, except in the puppet booths, so the live actors had to go back to their origins as jugglers, tumblers,

1 An English country fair c. 1820 showing *commedia dell'arte* influenced characters barking outside a booth. Colombina remains a traditional *danseuse*, Pedrolino is on buskins, and the figure on his knees may be a *zanni*. Note the audience queuing up the steps.

dancers, singers and pantomimists. This was the nature of the *commedia dell'arte* which crossed the Channel to the English fairs, where it was commonly used for 'barking' outside the booths as a catchpenny box-office attraction, with more legitimate and less fantastical fare being played within. When English spectators attended a Pantomime in a theatre in winter and saw Clown, Pantaloon, Harlequin and Colombine dance on at the end after the transformation scene, they were renewing acquaintance with figures last seen on a summer's day before going into a tent to watch a play.

Throughout the twentieth century there have been many revivals of *commedia dell'arte* based on attempts as enthusiastic as that at Nohant to revive the Masks. Some, but by no means all, of these essays are discussed in Part III of this book, along with experiments in the invention of new stock characters on the assumption that the old ones have lost their social relevance. Such endeavours seek to go beyond resurrection of a supposedly dead form, hoping new life will spring from the turning over of old roots. The distinction between reconstruction and renovation will be a constant throughout, and I have had the opportunity of conducting experiments along both lines with students, whose contribution to the growth of the body of information which forms this work is incalculable.

Commedia has also disseminated itself into other art forms and aspects of twentieth-century cultural consciousness: Stravinsky, Diaghilev, Cocteau, Picasso, Busoni, to name but a few, have all used it as a working base. Many of its techniques have re-emerged, without scholarly prompting, in the silent films of Chaplin, Keaton, Laurel and Hardy *et al.*, and in the talkies of the Marx Brothers. And in order for this to happen, the techniques of Italian, Jewish and Irish humour had first been melded in the pot of vaudeville. The present concern, however, is with the platform stage rather than the silver screen, and studying it will involve initial examination of European origins rather than New World evolutions.

Until its unification in the nineteenth century, Italy, like Europe today, consisted of an association of sovereign states. As a pan-Italian form, the *commedia dell'arte* had, therefore, necessarily to develop in a polyglot manner, using a vocabulary drawn from the northern city states and from the regions of the south. Its characters represent basic types from those states, each speaking in a dialect/language largely incomprehensible to the inhabitants of the others. There were, in effect, three divisions: the north, providing the 'four Masks' – Arlecchino and Brighella (Bergamese), Pantalone (Venetian), Il Dottore (Bolognese); the south – Pulcinella, Tartaglia, Coviello and Il Capitano (Neapolitan or Calabrese); and Tuscany, which provided the literary tongue befitting the manners of the Lovers and the female servant. As the Commedia players strolled from state to state, local characters would come into greater prominence in the scenarios chosen, carrying a higher burden of speech, often at the expense of the other masks who became less sympathetic, the butt of humour in the way

that *stranieri* often are. But the main language of all the Masks was action –
the Esperanto of the stage.

Thus the preoccupation of the first part of this book is with the period of
initial growth of *commedia dell'arte* in the the second half of the sixteenth
century and its flowering of the early part of the seventeenth. During these
years, Commedia, emerging as it did out of Carnival, was of an occasional
nature: like fairground showmen, companies, particularly the minor ones
(about which we know very little), would follow an annual celebratory
calendar and a complementary touring schedule. The 'great' companies, the
Gelosi, the Confidenti, the Accessi, the Uniti, the Fideli, would be required
at events of national as well as local significance. The Gelosi were called to
Paris, for example, to celebrate the wedding of Henri III's daughter in 1572,
but were captured around Lyon by Huguenot insurgents. Ransom was set
as the release of 1,000 recently captured prisoners, a price which the king
readily paid rather than lose face at the nuptials. Tommaso Garzoni (who
rarely had a good word to say about anybody) gives an inglorious picture
of the reality of life on the road in the 1580s for a less exalted troupe:

> Thanks to them, the art of the comedy lies buried in the mud,
> lords banish them from their lands, the law holds them in con-
> tempt, different nations scorn them in a variety of ways and the
> whole world, as if to punish them for their improper conduct,
> rightly rejects them. Thus you find the companies split up: the
> Signora is in Parma, the Magnifico in Venice, the Courtesan in
> Padua, the Zanni in Bergamo, Gratiano in Bologna, and licences
> and permits have to be sought on every side if they wish to act
> and earn their living, because everyone is sickened by this vile
> race that spreads disarray everywhere and introduces a thousand
> scandals wherever it goes. This is the reason, according to Valerio,
> why the city of Marseilles never wishes to suffer the presence of
> strollers and buffoons. When they enter a city, immediately a
> drum makes it known that the gentlemen players have arrived.
> The Signora, dressed as a man and with sword in hand, advances
> to survey the field, inviting the public to a comedy or a tragedy or
> a pastoral in a palace at the Pilgrim Inn, to which the mob, by
> nature eager for novelties and curiosities, immediately rushes to
> get seats and, paying for its entrance money, enters the hall that
> has been prepared. Here you find a fit-up stage and a scene
> crudely depicted in charcoal; you put up with an opening concert
> like that of asses and hornets; you hear a prologue from a charla-
> tan; a clumsy tune like Brother Stopino's; an action as painful as a
> malady, and murderous interludes; a Magnifico not worth a toss;
> a Zanni who's a goose; a Gratiano who squitters words; a daft,
> witless Courtesan; a Lover who saws his arms at every speech; a

2 Pierrot, Colombine and a Captain/Harlequin and Colombine in a 1923 art deco confection by John Austen illustrating *The Adventures of Harlequin* by Francis Bickley.

Spaniard who can say nothing but 'Mi vida' and 'Mi carazon'; a Pedant who drops into Tuscan at every line; a Burattino who knows no other gesture than to put his cap on his head; a Signora like a monster in her speech, dead in her delivery, soporific in her gestures, at perpetual war with the Graces and locked in a major altercation with Beauty.[12]

One wonders what Garzoni would make of the average 'sitcom'. Somehow the popularity of *commedia dell'arte* survived his onslaught and, since then, every era has tended to reinvent Commedia in its own image, often relying solely on an increasingly simplistic reinterpretation of the confection of its predecessor. Eventually such a mixture was bound to become so dilute as to be ineffectual.

Recently it has been a fashion to proclaim the *commedia dell'arte* a theatre of proletarian protest against oppression, an idea first put forward in 1914 by Konstantin Miklashevski.[13] . . . There is even less to justify as *commedia dell'arte*, a movement arising at the end of the last century, which sought to borrow its characters as symbols of the artist/poet in his struggle against philistinism; or that for the Pierrots, Harlequins and Colombines of the 1920s that flitted so charmingly across a moonlit stage or an Art Deco mantelpiece.[14]

My plea, then, is for a reinterpretation based on what is known of the root form: it is thus not merely chronology that leads next to a discussion of origins.

I have standardised the use of *commedia dell'arte*, even when quoting from others, as Italian and have accepted Commedia (as being a species of Comedy) into English. Scenario has already been received and for this reason I use a plural of scenarios, not 'scenari'. *Lazzi*, although becoming current in English (possibly more so than in contemporary Italian!), I have left italicised since the singular form *lazzo* is rare and I find 'lazzis' unnecessary. The word Mask is given an initial capital when referring to a Commedia character, not when referring to a mask as a physical object. Similarly, Zanni when referring to the Mask as a character, *zanni* when meaning the type in general.

All translations are my own unless otherwise stated.

Part I

The *commedia dell'arte*

# Origins

In certain fiestas the very notion of order disappears. Chaos
comes back and licence rules. Anything is permitted: the
customary hierarchies vanish, along with all social, sex, caste and
trade distinctions. Men disguise themselves as women, gentlemen as slaves, the poor as rich. The army, the law and the clergy
are ridiculed. Obligatory sacrilege, ritual profanation is commit-
ted. Love becomes promiscuity. Sometimes the fiesta becomes a
Black Mass. Regulations, habits and customs are violated.
Respectable people put away the dignified expressions and
conservative clothes that isolate them, dress up in gaudy colours,
hide behind a mask, and escape from themselves.[1]

OCTAVIO PAZ

The professional name

In order to clear the ground to begin discussion of the origins of *commedia
dell'arte*, scholarly caveats as to what the phrase itself means and how to
translate it need reiteration. For example:

> The name *commedia dell'arte* is difficult to translate. Literally it
> approximates 'comedy of the artists', implying performances by
> professionals as distinguished from the courtly amateurs. This
> form has been given other names which are more revealing of its
> nature and characteristics. These include *commedia alla maschera*
> (masked comedy), *commedia improvviso* (improvised comedy), and
> *commedia dell'arte all'improvviso*.[2]

Moreover, in fact

> the very term *la commedia dell'arte* was never used of the activities
> of actors or professional acting companies until the eighteenth
> century, when we find Carlo Goldoni employing it to distinguish
> the masked and improvised drama from the scripted comedy
> that as a dramatist he himself favoured. . . . Earlier terms used
> of the professional players and companies tend to be rather
> more specific: *la commedia degli Zanni, la commedia a soggetto,
> la commedia all'italiana,* or *la commedia mercenaria.*[3]

The actual phrase is not used by Andrea Perrucci in his *Dell'arte rappresentativa, premeditata ed all'improvviso,* written as late as 1699. To his *all'improvviso* one could add, from other period sources, *commedia non scritta, sei maschere,* and, outside Italy, simply Italian Comedy.

But once noted, these earlier alternative terms can be ignored: what is important is to distinguish a genus (which we now call *commedia dell'arte*), that was professional, masked and initially publicly improvised on temporary outdoor platforms in simple costumes, from the contemporaneous *commedia erudita,* which was acted by amateur *dilettanti,* scripted and performed without the mask and in elaborate costume on the private indoor stages of the courts. *Arte* can be translated into English not only as 'art', but also as 'craft' and 'know-how'. Dario Fo underlines that it also indicates licence: the granting of professional and therefore protected status:

> *Commedia dell'arte* means comedy performed by professionals, those
> who are recognised as artists. Only artists recognised by the author-
> ities were classified as Commedia actors. The word *arte* in fact
> implied the incorporation of the dramatic arts; it brought together
> those who were authorised to perform for the counts, dukes, etc.[4]

For Fo, then, the nomenclature *commedia dell'arte* indicates a social rather than an artistic phenomenon, meaning above all the association of professionals. It was through such association that comedians pledged themselves to mutual protection and respect, commensurate to the closed shops of the medieval English guilds. In Italy too, individual 'professional' actors had probably been employed by other guilds to feature in their annual religious plays. By the mid-sixteenth century such individual performers were in search of a form which would enable them to band together. In understanding the significance of *dell'arte,* therefore, one needs perhaps to imagine companies creating a form of theatre called 'Equity' rather than that which we now call a trade union. The first known contract within such a company reads, in part, as follows:

> The undersigned companions, namely Maprio known as Zanini
> from Padua, Vincentio from Venice, Francesco de la Lira,

Hieronimo from San Luca, Zuandomengo known as Rizo, Zuane from Triviso, Tofan de Bastian and Francesco Moschini, desiring to form a fraternal company, which will last until the first day of next Lent in 1546, and will begin on the eighth day of next Easter, have decided and deliberated, in order that the company continue fraternally until the aforesaid day, without bitterness, rancour or dissolution, to make and observe between themselves . . . the following articles, under pain of forfeit of the undermentioned moneys.

Firstly, they have with common accord elected Maprio as their leader. . . .

Item, that if by any chance one of the aforesaid companions should fall ill, that he be aided and assisted by means of the common purse. . . . .

Item, that if the company is required to tour, all members be obliged to do so and that all agreements made should be by the aforementioned Zanini.[5]

And the list goes on to include details of the keeping of the cash box and the communal ownership of the horse. As well as such internal safeguards, *dell'arte* members were also able to call on external protection from local authorities if rogue companies materialised on their patch and, for this reason, written permission to perform was often sought in advance by an itinerant troupe. Famous companies could also use their connections to oust the competition; for example, Isabella Andreini of the Gelosi wrote to the governor of Milan:

in so far as they intend to erect a stage in the public square in order to play comedy, or rather to ruin it, we accordingly beg that you write to Sig. Podestà telling him that you do not consent to their doing so.[6]

Fo concludes, in his *Manuale minimo dell'attore*, that history has not perhaps settled on the most accurate locution:

I find correct, in fact, the idea proposed by some scholars, of calling this genre, instead of *commedia dell'arte*, more specifically 'comedy of the comedians' or 'of the actors'. The entire theatrical transaction rests on their shoulders: the actor as histrion and author, stage manager, storyteller, director.[7]

The amateur connection

There was interaction, other than patronage of the Players by the Gentlemen, between the *commedia dell'arte* and the *commedia erudita*. In plotting their scenarios in particular, the Commedia troupes seem to have adopted much from the latter form which, in turn, attempted little which did not derive from Plautus and Terence – for example *Calandria* by Cardinal Bibbiena, which, like Shakespeare's later *Comedy of Errors*, is based on Plautus' *Menaechmi*. Also, as the professional improvised comedy looked to extend its range, it imported a basis for the roles of the Lovers from the repertoire of the amateurs, who in turn had developed the limited possibilities afforded by the Roman comedies (where women of social standing were not allowed to be portrayed). The Miles Gloriosus (boastful soldier) was similarly appropriated.

There is, however, a historical problem in that the first recorded instance of something approaching a fully developed Commedia performance is in fact of one given by *dilettanti*. The composer Massimo Trojano wrote the following description in dialogue form of a court performance in which he was involved in Bavaria in 1568:

> *Fortunio*: . . . in the evening was presented an Italian comedy, in the presence of all the ladies of high rank. Even though the most part of them could not understand what he was saying, Messer Orlando Lasso – the Venetian Magnifico, with his Zanni, played so well and so agreeably that all their jaws ached from laughing.
>
> *Marinio*: Be good enough to relate the subject of the comedy to me.
>
> *Fortunio*: The previous day, his Lordship, the Duke William of Bavaria, had the notion of attending a comedy the next evening. Having summoned Messer Orlando Lasso who he knew to be a man of general resourcefulness, he asked that one be instantly prepared. The latter, not wishing to refuse anything which would please his good master . . . relayed the whole request to Massimo Trojano and thought up an appealing subject. They made up the scenario together. In the first act, the prologue was read by a peasant from Cava, dressed so comically that he could have been taken for the messenger of laughter.
>
> *Marinio*: Tell me, how many characters were there?
>
> *Fortunio*: Ten, and the comedy was in three acts.
>
> *Marinio*: It would be very interesting to know the names of all the actors.
>
> *Fortunio*: The estimable Messer Orlando Lasso played the role of

Magnifico Messer Pantalone de Bisognosi; Messer Gio Battista Scolari de Trento played the Zanni; Massimo Trojano played three roles: the prologue under the guise of a stupid peasant, that of the Lover *Polydoro* and that of the jealous Spaniard, under the name of *don Diego di Mendoza*. Polydoro's valet was don Carlo Livizzano and the valet of the Spaniard, Giorgio Dori, from Trento. The courtesan *Camilla*, in love with Polydoro, was the marquis de *Malaspina*, her serving maid was Ercole Terzo, who also played a French valet. Coming back to the comedy, after the prologue was read, Messer Orlando had a pleasing madrigal sung by five people, whilst Massimo who had just played the peasant changed into the costume of red velvet with gold braiding above and below the waist, a hat of black velvet trimmed with magnificent sables, and appeared on stage accompanied by his valet. He thanked his happy stars and said he was proud to live in a kingdom where love, abundance and joy held sway; but then the Frenchman appeared, the valet of his brother Fabrizio, sent from the country with a letter containing very sad news. Polydoro read the letter out loud, sighing deeply, called Camilla, explained the reason for his departure, embraced her and, having thus made his farewells, departed. From the other side of the stage Messer Orlando then appeared dressed as a Magnifico, in a camisole of red satin, red Venetian stockings, a black cloak which came right down to the ground and his face covered with a mask that made people laugh at first sight. He held a lute in his hand and sang and played:

> Whoever walks this street without a sigh
> He is a happy man.

After having sung twice, he put down his lute and began to lament over his love, saying 'Oh, poor Pantalone, who cannot pass this street without making the air resound with sighs, without soaking the ground with tears!' Everyone laughed till they could do no more, and all the time that Pantalone was on stage, all you could hear were bursts of laughter, and, above all, my dear Marino, when Pantalone had spoken both by himself and with Camilla, Zanni appeared, who had not seen his Pantalone for several years, and who, walking carelessly, bumped hard into him. They started to quarrel, then they recognised each other and Zanni, mad with joy, seized his master by the shoulders and began turning him round like a windmill as fast as he could, after which Pantalone did the same to him. Eventually they both found themselves flat on their backs. Getting up, they talked about one thing and another, after which Zanni asked after his old mistress, Pantalone's wife, and learned in reply that she was already dead. They both began howling like wolves, and Zanni cried as he remembered the macaronis and the sauces that she prepared for him to eat. After a good cry, they cheered up again, and the master commanded his valet to carry some chickens to Camilla, his beloved. Zanni promised to speak in his favour, but did just the opposite. Pantalone left the stage and Zanni, very timidly, approached Camilla's house. She became attached to Zanni (which is not surprising, since women often leave the good for the bad) and invited him to come into her house. Here a musical piece could be heard executed by five viola da gambas and as many voices. Imagine how funny that was! By God, in no comedy that I have seen has so much sincere laughter been heard!

Marinio: It has to be admitted that all that is very droll and amusing. Tell me more, for I am most interested.

Fortunio: In the second act Pantalone appeared, surprised that Zanni was so long in bringing him a reply. Then Zanni appeared with a letter from Camilla saying that if Pantalone wanted to gain her affection, he should dress in the costume that Zanni would provide for him. They both went off gaily to change clothes. Then the Spaniard came on 'with his heart plunged into that ocean of fury which is known as jealousy', and he recounted to his valet the great deeds he had performed and how many hundred men he had slain with his own hands in the barque of Caron. And now a mere woman had stolen his courageous heart. Drawn by love, he made his way to Camilla and asked her to let him in. Through clever wheedling, Camilla managed to obtain a necklace from him and promised him a rendezvous for the same evening. The Spaniard departed, happy. Then Pantalone appeared, dressed as Zanni and Zanni in his master's clothes. They put their heads together for a long time with Pantalone asking his valet's advice as to what he should say. Finally they both went into Camilla's house. Then music was played with four voices and two lutes, a mandolin, a recorder and a bass viola da gamba.

In the third act, Polydoro, who was Camilla's protector, came back from the country, entered the house and found Pantalone inside dressed in simple clothes. To his question 'Who is this?' came the reply that he was a porter and that Donna Camilla wanted him to carry a trunk full of clothes to her sister Doralice in Santo Cataldo. Polydoro believed this and said he should do so immediately. The ageing Pantalone was not able to pick up the trunk; he began to argue and finally revealed that he was of

3 A few years after the amateur performance at the Bavarian court, professional
Commedia troupes began to tour Southern Germany. On the walls of the bedchamber of . . .

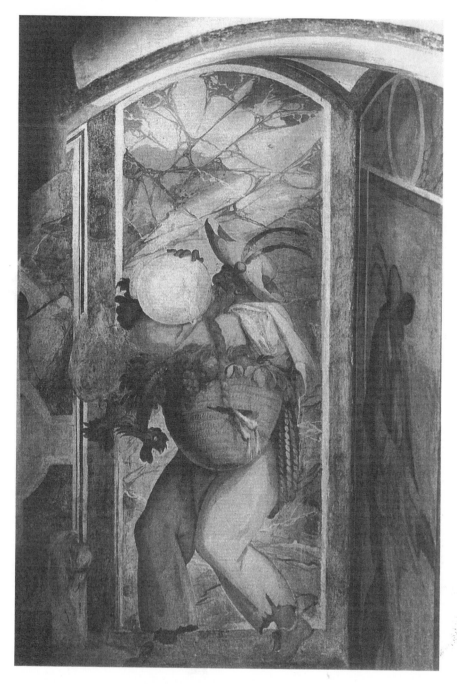

. . . William IV in the castle of Trausnitz are a series of frescos by Alessandro Scalzi, known as 'the Paduan', probably recording performances by one of them and, therefore, . . .

. . . almost contemporaneous with Trojano's reminiscences. Shown are Pantalone and Zanni serenading, Zanni carrying gifts to the courtesan and Pantalone, followed by Zanni, going to fight Capitano.

noble birth; but Polydoro, furious, seized a stick and thrashed him so soundly (to the great amusement of the audience) that he would not have forgotten it for a long time. After poor Pantalone had taken to his heels, Polydoro, angry with Camilla, went back into the house, whilst Zanni, who had heard the blows, hid in a sack which he found there. Camilla's servant tied the sack in such a way that Zanni could not get out. Meanwhile, the Spaniard arrived, for it was the hour of his rendezvous with Camilla. He wanted to enter the house, but Camilla told him that Polydoro had returned. Enraged at this new obstacle, the Spaniard drew and, raising his eyes to heaven, pronounced with a sigh 'Ahi! Margodemi!' But he stumbled on the sack with the unfortunate Zanni inside, and fell flat on the floor, his valet going down with him. Getting up in a rage, he undid the sack, made Zanni get out and whacked him all over with his own bat. Zanni fled and the Spaniard and his valet followed. Then Polydoro came on with his valet and Camilla with her maid. Polydoro said that she should get married since, for certain reasons, he was no longer disposed to keep her. She refused for a long time, then eventually decided to marry Zanni. On these words, Pantalone entered carrying several weapons followed by Zanni with two blunderbusses behind his back, a sword and buckler in his hand and a rusty helmet on his head. They were looking for the man who had belaboured them with blows and fired several imaginary rounds at an imaginary enemy. Camilla advised Polydoro to speak to Pantalone. The latter, seeing Polydoro, pointed him out to Zanni. Zanni decided that it was Pantalone who should mount the first attack, but Pantalone was of the other opinion. Having realised what was going on, Polydoro called him by his name 'Oh, Signor Pantalone!' and drew his sword, whilst Zanni was not sure which weapon to employ; a comic battle then took place, which lasted quite a while. Finally Camilla held back Pantalone and the maid restrained Zanni. Peace was concluded; Camilla married Zanni, and on the occasion of the marriage, they danced Italian dances, and Massimo, having excused himself in the name of Messer Orlando in that the comedy was not worthy of the dignity of princes, bade a respectful goodnight to everyone, and all went to bed.[8]

And this was not an isolated instance, a wild Bavarian folly: in his *Diario di Fernandino I e Cosimo II*, Tinghi speaks of comedies being played at the court of Florence by professional actors (whom he calls *zanni*), but then also writes of similar shows being provided by amateurs.

Various points are worth noting from the above description, other than

Trojano's self-esteem as an occasional comedian. The courtesan and her maid are played by men in front of a seemingly largely female audience; there are no Lovers, only lusters, and there is a Spanish Capitano, but he is not a coward, thus revealing how little *commedia degli zanni* had borrowed from *commedia erudita* by this date – at least among expatriates in Bavaria. On the other hand, although Trojano and Lasso were both composers, this is no reason to assume that more music than usual in a Commedia was inserted, merely that it seems to have been played and sung by separate musicians rather than by the characters themselves (with the exception of Pantalone's little song).

If the Gentlemen could thus imitate the Players and improvise from scenarios (without mixing genres with their own), surely, then, the professionals could have acted from scripts? In the provision of occasional pastorals and tragedies they may well have done so to some extent, but to have based their Commedia playing on the memorising of lines would have been a hindrance rather than a help. The texts which have survived (several of which are given in extract in the sections on the characters later in this book) were mainly written down after the event rather than before it, as Gherardi did, for example, in his *Le Théâtre italien* (1700).

Given the difficulty that many actors have in improvising, it may seem strange to consider a script as an encumbrance, but that is what it would have been for such actors on an outdoor stage engaged in a live, give-and-take relationship with a popular audience. The crucial difference between early *commedia dell'arte* and the *commedia erudita* was not that one was a profession and the other a hobby, or that one was for the nobs and the other for the plebs, but that one was initially an outdoor form, breathing the fresh air of invention, and the other indoor and sustained by artifice.

The market place

Commedia dell'arte was born, some time around the middle of the sixteenth century, in the market place where a crowd has to be attracted, interested and then held if a living is to be made. Zanni, for example, speaks in a loud, coarse voice because his comic type is based on that of the Venetian market porter who had to make himself heard offering his services above the clamour of the piazza and the rest of its traders, if he was not to go hungry.

A modern performer wondering where to start a practical study of Commedia can do no better than listen to a barrow boy or a china salesman pitch his goods from a van in an outdoor market. His direct relationship to his public, based on a humorous sense of collusion – the implication that the crockery is only cheap because it is 'dodgy', whereas, in fact, it is just cheap – has an ancestry as old as such markets themselves: such a figure is a charlatan, otherwise known in English as a mountebank, with Italian cousins known variously as *ciurmadori* and *ciarlatani* as well as *montimbanchi*. A *banco* is a trestle stage, which the charlatan would mount (the van mentioned above usually has a platform built into it) and on and off which his acrobatic assistants could leap in their capacity as *saltimbanchi* (*saltimbanques* in French). The charlatan himself has antecedents: he is a shaman, an astrologer, almost a magus whose incantation puts the audience into a kind of trance from which only the waving of money can release them.

Antonio Fava in his school teaches that the charlatan can be of seven kinds:

1. The medicinal quack selling patent cure-alls, especially in Venice, the city of spies and domestic skulduggery, where antidotes to poisons were much in demand!
2. The mystical pedlar of exotica, supposedly from the Far East.
3. The inventor with an amazing patent device.
4. The religious fanatic declaring 'the end of world is nigh'.
5. The sex-monger offering forbidden pleasures.
6. The magician and illusionist.
7. The pathetic type, a virtual beggar but with a specialism, as in *The Beggar's Opera*.

All such types wandered from country fair to city Carnival throughout the sixteenth century, setting up wherever they could draw a crowd that might escape the attention of civil or ecclesiastical officers. By the early seventeenth century, they seem, according to one eyewitness account, in Venice at least, to have been more tolerated:

> I hope it will not be esteemed for an impertinencee to my discourse, if I next speake of the Mountebanks of Venice, seeing amongst many other thinges that doe much famouse this Citie, these two sorts of people, namely the Cortezans and the Mountebanks, are not the least: for although there are Mountebanks also in other Cities of Italie: yet because there is a greater concurse of them in Venice than else where, and that of the better sort and the most eloquent fellowes; and also for that there is a larger tolleration of them here then in other Cities.[9]

For example Milan where, in 1565, the governor prohibited all 'Masters and players of comedie, herb-sellers, charlatans, buffoons, Zanni and mountebanks' to play on church feast days or in Lent or on stages near the church except after service 'on pain of whipping'. But Venice was the centre to visit, with the charlatans of St Mark's Square a tourist attraction similar to present-day Speakers' Corner in London's Hyde Park:

> Therefore they use to name a Venetian Mountebank . . . for all the coryphaeus and principal mountebanks of all Italy. . . . Surely the principall reason that hath induced me to make mention of them is, because when I was in Venice, they oftentimes ministred infinite pleasure unto me. I will first begin with the etymologie of their name: the word Mountebank (being in the Italian tongue *Monta'in banco*) is compounded of two Italian words *Montare*, which signifieth to ascend or to go up to a place, and *banco*, a bench, because these fellowes doe act their part vpon a stage, which is compacted of benches or formes, though I have seene some fewe of them also stand upon the ground when they tel their tales, which are such as are commonly called *Ciarlatanoe*'s or *Ciarlatans*, in Latin they are called *Circularores* and *Agyrtae* which is derived from the Greeke worde which signifieth to gather or draw a company of people together. . . . The principal place where they act is the first part of Saint Mark's street that reacheth betwixt the West front of Saint Mark's Church, and the opposite front of Saint Germinian's Church. In which, twice a day, that is, in the morning and in the afternoone, you may see five or six severall stages erected for them. . . . These Mountebanks at one end of their stage place their trunke, which is replenished with a world of new-fangled trumperies. . . . While the musicke plays, the princi-pall Mountebanke whiche is the Captaine and ring-leader of all the rest, opens his trunk and sets abroach his wares; after the musicke hath ceased, he maketh an oration to the audience of halfe an houre long, or almost an hour. Wherein he doth most hyperbolically extoll the virtue of his drugs and confections . . . though many of them are very counterfeit and false. Truely I often wondered at many of these naturall Orators. For they would give their tales with such admirable volubility and plausible grace, even extemporere, and seasoned with that singular variety of elegant jests and witty conceits, that they did often strike great admiration into strangers that never heard them before. . . . After the chiefest Mountebanks first speech is ended, he deliuereth out his commodities by little and little, *the iester still playing his part* [my italics] and the musicians singing and playing on their instruments.[10]

According to this English tourist, Sir Thomas Coryat, a charlatan could play to up to a thousand people at a time. He noted in particular a snake charmer and a blind black man playing the bones. The offer price for their

4 Charlatans in the piazza San Marco, Venice. Seventeenth-century engraving by Giacomo Franco. In the foreground a snake-charming mountebank with *innamorati*, Pantalone and Burattino.

'trumperies' would start at ten crowns and then descend so low as four gazets – apparently something less than a groat. However much that was, it presumably comes to the same as the one pound at the end of today's sequence which begins 'I'm not asking five pounds, I'm not asking four pounds'.

But who was the 'iester', and what part did he play? The playwright Carlo Goldoni in his *Memoirs*[11] speaks of a certain Buonafede Vitali who sold his drugs with the aid of 'the four Masks', (Pantalone, Il Dottore, Brighella and Arlecchino), whose business it was

> to collect the money thrown to them in pocket-handkerchiefs, and to return the handkerchiefs filled with pots of ointment and boxes of pills to the purchasers, after which they performed plays in three acts with a certain kind of pomp under the light of wax candles.

A full mountebank performance, then, might have begun with busking by the Masks, leading to the introduction of the mountebank, who would

5 Mountebank outside Notre Dame with Pedrolino and Arlecchino. Arlecchino's seeming affinity to the Monkey King of the Peking Opera may, it seems, have no more of an Oriental origin than the actual monkey who often seems to have joined him in his 'iests' when working with a charlatan. The latter sometimes used a monkey only, like an organ grinder.

deliver his pitch with the aid of his masked *saltimbanque* assistants leaping on and off the stage to complete transactions or using their juggler's skills to throw the goods precisely to the person who had paid. When the audience were judged to have been sufficiently tapped, they would have been rewarded with a Commedia performance. As with the escapologists one sees today in the Place Beaubourg in Paris, for example, their act would presumably not have taken place until sufficient customers had been parted from their loose change. Originally *zanni*, these *saltimbanchi* later adopted the personae of other Masks – Arlecchino, Brighella, Pedrolino, etc.

 Carnival

The other major outdoor source from which Commedia was formed is even harder to document:

> When the older records are searched for evidence of traces in the steps of the actors' upward progress, the earliest are found to be a few tantalisingly scant and unsatisfactory notices, scattered chiefly in accounts of Carnival gaieties and for the most part mere allusions in the letters of princes to some buffoon whom they have taken from his companions and established as court fool.[12]

And Allardyce Nicoll warns:

> the currently fashionable view rejects the supposedly Roman sources and attributes the rise of the Commedia to *(a)* the development of Carnival elements, *(b)* the attempt to make popular the academic comedies of the time or *(c)* the desire to find a means of social satire. . . . Historical evidence is strained, and Ireneo Sanesi does well to emphasise the need of sticking to the facts and of carefully questioning a number of commonly repeated statements.[13]

The problem is that the evidence of recorded history is usually that sanctioned by people who could read and write. The Renaissance was a period of rapid oligarchical cultural advancement in which no ink seems to have been wasted on documenting the traditional popular calendrical manifestations of Carnival. What we lack is an eyewitness account from the early sixteenth century commensurate with the following description of the last three days of Carnival in Rome in 1826:

I now ... present some little scenes which take place in the streets of Rome. And that I may succeed in this, I beg that in imagination you will transport yourselves with me to some place in the neighbourhood of the Corso, where our theatre is set up.

It is two o'clock in the afternoon, and no one is yet to be seen. The sky is overcast, but the weather will be safe; it will not snow.

Behold! here already is a Pulcinella, playing a trumpet, leaping and talking. Let us listen. He complains of the indolence of the masks; it is after two o'clock, and they are not yet ready; a very little more would induce him to beat them. He departs quite angrily, protecting his better half, who leans upon his arm.

Suddenly there is a great noise; a Harlequin, walking on tip-toe, lantern in hand, leads the way for a *Quacquero*[14] and his lady, the *Quacqueressa*; with him comes a *Bajaccio* under an open sunshade. What the devil's this, my friend, a sunshade and a lantern? Night and sunshine? Yonder our desolate Pulcinella is returning, and he who lately was lamenting is now at the very summit of hilarity; he has just met another Pulcinella, to whom he relinquishes his wife. Reciprocal joy. Here comes an *Abbataccio* and here two or three *Quacqueri, Poverelle, Sbiri, Micheletti*; and last a Captain Fracasso in argument with a Tartaglia: 'If you you don't return at once to the galleys I will cut you in two, piece of a thief!'

(To which, with much stammering, Tartaglia replies that he has got the wrong man.)

Turn now to this *Abbataccio*, a book under his arm, who with the assistance of other masks has just seized upon a poor imbecile of a peasant, who has come to see the Roman Carnival, and who certainly never expected to become an actor in this farce: 'You are my debtor', he bellows at him, 'these last two years, these last two centuries. Your grandfather, great-grandfather, great-great-grand-father, or, if you prefer it, your archi-great devil of a father, who was my man of affairs, wrote me a bill of exchange. Don't you believe it? Do you deny the patent truth? I am going to show it to you.' With that he opens his book, which turns out to be nothing but a flour box, blows into it, and thus almost blinds the poor peasant, who was gaping at him. He becomes the butt of the laughter and ridicule of all who are present. A mask in the dress of a groom comes to rub him down; the sweeps sweep him, and a fool mystifies him. The peasant attempts to depart, but at this moment a Doctor, an Apothecary and some Matassins insist upon offering him their services. 'He has turned pale,' cries one, pointing to his flour-covered face, 'he is about to die.' He gets away at last and darts round a corner of the street, followed by his mockers, of whom heaven alone knows when he will succeed in ridding himself.

6 *Pulcinellas in a Carnival Procession*. Sepia wash from a cycle of Pulcinella drawings by Domenico Tiepolo, c. 1790.

What is this noise? What is happening? 'A Spectre, a Spectre!' (*una Fantasima!*) cries someone, and you behold the Pulcinelli, Arlecchini, Brighelli, Pantaloni cutting a thousand capers of terror. Captain *Ammazzasette* (Rodomont) puts his hand to his sword and runs to meet the phantom, which lengthens itself almost indefinitely, and then disappears, to the great shouts of the assembly.

Observe this crowd, listen to this noise! Here comes the cause of it: a well-harnessed donkey, bearing the king of the Polichinelles with two little Polichinelles, his sons, seated in the panniers. The court, consisting of thirty or forty Polichinelles, escorts him, playing all conceivable instruments. This general masquerade is extraordinary, capricious and very droll. Consider that no two wear the same head-dress; one wears a huge wig, another a basket, some an evil hat, others go with shaven heads, and yet another bears a cage with birds in it.

Along the Corso, from end to end, the people swarm like ants. There is no window that is not crowded with sightseers. And how varied is the assembly! Here ranks, ages and sexes are all intermingled and confounded. Joy, gaiety and good humour rule; pleasantries, practical jokes, laughter, nosegays and clouds of flour on this side, and a rain of flowers on the other, long queues of carriages filled with masks, and ancient coaches on which the youthful nobility of Rome is representing the abduction of Proserpine. Next we see women disguised as officers, as sailors, as natives of Frascati or Albania. Two squadrons of ancient warriors on cardboard horses engage furiously in combat, and so on. The revels conclude with races of unfettered and unmounted horses down the middle of the Corso. Such is the Roman Carnival until the hour of the Angelus, at the sound of which everyone unmasks, and all go to conclude the day at the theatre, at a soirée, or at home. Shrove Tuesday being the last day, the Angelus bell is impotent to command obedience; all retain their masks and then begins the scene of the *Moccoli*, too well known to need reporting here.[15]

As with the revived Venice Carnival of today, these Roman festivities of the first quarter of the nineteenth century already seem rather arch, hardly spontaneous in their licence and at worst a pretext for Hooray Henries to have fun at the expense of the lower classes. It is, however, clear that the Commedia Masks still held their popularity in the street, although they had disappeared from the stage many decades previously. What fun to play at these figures which had for so long been the preserve of the professionals, one might think. But although some characters were invented or creatively developed from stock sources by the actors of the sixteenth and seventeenth centuries, most of the Commedia masks thronging the streets in the Carnivals of the nineteenth and twentieth centuries are indubitably returning whence they came.

When one has said that the *commedia dell'arte* is a manifestation which comes from tying dressing-up together with improvisation, one has already directly arrived at the ritual nature of several cultural processes whose origin stems from Carnival. In Carnival we find the masks, the language, the triviality, the satire, the mimicry, the acrobatics, in one word all the elements which have passed into the tradition of improvisation together with the nomadism which has constituted one of its immutable characteristics.[16]

We think of Carnival today as a single fantastical procession, but in origin it was a valediction to *carne*, a ritual indulgence in the consumption of the last meat available in dried or salted form at the end of winter, a pagan rite of passage between the old year's sustenance and the new, between waxing and waning, between, as the Christian symbolism now had it, the Devil and Christ, Carnival and Lent. It thus may have involved two processions, not one, ending in one or more confrontations in suitable parts of the town:

> The quack doctor besides selling his wares sometimes took part in
> one of the crude farces or *contrasti* given on the street stages.
> Perhaps the oldest theme in which he found his place is the
> struggle between winter and summer, personified in the *Contrasto
> between Master Carnival and Lady Lent*; each of the leading charac-
> ters appropriately dressed salutes the other in foully abusive
> language till both fall to blows to decide their contest. Carnival
> must die of course but not until he has called in Doctors and
> magicians, heard and even attempted their burlesque prescrip-
> tions, and made a ridiculous will, leaving to his sisters his 'credits
> never acquired', to his wife 'property not yet bought' and to
> others still less desirable gifts; then amidst howls of grief from
> members of the family, Lent summons her enemy's soul.[17]

The inherent battle was also that between asceticism and artistic licence,
censorship and freedom of expression, a tension which is also inborn in
commedia dell'arte. The week prior to Lent was known as Devil's Week in
Holland, and throughout Europe the Devils which featured prominently in
the Mystery Cycles were also let loose in the streets of Carne-vale to play
pranks on the citizenry. For present purposes it is not necessary to resolve
the argument as to whether Arlecchino has a medieval devilish ancestry as
the head of the impish rout, Hellequin, Herlequin or even Harlequin.[18] What
we do know is that at the Roman *mardi gras* of 1555/6 Joachim du Bellay
saw a certain Marc'Antonio and Zanni 'bouffoner avec un Magnifique à la
Vénétienne' and that three years later Anton Francesco Grazzini, a
Florentine poet and dramatist, published a Carnival song, a duet for
Pantalone and a chorus of *zanni* which most scholars agree to be the first
satisfactory evidence of *commedia dell'arte*:

> We play the Bergomask and the Venetian
> Touring the country's every part
> Acting comedy is our art.
> And today we're doing Florence
> As you can see, Messer Benedetti
> All Zanni are we
> And perform most excellently.
>
> The other favourite players,
> Lovers, Ladies, Hermits, Slayers,
> Are all for now home-stayers.[19]

In other words, the entire company are out playing *zanni*, busking for the show which is to be given tomorrow 'when we're in our own hall'. Although this is a Carnival song to be sung in the streets, it is also an advertisement for a professional performance of 'new plays in our style, that when you hear them delivered, you'll almost die from laughing'. The song ends with the claim that lastly they will show a beautiful and well-made scene, 'during which Caninella and Zanni will act and delight you, so if you want to have a good time, laugh and have some fun, come tomorrow and find us in our hall'. The evidence thus points to at least a mid-sixteenth-century interaction between the popular street celebrations of Carnival and professional performance (indoors, given the time of year) by itinerant troupes.

The *contrasto* between Pantalone and Zanni, though not as central to Carnival as the clash between the heads of the opposing processions, may well have been one of the basic ingredients adopted by the *commedia dell'arte* for improvised performance throughout the year.

> As early as 1518/19 Pontano describes an entertainment played outdoors by masked actors, but whether or not Zanni and Pantalone were among them he does not say. From that time on, however, Zan, or Zanni, or Zoan, 'Bergamask servant', begins to appear in written plays, 'ludi zanneschi' to be mentioned vaguely among courtly amusements and Zanni with various companions to be noted in the accounts of Carnival merrymakings.[20]

The dialogues between Pantalone and Zanni called for in Trojano's scenario (which are in part developed into scripted form in the extracts given on p. 72) represent a *fons et origo* of comedy, the battle between authority and the underdog, rich and poor, privileged and dispossessed. Those in the middle of the class scale confirm their status by laughing at its extremes, either playing the Masks themselves or paying professionals to do it for them, and, after the release of tensions through Carnival/Commedia, social balance is restored. Despite his wealth Pantalone, in his lonely and irascible dotage, is not to be envied after all, neither are the *zanni* who, although they are spirits of the earth (and possibly further down), once again are left with nothing but their limited wits to survive on.

The 'iesters', then, who banded together to form the *commedia degli zanni*, later to be known as the *commedia dell'arte*, were *saltimbanchi* who developed their first shows out of crude Carnival *contrasti* between themselves and the oppressor figure of the Magnifico Pantalone. Subsequently they went in search of other Masks in order to evolve more complex comedic improvisations: the origins of each of these are given in the chapters on the characters.

The mask

The mask is a terrible, mysterious instrument. It has always
given me and continues to give me a feeling of fear. With the
mask we are on the threshold of a theatrical mystery whose
demons reappear with static, immutable faces, which are at the
very roots of theatre.

GIORGIO STREHLER[1]

 Persona versus personality

A masked man had no right to bear arms during Carnival season in
medieval Italy because he was considered to have divested himself of his
own identity by assuming another persona, for whose actions he was therefore not responsible. Similarly, in *commedia dell'arte*, by virtue of its derivation from Carnival (as has been argued in the previous chapter), personality
disappeared to be replaced by type: the personality of the actor is thus over-
taken not by an author's scripted character, but by the persona of the mask
to be played.

In fact, to speak of the persona of a mask is tautologous since its
etymology comes from the Latin: 'Persona, I *A mask:* hence II, *The person part
or character played by an actor.* III *The part or character sustained by anyone
in the world:* also *a person who sustains a character.'*[2] In the liminal phases
of life such as Carnival and Fiesta, persona, because it is of all times and
all places, readily overcomes personality, which is time and place specific.
There is no point, therefore, in looking for values in *commedia dell'arte*
which it cannot provide, such as psychological realism or comedy of
manners. That is why playwrights, as they assumed creative control of
the European stage, found the use of masks limiting: Carlo Goldoni, for

example, came to the conclusion that 'the soul under a mask is like a fire under ashes'.[3]

It is true that a mask has no individualised past when it appears, only a present presence as a Mask. In Commedia, 'Mask' refers to character type and is inclusive of each individual mask. Thus the Lovers are still 'Masks' even though they do not wear actual masks. In Italian they are among the *tipi fissi*, 'fixed types' which, although they can gain human significance from the context in which they find themselves, can never be mistaken for the representation of actual human beings. A Commedia plot, therefore, moves forward from its *point d'appui*, not back into the investigation of past events, and from that point on, one action begets another – but not as a series of psychological consequence. The Mask remains what it seems and at the end of the play it is returned to its box unaffected by the game which has been played with it. Catharsis is not therefore possible and the *all'improvviso* form does not lend itself to tragedy. Laughter is dependent on stereotyping, on objects of derision being less than human and objects of amazement more so.

In *commedia dell'arte* the isolation of, say, avarice in Pantalone or of intellectual pretension in Il Dottore, is completely crystallised in their masks. As an actor you must work within the limitations of persona and cannot escape into the complexities of personality. In a sense you are the prisoner of the mask, and you must play out your part in terms of the statement *it* makes, rather than in terms of some complex of emotions that go beyond that statement. Actors must 'live up' to the mask. As soon as they can no longer do so, either because society no longer finds it relevant or because the *arte* which sustains it is in decay (as it was in Goldoni's time), they must surrender creative autonomy to the writer in order to continue to earn a living.

Each Mask represents a moment in everyone's (rather than someone's) life. That is not to say that the fixed types of Commedia are simplistic or reductive of life: each contains and expresses at least one paradox and its seemingly obvious physicality usually implies a metaphysical quality which it may take an actor years to acquire. For example:

> Arlecchino, the simpleton from Bergamo, the servant of a skinflint of a Doctor, is obliged, through the meanness of his master, to wear a costume made of different coloured patches. He is a foolish buffoon, a roguish servant who seems always to wear a cheerful grin.
>
> But see what is dissembled by the mask: Arlecchino, the all-powerful wizard, the enchanter, the magician; Arlecchino, the emissary of the infernal powers.
>
> The mask may conceal more than two aspects of a character. The two aspects of Arlecchino represent two opposite poles. Between them lies an infinite range of shades and variations. How

does one reveal this extreme diversity of character to the spectator? With the aid of the mask.

The actor who has mastered the art of gesture and movement (herein lies his power!) manipulates his masks in such a way that the spectator is never in any doubt about the character he is watching: whether he is the foolish buffoon from Bergamo or the Devil.

This chameleonic power, concealed beneath the expressionless visage of the comedian, invests the theatre with all the enchantment of chiaroscuro. Is it not the mask which helps the spectator fly away to the land of make-believe?

The mask enables the spectator to see not only the actual Arlecchino before him, but all the Arlecchinos who live in his memory. Through the mask the spectator sees every person who bears the merest resemblance to the character.[4]

Meyerhold wrote that analysis of Arlecchino before the Russian revolution when, at the same time as experimenting with *commedia dell'arte*, he was developing his system of bio-mechanical training as the basis for a contemporary art of gesture and movement. Other early twentieth-century directors, such as Jacques Copeau, also understood the need for a technical training which could provide new foundations for such old mastery, since its requirements were clearly incompatible with the cult of personality on which the prevailing theatrical star system was based.

The actor who plays in a mask receives the reality of his character from a cardboard object. He is commanded by it and must obey it willy-nilly. No sooner has he put it on than he feels an unknown being spread into his veins of whose existence he had no suspicion. It is not only his face which is modified, it is his entire being, the very nature of his reflexes where feelings are already preforming themselves that he was equally incapable of feeling or feigning when bare-faced ... even the tone of his voice will be dictated by his mask.[5]

Surrendering to the mask necessitates a non-egotistical working base, a state of availability of mind and body, or rather mind in body, which, thanks to the experiments by Jacques Copeau and Suzanne Bing in the Vieux Colombier School and developed by Jean Dasté and Jacques Lecoq, has become known as 'neutrality'. The 'great' Commedia actors tended in fact to 'become' their masks, and their biographies often became inextricably intermingled with the characteristics of their Mask.[6] Antonio Fava teaches that when the mask is raised after performing, it should seem as if the actor's face is still formed by it, wearing its imprint, if no longer its actual contours.

Dario Fo finds such a demand at times intolerable, which is not surprising since his face has become a trained instrument in its own right:

> Firstly, wearing a mask can, in an actor, induce anxiety deriving not so much from the use itself as from the fact that the mask restricts both the visual field and the acoustic-vocal range. Your own voice seems to be singing at you, stunning you, ringing in your ears and, until you master it, you cannot control your breathing. The mask feels like an encumbrance and can easily transform itself into a torture chamber.
>
> That is the first reason. Then there is a second which is mythical, magical almost. A singular sensation afflicts you when you take off the mask – this at least, is my reaction – the fear that part of my face has remained stuck to it, or the fear that the face has gone with the mask. When you remove the mask after having had it on for two or three hours, you have the impression of annihilating yourself.[7]

Animal magic

The advantage that the schools of Lecoq and Fava have over Copeau and Suzanne Bing's early experiments is that their masks are not made of cardboard. From experience I would say that Commedia masks have to be made of leather, and it is only possible to make the most rudimentary discoveries in ones made of cardboard, papier mâché, celastic or fibreglass. One of the reasons for this is primordial:

> One of the earliest pieces of evidence for the use of masks dates back to prehistoric times, to the walls of the cave 'des deux frères' on the French side of the Pyrenees. The painting, a hunting scene, has been drawn with astonishing skill and depicts a herd of wild goats grazing in a field. The group appears, at first sight, quite homogeneous, but, on close inspection, it becomes clear that one of the goats has, instead of the cloven hoof, a man's legs and feet. And not four, but only two. The hands which can barely be seen from beneath the animal are gripping a taut bow and arrow. The creature is evidently a man, a hunter in disguise. On his face he has a goat's mask with horns and a beard, and the area from the shoulders to the small of the back is covered by a goat's skin.[8]

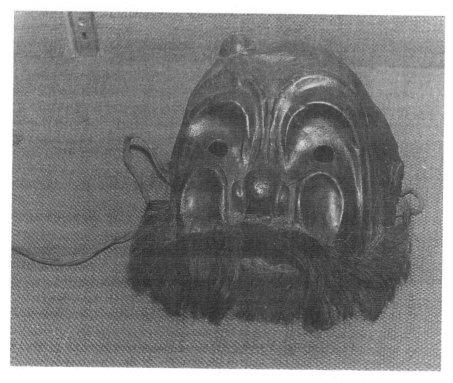

7 Probably the earliest extant Zanni/Arlecchino mask: is the hair a vestigial remains of primitive animal disguise carried forward into carnival and thence to Commedia?

Much of this statement by Dario Fo is inaccurate: the cave is 'Les Trois Frères', the wild goats are in fact thirty bison, ten horses, four ibexes and one reindeer, and the 'hunter' is more often thought to be a sorcerer and his bow to be one of a musical variety. However, with his actor's instinct rather than scholar's iconography, Fo is undoubtedly right in the conclusion which he draws:

> the transformation of oneself into an animal plainly required a certain skill because it is never enough just to pull a mask over your nose or toss a smelly piece of animal skin over your shoulders. The real problem is to imitate the movements of the goat or whatever animal one is intent on capturing, and these movements vary according to the situation. The rite of dressing up in animal skins is linked to the culture of almost every race on earth.[9]

And the sorcerer of 'Les Trois Frères', with his fringed beard, lightfooted motion and trunk held firm by a lowered centre of gravity, bears more than a passing resemblance to the earliest extant mask of Arlecchino and to woodcuts and engravings made before the use of balletic stances influenced the physical playing of the masks. Such a prehistoric ancestry for Arlecchino is, of course, highly speculative, but not perhaps more so than the claims of Sand, Duchartre and others that the antecedents of the Masks are to be found in terracotta statuettes of characters from the Roman Atellan farce or vase-paintings depicting ancient Greek *phylakes*.

Such animal mimicry is at the source of many, if not all, of the masks of the *commedia dell'arte*, but they are the animals of the domestic scene such as cats, dogs and even monkeys, as well as of the farmyard, such as chickens and pigs, rather than of the plains of the hunter-gatherer. Fo calls them the masks of the 'below stairs' classes. On the other hand, the aristocracy in Commedia, the Lovers (though not their fathers), cannot be seen to be demeaned by zoomorphism and thus appear unmasked, paradoxically revealing the artificiality and immaturity of their existence.

The other reason for leather is that it is practical. Italy is a hot country. Playing Commedia is a sweaty business. A new leather mask is like a new shoe or a new glove, only gradually will it take on the identity of its wearer and become something comfortable rather than alien to wear. Simply, the two skins learn to co-operate rather than conflict. In order to achieve this, the mask needs to be your size, not someone else's – preferably hand-made to your own lath or, in mask-making parlance, 'matrix'. Such a mask can 'absorb your sweat as well as live in symbiosis with your body heat and breathing rhythms'.[10]

Yet however much symbiosis is achieved, the mask will retain mysteries which cannot be incorporated. One of these is the red warts which erupt on the masks of, in particular, Zanni, Arlecchino, Pantalone and Pulcinella. Antonio Fava applies three criteria in his research: sociological, cultural and practical. Applying this to the warts on the mask, sociologically he considers they refer to the boils and skin diseases of poor people on inadequate diets, culturally they are vestiges of the horns of the Carnival devils from which they derived, and practically they are a way of accommodating imperfections in the leather during the mask-making process. Dario Fo adds a fourth possibility:

> A very similar sign can be seen on many oriental masks, perhaps under the form of a golden disk or of a coloured mark between the eyebrows. . . . Other masks indicate demonic figures, and sometimes even have a stone or a coloured crystal set in a swelling on the forehead. Evidently this is also a kind of third eye, which allows the holy man, or demi-god or demon to see beyond the bodies of men and into the very depths of their being. The third eye can also be found in Chinese and some Japanese masks.[11]

Acting in the mask

One of the first rules of carpentry is to learn to 'let the tool do the work'; the same is true of masked acting. In both cases there are two things to be learned: what the work is and what the properties of the tool are. Once such an apprenticeship is over, the craftsman, having selected the right tool for the job, needs to supply no more personal effort than is necessary for its accomplishment. The first thing to appreciate in learning to 'let the mask do the work' is that facial expression is replaced by what is known as 'the gaze' of the mask. A badly made mask does not have one – in fact it is not a mask at all and might as well be thrown away, or hung on a wall (if it has any decorative value). A real mask should never be hung on a wall, unless its working days are over, since its gaze will be diminished by unanimated familiarity. A real mask will gaze immediately it is put on by no matter whom. The first second of wearing it is easy; it is as if the mask switches itself on. The difficulty lies in then letting it sustain its expression. In the early stages of learning the gaze will soon be lost, the mask betrayed as inanimate by the wearer's desire to make it express something which comes from his or her own experience rather than the characteristics of the mask. Even so, the mask will not want to be taken off, it is a possessing spirit which would rather put up with the inappropriateness of your actions than return to the limbo of suspended animation. The longer the nose of the mask, the more stupid it is and the more necessary it is to reduce the range of your own thought processes in order to let it play, rather than have to suffer your cleverness at its expense.

In order to understand how its gaze works, it is important to appreciate that the mask has only one eye – which you need to imagine as situated at the end of the nose. If the eye-holes are correctly placed for the wearer, a kind of tunnel vision is set up, a constant reminder that the mask's expressive range is also limited. The world ceases to have dimension and the only means of finding your way around it is to 'follow your nose'. The neck has to become alive in a manner that is rarely demanded of it in the three-dimensional world where the eyes shift their focus with only minimal alterations of head position – if major changes in attention are needed then the whole body is required to make a sympathetic movement. In Commedia mask work the body is often required to be doing something different, working contrapuntally or even paradoxically. For example, your master calls: your body must go but your attention remains fixed on the spoonful of pasta that Pulcinella is offering you; Colombina enters, in a loving mood – you register this fact as your master calls again (not to go at once will mean a beating). The resolution of the master/Colombina choice is to go back and eat the pasta, but this action will not be comedic unless the mask has sustained the interest of its gaze during the physicalisation of the other two demands.

The shoulders are part of the trunk, of the body and its intentions, not of the neck and the gaze of the mask. This means training the cervical vertebrae to move with greater independence from the thoracic than is the case in everyday life. Movements of the neck have to stop at the seventh cervical and not be picked up by the first thoracic (the first vertebra to have ribs attached). The second cervical, the Axis, is the only vertebra to allow rotation and this must be completely free: not easy when a seventh of the body's weight, the head, is attached to the one above it, the first cervical, or Atlas. Proper training of the neck requires expert attention and actors who allow the mask to overexert their cervical vertebrae without proper preparation can need remedial treatment. Personal supervision is necessary, not printed instruction, so I will confine myself to suggesting that flexibility should be built up gradually, not as a sudden demand. Eventually some actions need

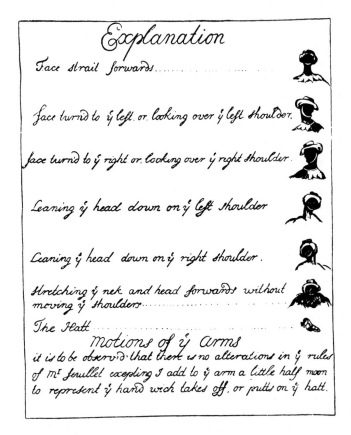

8 Head, neck and shoulder positions for the mask of Arlecchino illustrating *A Chacoon for Harlequin* by F. le Rousseau, dancing master, 1735.

to be quick, like the pecks of a ground-feeding bird, but training should prepare for such movements, not consist of them. The capacity for extension (both forward and back), torsion (to both sides) and tilting all need to be improved before working in the mask.

A technique which can then be practised in the mask is to stand centre behind a post and, keeping the body vertical, incline the neck to one side, tilting the head to retain the eyes in a horizontal plane; a lot of the action in Commedia is spied on by other characters and this is the correct gaze with which to do it. From the very beginning, Commedia mask work should include a sense of the spectator. The Masks live in the eye of the beholder, not of the actor. Mirror work is therefore prohibited since it leads to self-consciousness. In working the mask for the spectator (in practice it is useful if this is a co-worker with whom you can swap tasks, since you can learn as much from observing the mask and commenting as you can from wearing it yourself), develop a concept of the 'little mask': this means that one eye and the nose should always be visible: less than that and the mask dies for the spectator. This needs to be taken into account especially when making an exit or working with an upstage focus.

The masks are monochrome, thus avoiding any attempt at naturalistic, expressionistic or indicative painting in order to suggest character. This is another reason why leather is the only appropriate material: anything else seems to need painting in order to make it come alive and in doing so the maker is placed immediately in the realm of individual aesthetic choice rather than traditional form. Different masks are now associated with different colours, black or red (Hell), or green or brown (peasant, rural, earth colours). But originally the likelihood is that they were all a natural light tan colour and became blackened through being used in bright sunlight.

The masks inherited from Carnival were full-face, and initially experiments were made with hinging the jaw in order to allow speech, but this makeshift was soon abandoned in favour of the half-mask. As a result the lower face has to be trained to adopt a limited expressive range incorporating the same sculptural volumes as those afforded by the mask. The mouth and jawline are usually treated in some way, either by make-up or, as in the case of Arlecchino, winding black material round from the top of the head.

The actor's hands should never touch the mask because they are the only uncostumed, unmade-up part of the body in Commedia. Even the Lovers, though not masked, are exaggeratedly made up. The natural should not come into contact with the grotesque, the polychromatic with the monochrome.

> For a start, the mask imposes a particular obligation: it cannot be touched. Once you lay a hand on that thing drawn over your face, it vanishes, or appears contaminated or nauseating. Seeing hands on a mask is damaging and unbearable.[12]

Once this taboo is observed, the position of the hands in relation to the gaze of the mask is crucial and the planes and articulations to be used vary from Mask to Mask and have to be learned as part of the apprenticeship to each. But the hands are not the starting point but the finish of an articulation which begins in the centre of gravity; this, for all except the Lovers, is contained within the pelvic girdle, and controls the movements of the legs and feet as well as the arms and hands. The gaze of the mask is connected to the gut, through the respiratory process, not to the brain via the optic nerve.

 # The rediscovery of the mask

In 1948 in Padua, Amleto Sartori, in discussion with Jacques Lecoq and Gianfranco de Padoue about masks, decided to try to reconstruct the techniques of making leather ones. Leather had not been used since the 1700s, since Goldoni's abandonment of the mask, in fact. It was partly due to his efforts that the use of the mask in the theatre declined, although it became fashionable to wear them in the street, especially in Venice (and not just at Carnival time). But those incognito masks of street and ball were made of silk and other precious fabrics, with golden threads and pearls sewn into the edges, as ostentatiously ornate as the rich people who wore them. After over a year of research, Sartori's only result 'was a frail, inexact notion of the book-binding technique used in Venice in the first half of the Cinquecento'.[13]

Three years later, in 1952, Lecoq went to Milan to found the School of the Piccolo Teatro: 'It was in a café near the theatre one sunny day, under the shade of the stone canopy, that I introduced Sartori to Strehler and we talked about the masks that he had made so far.'[14]

The Piccolo had already performed the first version of *Arlecchino servitore di due padroni* (*The Servant of Two Masters*). Strehler recalls:

> The actors . . . played in pathetic masks made of gauze and painted cardboard. We made them ourselves. They were infernal, awkward, unhappy things. The contours quickly bit into your flesh and visibility was relative and obscured. Fastened, as they were, straight on to the face, with a primitive system of elastic, without any suppleness, the masks did not permit the eyelids to move. The eyelashes of the actor brushed against the edges and made the eyes weep continuously.
>
> The actors, each on their own personal initiative, began to pad them with peculiar pieces of wadding held on with sticking plaster. Thus the inside of the mask began to take on an altogether

poetic quality. Then, as they were worn, the sweat of the actors penetrated the cardboard and made the glue melt.

By the end of the play we were holding in our hands a few little black sweat-soaked patches which would not regain their shape until the next day. There was also the personal drama of the actors who could not 'feel it' in such a mask.[15]

Marcello Moretti, as Arlecchino, had ended up playing without the mask, painting his face black, since he was onstage a lot and in continuous movement. But it was not just that he could not wear the mask; he would not

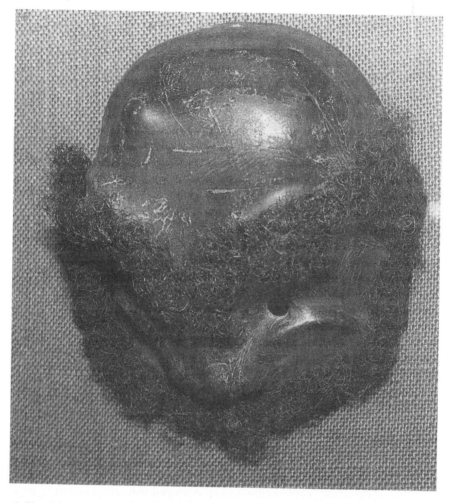

9 The Arlecchino mask in the Musée de l'Opéra on which Strehler and Sartori based their first experiment.

because he felt that he lost expressiveness rather than gained it. To try to convince him that physiognomical expression was unnecessary to the character, Strehler took him to Bologna to meet a very old actor, the last in a line of generations of Arlecchinos, only to discover that even he had played without the mask.

Sartori now offered to attempt to make proper leather Commedia half-masks. Lecoq remembers

> accompanying him to the Museum of the Opera in Paris to look at the ancient mask of Zanni. We looked at it closely to see how it was constructed. Shortly afterwards the first mask of Arlecchino took shape. We tried putting it on and making it live, but in vain. It did not work. The glass exhibition case had not succeeded in keeping it alive. I still keep that mask at home, hanging on the wall of my studio, which is a sad fate for a mask. A mask can be technically well-made, beautiful to look at, but impossible to work in.[16]

By the time *The Servant of Two Masters* was brought back into the Piccolo's repertoire later in 1952, the masks were made of leather. An eyewitness to the process had been Amleto Sartori's son, Donato:

> I was still very young when I began to follow the theatrical adventures of Arlecchino. . . . My father had to do a plaster cast of Moretti's face in order to construct the mask. The following scene, as spirited as it was funny, ensued: Marcello was lying supine on a model's bench while my father poured quick-setting plaster over his face as was the usual procedure. All of a sudden Moretti began shouting and jumped up sputtering plaster all over. He had had a sudden attack of claustrophobia. We all just stood there in amazement. And so that was the beginning of my father's relationship with Moretti.[17]

When the first masks were given to the actors to try, 'They were still heavy and quite rigid, but they were made of a fundamental substance: leather. The material was now no longer hostile to the face of the actor.'[18]

As soon as they saw these masks in the rehearsal room, the actors, including Moretti, began to be convinced. But the eye-holes were too small for him. In rehearsal, the tiny field of vision afforded by the traditional small round eyes of the Arlecchino mask led to another attack of nerves:

> It happened when Marcello was practising yet another dangerous acrobatic leap. My father was, as usual, in the stalls, taking notes and sketching ideas as he followed the rehearsal. Marcello felt his

concentration suffocated by the narrow space the mask left for the eyes, and was continually making jerky movements in order to see where he would end up, just as the original Arlecchino was meant to do. He was very ill at ease and soon lost his patience. Without saying a word he took off the mask and enlarged the eye-holes with a large pair of scissors that were lying on the stage. Then he put the mask back on and was calmly about to begin practising the leap again when my father, who had witnessed the whole scene, incredulous and without the breath to utter a sound, let out an enormous yell, calling Moretti a madman. The incident did lead to a happy conclusion: the cat-like Arlecchino was born. The eyeholes became wider and elongated giving the face a feline expression which Moretti's sleek agility effectively confirmed.[19]

This mask was later to change as the production itself developed over the years.

> Sartori's theory on the subject of Arlecchino was that you could have a mask of a 'cat' type, a 'fox' type or, a 'bull' type (useful definitions for fundamental mask expressions); this engrossed Marcello like a child. He wanted his first mask to be of the 'cat' type since 'cats are more agile'. . . .
> So Marcello covered his face for the first time, with a brown mask of the 'cat' type, only to then pass on to the 'fox' and finally (his triumph) to a fundamental type of primitive Zanni, softened naturally by the rhythm and style of Goldoni's *The Servant of Two Masters.*[20]

In fact the 'cat' mask is Truffaldino, an Arlecchino derivant who did not appear until 1620 and did not become fashionable until the Italians' enforced return from Paris. By the time of Moretti's death, then, his character had regressed to

> Arlecchino in his full vigour, obscene, violent, charlatan . . . the archaic Zanni, the servant-buffoon, a character that still has its roots visibly in the humus from which he originates. The mask representing him openly wears the signs of his malice. Aggressive expressions of shrewdness and spite, with prominent cheekbones, a thick bumpy forehead, and heavy eyebrows. It's covered with warts, atrophied vestiges of antique cuckold horns [another possible derivation of the wart, but, I would have thought, more pertinent to Pantalone]. The eye is almost lost, small and cavernous in the compact mass, a tiny opening dug into the darkness of the character's animality. Because it limits his visual field, the

actor is forced to make abrupt, monkey-like movements before jumping or grasping.[21]

When the show was over, the actors to begin with continued their former practice of throwing the masks into the wings in order to take their bow. Gradually, unprompted by Strehler, they found ways of holding on to them or pushing them up: Sartori's masks were never again found on the floor, always in pride of place on the prop table.

Making a leather Commedia mask

In the appendix I offer some notes on how to make a leather mask; although the Sartori secret is out (the information given here is being used by many mask-makers these days), the reader should not assume that a successful product can be arrived at merely by following these suggestions, which are based on our own experience at Exeter University Drama Department and on the work of Françoise Malaval in France.[22] Learning this craft is a long process and, for anyone not already skilled in woodcarving, even longer. If you or your institution need immediate access to masks which work, then you will need to contact a mask-maker. If you want, either as an apprentice or as a purchaser, to go to the source, then Donato Sartori is continuing and developing his father's vocation at the Centro Maschere e Stutture Gestuale in Abano, near Padua. These notes offer, then, a basis on which to begin an apprenticeship, in the same way that those which follow in the next chapter offer the elements of technique necessary for playing the Masks which the masks become when worn. At a minimum level they at least reveal enough of the craft for the actor to be able to understand and respect the processes involved. It is, perhaps, worth quoting Charles Dullin on the need for such respect since, regrettably, it does not always seem to be instinctual:

> A mask has its own life. . . . Nothing annoys me more than to see a student leap upon it like a draper's assistant grabbing a carnival mask. I feel that he commits a sacrilegious act, for in fact the mask has a sacred character. It summons a public of initiates – not the crowd which seldom regards it as anything but an instrument of buffoonery; nor schoolmen who exploit it for academic purposes, wanting to go backward, to restore vanished forms. . . . The use of the mask in the modern theatre must be made from the whole cloth. It lays down conditions for a dramaturgy that has yet to find its poet.[23]

Playing Commedia

The inspirational actor is content to rely exclusively on his own mood. He refuses to bend his will to the discipline of technique. The inspirational actor proudly claims to have rekindled the flame of improvisation in the theatre. In his naïveté he imagines that his improvisations have something in common with the improvisations of traditional Italian comedy. He does not realise the improvisations of commedia dell'arte have a firm basis of faultless technique. The inspirational actor totally rejects technique of any kind. 'Technique hinders creative freedom' is what he always says.[1]

MEYERHOLD

Staging

I write 'playing' rather than 'acting' advisedly. If *commedia dell'arte* were a game it would be an outdoor one. As soon as a few basic skills in acting a Mask have been acquired, I suggest you send it out into the fresh air to play with its friends. The primal energies of Commedia can successfully be released into the nocturnal, darkened rooms we call theatres, but only after their potential has been fully developed in the full light of day. In the end, or rather the beginning, the only way to learn to play Commedia is to go outside, put on a mask, stand on a box and give it a try. Many of an actor's normal preoccupations will immediately be found to be irrelevant. The need to develop further technique becomes real rather than academic. Even if you are only playing in a park to two drunks, a barking dog and a small child who has lost its parents you will learn more about the necessary scale and clarity, immediacy and impetus of Commedia from fifteen minutes of 'having a go' than from fifteen days of self-doubt in a rehearsal room. Further training and practice are then obviously essential, but one learns not to undertake the kind of over-specific rehearsal which is inhibiting to spontaneity and liable to create a false text which will let you down in performance.

To play outdoors you will need, apart from masks, costumes and props, at least a mountebank-style platform and a curtain from behind which to enter. Already there are decisions to be made: how wide, how deep and

10 Detail of *The Fair at Impruneta* by Jacques Callot. Although a mountebank rather than a Commedia performance, the amount of infrastructure afforded the platform, unusually here seen from behind, is typical of all such illustrations.

how high? For the inexperienced it is far better for the acting area to be too small than too large: in a limited space the Masks have to relate to each other visually and make meaningful compositions, and they will also be able to sustain *tempi* more readily. Width is more useful than depth: it takes a lot of experience to work a mask (with its narrow field of vision) for the audience, at the same time as relating to someone playing some distance behind you. It is also easier to create an illusion of space on a crowded stage than to create a crowd from a handful of characters in the middle of indeterminate space.

The platforms of the piazzas and the fairgrounds were high by today's standards: the public were used to being on their feet all day and were quite happy to stand to watch the show. Stages needed to be raised accordingly almost head-high so as to provide overhead sightlines and attract 'walk past' spectators. One surmises that this also gave the actors some security from interference. I have, however, yet to see a period engraving which gives more than a token suggestion of the trestle structure necessary to raise a platform to such a height: if the actual carpentry was so flimsy, the actors' personal safety cannot have been very great.

In erecting platforms today you can usually assume that the spectators will be seated, either on the ground or on chairs. The playing surface can then be as low as 2 feet high, although a metre is preferable. The placing of the platform within the playing space is crucial, not only in terms of the visual actor/spectator relationship (don't forget that the sun must be in your eyes, not the audience's), but also the auditory one. It is invaluable to be able to bounce your voice off a wall or a building behind the spectators, even if it is some distance away. Incidentally, nobody ever speaks in a low voice in *commedia dell'arte*, except for stage whispering when called for by the scenario. If you use wooden rostra you will soon discover another basic law: Commedia is played with extreme lightness of foot – it is virtually an aerial form since nothing kills comedy more than the booming and clonking of feet on planks or rostrum lids.

As to the curtain: it needs to be about 7 feet high (enough to provide a background to all but the most elevated action, but not too high for appearances 'above' on a set of steps). It should preferably have a centre opening, and a useful sophistication is to have slits at head height for Masks to poke through in order to spy on the action. Some kind of offstage, out-of-sight area is needed behind, and one of the simplest ways of providing this is to have the curtain carry round in a rectangle. The front curtain should be less wide than the stage in order to allow for exits to be made round the ends. When exiting it is best practice to go beyond the end of the curtain and then turn onstage, taking the gaze of the mask via the audience, before going off behind. This will feel artificial at first but reads perfectly well to the spectator, whereas showing the back of your head betrays the mask.

When playing outdoors even the slightest breeze will turn the curtain into a sail, no matter how much chain you put into the bottom hem. For this reason you need at least 50 per cent fullness, lining and even inter-lining. Resist the temptation to fasten the bottom edge down, however: it only leads to disaster. It is much better to let the material be lively and play with it rather than against it.

The basic locus of *commedia dell'arte* is a street, with either side of the stage conventionally representing a house, usually Pantalone's to one side and Il Dottore's to the other; in indoor theatres these become set-pieces with a downstairs door and an upstairs window. When playing outdoors, use simply the ends of the curtain and one or two pairs of steps behind, enabling characters (usually the female Lovers) to appear above. The change to an interior setting can be indicated by the addition of a chair or stool.

The scenario

After a platform and a back curtain you need a scenario, literally 'that which is on the scenery', i.e. pinned up backstage. All it consists of is a plot summary, the bare bones of who does what when. The most readily available scenarios in English are Flaminio Scala's *Il teatro delle favole rappresentative*,[2] but they have been dressed up as literary creations and are too baroque for contemporary performers to attempt whole. Start with something plainer. For example, here is the first act of a scenario by Basilio Locatelli, *A Play within a Play*:

> *Pantalone and Arlecchino.* Pantalone says that he intends to give his daughter Sylvia in marriage; Pulcinella has asked for her hand and he wants her to accept.
>
> *Pulcinella*, from the house. He overhears that Pantalone is disposed to give him Sylvia for a wife. *Lazzi.* They come to an agreement on the dowry. Pulcinella calls
>
> *Sylvia*, from the house. She realises that she will be given in marriage to Pulcinella. She refuses. *Lazzi.* Finally, by dint of threats, Sylvia gives way and touches Pulcinella's hand. Sylvia, rebellious, re-enters the house. Pulcinella says he will go to the office for the marriage contract and will await Pantalone there; he leaves. Pantalone tells Arlecchino to go and warn the comedians and tell the relatives that a comedy will be played and everyone will make merry. Arlecchino goes on his way; so does Pantalone.
>
> *Flavio*, from the street. He says that, in order to see Sylvia whom he loves, he has left Padua University, where he was sent by his father. Knocking.
>
> *Sylvia*, from the house. She recognises Flavio, who is incognito, having changed his name since leaving Padua. He is wearing a false beard. Sylvia is in despair because Pantalone, her father, wishes to give her in marriage to Pulcinella. Flavio sorrowfully tells her to be of good heart and he will try to upset all the arrangements. He leaves. Sylvia goes back into the house.
>
> *Pantalone*, entering from the street, says that the marriage contract has been drawn up and that Pulcinella wants the wedding to be very soon. Enter
>
> *Arlecchino* and *Il Capitano*, from the street. Arlecchino tells Pantalone that he has informed all the relatives and that he has brought with him the leader of the comedians, Il Capitano. Pantalone asks him what part he plays. Il Capitano says that he

plays the part of the Lover. Pantalone laughs at this, saying: 'Look at this ugly mug who plays the Lover!' In the end they agree to play a comedy for 10 scudi; Pantalone gives him a deposit on the price. Il Capitano says he will call his companions, and leaves. Pantalone has all the preparations made and the seats arranged in the open. He says he is looking forward to it. All enter the house.

Pulcinella, from the street. He is filled with joy about the wedding and the festivities. He says he would like his daughter Franceschina to enjoy the wedding. He knocks.

Franceschina, from the house. She has heard that her father, Pulcinella, wants to take a wife without first finding her a husband and wants her to attend the wedding and the comedy.

Pantalone, *Sylvia*, and *Arlecchino*, from the house. Pantalone embraces his future son-in-law, Pulcinella, and they make merry. Sylvia, against her will, receives them. Then they sit down, having understood from Arlecchino that the comedians are now ready.

Il Dottore then enters from the street, having come to listen to the comedy. They welcome him and he sits down. After which

Flavio enters from the street and sits himself near the others to hear the comedy. Orders are given for the comedy to begin. Enter

The Prologue, spoken by *Pedrolino*. After some music has been played, he calls for silence, because a comedy will be played *all'improvviso*. Enter

Oratio. He speaks of his love for Isabella, daughter of Il Capitano. He says that he wants to ask her father for her hand in marriage. He knocks.

Il Capitano, from the house, having overheard everything Oratio has said, comes to an agreement with him about the marriage. At this, Sylvia drops a glove.

Flavio immediately runs to pick it up. He kisses it and hands it back to Sylvia. Pulcinella rises, telling Flavio that he will have to settle accounts with him. There is much noise and confusion; everyone runs away, some by the street, others into the houses.

Although not numbered, the scenes are 'French', that is to say separated by changes of personnel onstage. The lay-out is such that an actor can easily see what action he or she is involved in. But there can be quite a panicky queue round the scenario, so I recommend writing down your personal through line for your Mask separately and keeping it handy somewhere else. Domenico Biancolelli (known as Dominique), the Arlequin of the Italian troupe in Paris between 1662 and 1680, seems to have done just that. Here are a couple of examples of his performance notes:

In this scene I call Diamantine and beg her pardon, I say that someone wants to kill me, that she must hide me and that I will tell her all, she says she will shut me in the flour bin, I agree and tell her that I don't want to get in there because if the old cook finds me covered in flour she will take me for a sole and try to fry me.[3]

And:

I arrive on stage. I find Trivelin there on the ground, and thinking him dead I try to pull him to his feet, dropping my wooden sword, which he seizes and uses on my buttocks. I turn without a word, and he gives me a kick in the back and I fall over, get up, pick him up, carry him, and prop him against the right cantonade. I turn away to the footlights, during which time he gets up and sets himself against the left cantonade. This *lazzo* is repeated two or three times.[4]

He includes his own action for each play in the troupe's repertoire, as well as that of other characters onstage at the same time. Sometimes he includes dialogue indications, occasionally whole sections of duologue. There are often insertions at the end of an entry, probably successful additions from later performances. Similarly there is one suggestion of *lazzi* to replace others which have not worked. He is not interested in plot, presumably because he knew he could get that from the scenario.

Scenario, like *commedia dell'arte*, is in fact a term which came into use late in the development of the form; earlier names were *canovaccio*, *centone*, *soggetto*, even *commedia*. *Canovaccio* (that which is on the canvas) is the word used by Antonio Fava to mean a short single plot sequence, rather than a three-act structure with sub-plots, and this can be a helpful distinction. For a group starting out it is far better to play a series of unrelated *canovacci* than attempt a full scenario.

The *canovaccio* is a simple synopsis, a technical indication of scenic content, a list of characters and the action to be accomplished by them, perhaps together with some hints about argument and dialogue. Examples are given for most of the major Masks in Part II of this book. A *canovaccio* can be driven by one of three desires: love, money or vengeance, whereas a scenario, if one accepts the working distinction, often includes all three in complications of plot and sub-plot.

In a full scenario, which almost invariably has three acts (among the hundreds of extant scenarios, there are only a handful of five-acters), there needs to be a proposition, a development and a solution within each act, within each scene of each act, and even within its composite dialogues, monologues, *lazzi*, *burle*, *concetti*, etc. Again an analogy can be made with

Japanese Noh which operates throughout on the principle known as 'Jo, Ha and Kyu', terms which can be roughly translated as Introduction, Exposition and Denouement.

> These three sections move at an ever-increasing pace and form the basic dramatic, rhythmic, and melodic basis of the Noh. A more literal translation might be 'introduction' (jo), 'breaking' (ha), and 'rapid' (kyu), suggesting some of these performance elements.[5]

A workable *commedia dell'arte* scenario structure for performance today might, then, look something like this:

ACT I

Prologue. Traditionally prologues had little to do with the actual entertainment, but were stock introductions by one of the characters, often Pantalone, Il Dottore or Colombina (see pp. 131–2). Sometimes they might be given by a minor character who would not appear in the action itself. For a present-day audience it might be better to have an introduction to all the characters (see Part III, The San Francisco Mime Troupe) or a company song setting the atmosphere and possibly the theme of the piece.

Exposition of events so far: an optional scene played out by the characters as background to the story.

First scene in the present – establishing a simple, uncomplicated normality.

First complications introduced and leading to a cliffhanger – ending on a reaction of surprise and despair.

ACT II

Résumé of first act, possibly as a musical interlude.

Continuation of a series of complications, each building on the other, with attempted solutions breeding even greater problems. And all with increasing tempo.

ACT III

Take up all complications so far and add more.

Another résumé (perhaps a monologue delivered by Il Dottore).

Extreme consequences of complications are reached: a solution is imminent.

The solution – the revelation and unmasking of any disguised characters.

Finale – a joyous celebration, forgiveness all round, possibly after a ritual beating or other comeuppance for Il Capitano or Pantalone.

The whole to last no more than two hours, including intervals which should be musical. Act I should take no more than thirty minutes. The résumés are important: you have to educate a modern audience in the conventions of Commedia at the same time as playing to them. Don't try to be funny all the time! The progress of a good scenario is from the physical to the metaphysical and back again.

As regards content, you may find arranged marriages, masters beating servants, the ridiculing of old age, attempted sexual harassment and other stocks-in-trade of the Renaissance aversive to contemporary sensibilities. By all means look for today's equivalents, and obviously the ones you find will depend to an extent on the political and social standpoint of your troupe – but be careful not to throw Mr Punch out with the baby's bathwater.

Non-improvised elements

The amount of improvisation to be done in performance can be over-estimated: all the exits, entrances etc. are fixed by the scenario and used to be gone through beforehand by the choregos or actor-manager (Italian *corago*).

> The *corago*, the leader or the *maestro*, the one most capable of instructing others, should rehearse the *soggetto* before it is performed so that the actors are familiar with the content of the play, know where to conclude their speeches, and can explore in rehearsal some new witticism or new *lazzo*. The person in charge of the rehearsal does not restrict himself to just reading the scenario, but explains the names and qualities of the characters, the argument of the play, the location of the action, the stage houses, the distribution of the *lazzi* and all the necessary details, taking care of the props required for the play, like letters, purses, daggers and such like, as listed at the end of the scenario.[6]

Furthermore, the stock-in-trade of each Mask remained the same from one piece to the next, consisting of individual *lazzi* (sight-gags), *burle* (byplay between characters), *battute* (stock repartees) and *concetti* (stock rhetorical passages). Even seemingly improvised dialogue would be more an extemporisation, using known structures or *meccanismi*. Monologues were also stock, taken from the *repertorio* or *zibaldone* (gag-book) kept by the actor for each Mask.

In order to act properly in improvisations, therefore, it is necessary to observe all the rules laid down for written plays. For in this respect neither form of acting is different in the theatre – neither in costume, voice, pronunciation, memory, gestures or acting. All that is necessary is that there be some preparations for acting with greater facility and measure, so that the improvisation conform as much as possible to a well-rehearsed performance.[7]

A modern practitioner, Carlo Mazzone-Clementi, suggests that changes of level are the key to not getting lost:

To perform *commedia* properly you must also have a concept of the levels of *commedia* style. *Andare a soggetto*, to go with the subject, is to accept a basic premise and, with your team, create in, around, over, under and through it. *Commedia a braccia*, indicates that the physical activity is measurable 'at arm's length'; in other words that the actors adapt their movements and positions precisely but spontaneously. . . . *Commedia all'improvviso* or 'all of a sudden' means just that: anything goes (or comes!).[8]

And another level comes from the *aparte* (asides) through which a continuous channel is kept open between some Masks and the audience.

The performance elements which are not to be done 'suddenly', i.e. improvised on the spot, need careful preparation, but not full-scale rehearsal. I recommend 'marking', i.e. going through the motions, but without performance energy, carrying the mask rather than wearing it, *sotto voce* rehearsals, or even armchair run-throughs where the stating of intentions replaces acting them out – anything, in fact, rather than full-scale repetition of the scenario as if it were a text. The elements need to be kept separate until they are brought together in live performance.

It was further necessary that [you] should stock [your] mind with what the actors called the *dote* of a play and with a repertory of what they called *generici*. The *dote* or dowry of a comedy consisted of soliloquies, narratives, dissertations, and studied passages of rhetoric, which were not left to improvisation. These existed in manuscript, or were composed for the occasion. They had to be used at decisive points of the action, and formed fixed pegs on which to hang the dialogue. The *generici* or common-places were sententious maxims, descriptions, outpourings of emotion, humorous and fanciful diatribes, declarations of passion, love-laments, ravings, reproaches, declamatory outbursts, which could be employed *ad libitum* whenever the situation rendered them appropriate. Each mask had its own stock of common topics, suited to the personage who used them. A consummate artist displayed his ability by improving on these, introducing fresh points and features, and adapting them to his own conception of the part.[9]

These prepared sequences, whatever terms a company may agree to call them by, and whether or not they are stock or have been specially invented for a particular scenario, need to be led up to and away from in performance in such a way that the audience do not notice that they have been preprepared.

 *Lazzi*

Such seamlessness is not needed, however, in the playing of *lazzi*, which are inspired by the action but do not further it. *Lazzi*, according to a doubtful etymology, comes from the Tuscan word *lacci*, 'tied', because these tricks are supposed to have tied the action together. Rather they are insertions, most useful when the action is flagging. But the word can also mean 'ribbons', in which case they could be seen as being superfluous but decorative additions. Perhaps the most useful concept implied in this derivation is the idea of tying your shoelaces: you stop what you are doing for a brief moment to do something physical at which long practice has given you skill.

> We give the name of *lazzi* to those sallies and bits of byplay with which Arlecchino and the other Masks interrupt a scene in progress – it may be by demonstrations of astonishment or fright, or humorous extravagances alien to the matter in hand – after which, however, the action has to be renewed upon its previous lines. In sum they are bits of uselessness which consist only in comic business invented by the actor according to personal genius.[10]

Lazzi and other flights of fancy should thus always return to their starting point, from which the action then continues as if nothing had happened. However, once an idea has been introduced it can never be worked at a lesser level or dropped without coming to fulfilment – if you start such an interruption, you must finish it, even if the audience are not laughing. The same goes for the introduction of extraneous objects (see p. 62). This is not easy for the person who is being interrupted, who needs to be ready to take the focus back, but not until the byplay is finished.

In fact in performing Commedia, readiness is all: you must be constantly prepared not only to interrupt and be interrupted, but also to be called on even when you are not onstage and you think the scenario is offering you a break. Anyone who is called onstage *must come at once*, and as many times as necessary; for example a master calls for Zanni, sends him off, then keeps stopping him and bringing him back for a further demand or to check that he has remembered the message right.

Being on the *qui vive* all the time can lead to hyperactivity in the inexperienced:

> There are in fact two pitfalls that must be avoided – too little ardour, or too much. Some players who are very conscientious, but sadly inhibited, keep to the letter of their part, and throw themselves into it so little that they freeze their protagonist. Others are so impulsive and so uncontrolled that they come on to the stage in a sort of frenzy, and while as soloists they are superlative and often extremely original, they are the despair of their fellow players. For example, they throw that which is needed in the following scene through the window and off the stage in a transport of folly: they carry off the armchair into which the heroine must shortly sink in a swoon; they drink with great gusto the potion that was to be swallowed as a poison by another character, while the unhappy actor who was working up into a wonderful death scene looks everywhere for it with increasing anxiety, and sees himself reduced to cracking his skull against the wall, if he doesn't happen to be wearing a dagger in that scene. The perfect player is he who can give himself up to the excitement of his role without forgetting the least detail, and without ceasing to be aware of what the others are doing or saying, in order to provoke the cue that he needs. He must at one and the same time be the ecstatic character of the comedy and the tranquil actor who watches and guides him.[11]

Improvisation

Suggestions as to practice improvisations for each Mask are given in Part II. The amateur actors at Nohant, starting as they did from scratch, made the kind of mistakes that it is helpful to be warned of:

> The strange thing is that, when you begin to improvise, far from having nothing to say, you find yourself overflowing with

dialogue and make scenes last too long as a result. The hidden danger in this genre is to sacrifice the development of the basic idea to incidents which stem from it. You must also be very alert, in order not to have several characters speaking at the same time, to the possibility of having to sacrifice what you were going to say as a result of something your partner has said, and also to revitalise the action when you sense him flagging; to bring the scene back to its objective when the others are wandering off the point and to stick to it yourself when your imagination is trying to persuade you to go off into dream-land. In spite of our good intentions, it happened more than once that the voice of those actors who had left the stage and become spectators would bring us to order, shouting 'get back to the scenario'. It was like a bucket of cold water being poured over your head, but we'd promised to obey it, so we obeyed it.[12]

The constant quest in improvisation is for form, not content. The wine is no problem: it is the skin to put it in which is needed if the audience are to be able to drink it. To change the metaphor, a foundation, once established, needs building on, not swapping for another. In fact the audience will not be satisfied until you have reached the chimney pot. As soon as you find a rhythm, a mechanism which works between your Mask and another one, don't lose it: it is more important to develop the form than it is to avoid speaking rubbish. In fact gobbledygook can be extremely useful. In Commedia it is called *grummelot*.

 # Grummelot

Dario Fo uses this technique a lot, though he calls it *grammelot*:

> *Grammelot* is a term of French origin, coined by Commedia players, and the word itself is devoid of meaning. It refers to a babel of sounds which, nonetheless, manage to convey the sense of a speech. *Grammelot* means the onomatopoeic flow of a speech, articulated without rhyme or reason, but capable of transmitting with the aid of particular gestures, rhythms and sounds, an entire rounded speech.[13]

Fo probably learned of it from Jacques Lecoq who certainly got it from Jean Dasté who had used it with the Copiaus (the touring troupe which emerged from Jacques Copeau's Vieux Colombier School), which called it *grummelot*. At that school it formed the basis of the second phase of improvisation training (the first being the miming of simple dramatic actions). Instead of adding text, Michel Saint-Denis recalls, they then used 'grummelots which gave – I really mean *gave* – the music of the meaning. The characters were merely indicated; one could recognise the fat woman, the trollop and the shrew, but that was all.'[14]

The technique was originally developed through necessity by the Italian players at the end of the seventeenth century, when they were banished from the Parisian theatres to the fairground booths. Since spoken dialogue was prohibited except on the legitimate stage, they were obliged to turn to oratorio, placards, scrolls and *grummelots*.

In training, once some of the basic physicality of a mask has been discovered, it will naturally want to make sounds, often quite babyish, before words become appropriate. The discovery of a vocal centre, the exploration of its sonority, and the correct mouth shape in relation to the half-mask through which to issue it, should all be developed before the use of actual words. The use of *grummelot* in terms of a country or region of origin can then be a useful next step, throwing in more and more words as the mask develops its particular vocabulary. This is a stage which can then be reverted to in later improvisation when at a loss for words, and which can even have a positive comedic effect when the going gets hectic in performance.

 # Concerted playing

Ensemble work is crucial to the success of a Commedia performance because the very best improviser can only play as well as partners can respond. A chain is only as strong as its weakest link.

> The Commedia actor never works alone. His virtuoso excursions must never proceed from his own ego. There must be a constant awareness of the whole. He must know and understand his partners, balancing and contrasting them, working together with such sensitivity and unity that we are caught up in their game before we know what has happened. Nonsense is more important than sense. . . . Trust and confidence, based on real, existing skills and knowledge of one another, must be present in a Commedia company. You are literally all in it together.[15]

I call this concerted playing after the English concert parties and Pierrot shows of the inter-war years, who used the term to indicate a style of playing with the full company onstage, and also for its musical connotations. In fact a Commedia troupe are almost never all onstage together, except at the end, but nevertheless a sense of collective playfulness and mutual support is necessary throughout and should communicate itself as an atmosphere to the spectator. There is no room on a Commedia platform for a selfish performer:

> Whoever refers to 'a good actor of the Comédie Italienne' is identifying a player with a personality of his own, one who depends more on the strength of his imagination than on his memory, and one who composes what he performs even as he delivers it; one who knows how to adjust to the player he acts with; one who can, that is, so perfectly marry his own words and actions to the words and actions of his colleague, that he can blend with the action of his companions and react as required, making all believe that his acting was premeditated.[16]

A good exercise in concerted playing is for a flea to make its way round the company: those laughing at the misery of others soon become afflicted themselves, while all have to keep a single, tiny but highly volatile focus. Eventually it starts to breed, leading to an orgy of frenzied scratching.

 Music

It would be strange if an Italian performance genre did not have musicality: in fact it is best not to think of Commedia as being action and dialogue with interposed songs and musical interludes, but as being inherently musical and constantly on the brink of tipping over into operetta. Most of the *zanni* can carry instruments and they should use them to provide an underlying score rather than for punctuation, though they can communicate directly through them rather as Harpo Marx does with his parphorn.

Properties

Props could be toured by strolling players, whereas settings could not. Actors would therefore be very familiar with the stock they had in their basket and with the comedic potential of each object. These were called *robe per la commedia*, and a typical list of requirements for a scenario reads

> A soldier's helmet
> Sword and buckler for Burratino
> A bucket with water
> A chamber-pot with white wine in it
> A club
> A lady's cloak for Pantalone.[17]

Indeed one way of creating the basis for a scenario is to improvise around some typical props. Ladders, letters, lanterns, syringes for enemas, boxes of jewels, goblets, rings and all kinds of disguising costumes might also be called for. Or the requirements could be simply

> A sign for the inn
> A large travelling bag
> A packet of letters.[18]

Such props should be as authentic as possible, not token or stagy. Objects should only be mimed in *commedia dell'arte* when speculating or fantasising – for example what would happen if Arlecchino were to hang himself, in which case he can mime the rope being thrown over a branch. Never work with the uncontrollable – for example balls or animals, which are likely to create their own chaos.

The stock characters

These are the subject of Part II of this book. It is difficult to find the right single expression for them: they are sometimes called Masks, sometimes Types, and so on. The critical point is that they are more stock than they are characters, cartoon figures, but by no means all drawn by the same artist. Mazzone-Clementi again:

> One can begin with the stock characters. Actually, I prefer the phrase 'comic prototype'. In *commedia* there are three levels of characterisation that build to the level of this comic prototype. The *caricati* are basically caricatures (the lovers etc.). They wear no masks and are essentially a part of the landscape. The *macchietta*, or 'little spot' (e.g. the funny messenger) is the equivalent of our

modern 'cameo' role. Then there are the pivotal roles known as *maschere*. . . . The rules of professional etiquette for these characters are clearly defined in a manner much like burlesque. A *caricato* is not entitled to get big laughs. The *macchietta* has a bit more freedom to 'warm the audience up'.[19]

And other divisions are possible, the hierarchical, for example. How should one list them and in what order? My approach has been to take a basic set needed for playing a full scenario, in rough chronological order of introduction into the *commedia dell'arte*: therefore *zanni* are discussed first, Colombina last. Characters not necessary to the set I have chosen are grouped under 'other types': this does not mean they are necessarily less important, but that if used they would normally displace one of the basic set. If you allow this to happen, beware – some of them are egocentric loners and can have a disruptive effect.

The headings within each work sheet are, I hope, self-explanatory.

Part II

The stock characters

The *zanni*

> Each character is the representative of a social class which, by the act of theatre, becomes the magical incarnation of all its class.[1]

> CARLO BOSO

Zanni

Name. Zanni is both singular and plural, the Venetian diminutive of Giovanni. It can be both a generic name, referring to all *zanni* or the name of an actual Mask when the character is not defined further as being Arlecchino, Brighella, Pedrolino, etc. In the sixteenth century it was also shortened to Zan as a prefix to further identification: Zan Paolo, Zan Ganasso, etc. In Italian, it is simply the name given to any unnamed character, a person whose actual identity you cannot be bothered to discover. I was once acquainted with a man who had the patronising habit of calling all non-Caucasians 'George'. My own name suffers the same utility, so I am familiar with such familiarity: 'All right, John!' However, by way of compensation, *zanni* also gives us 'zany' in English.

Status. Bottom of the pecking order. Zanni is that regrettably eternal unfortunate, the dispossessed immigrant worker.

Origin. A Bergamase peasant up from the country (Giovanni was the most common name in the mountains of the Valle Orobia) seeking to earn a living portering and odd-jobbing in the towns of northern Italy. When Bergamo was conquered by Venice, famine set in in the countryside, since the peasantry were not able to price their wares competitively: the markets were flooded with cheap imports based on slave labour from Greece, Turkey and the Middle East. Between them the two major city states of Venice and Genoa literally swallowed everything. 'Gnawing at the hinterland they killed off the indigenous markets. For tens of thousands this meant poverty and starvation. Behind [*zanni*] stands the terrible reality of a population uprooted and crushed.'[2] For many, migration to the very cities which had caused the disaster was the only option.

Garzoni described these migrant would-be workers as

> coarse fellows, simple and good natured enough, who come down from the mountains of Bergamo to fetch and carry for the rest of mankind. . . . They hawk food and wines about the city, the poorest are basket-weavers and others carry coals [and] they ply for errands in the square with sacks slung over their shoulders. . . . Nimble as cats they jump into the boat, throw out your cases, parcels, packages, and bundles and carry them off on their shoulders to the other end of the city.

And for ladies, he reported that they 'do their errands with their particular sweethearts'. 'As a mountain race,' he continues,

> the *facchini* [literally 'carriers of bundles', hence 'porters'] are as tough as timber, but not bulky, the sturdiest people you ever saw, and except for a few who have become lean with hardship, they are as round as the bottom of a barrel and as fat as the broth of macaroni. . . . Their dress is utterly uncivilised, and you can smell their sacking miles away. Their speech is so grotesque that the *zanni* who are like magpies to mimic a pronunciation or any other characteristic have adopted it in their comedies to entertain the crowd.[3]

Costume. Baggy, white, originally made of flour sacks.

Mask. Originates in the full-face Carnival mask parodying a *facchino*, but, with the development of the short plays known as *Zannata*, with improvised dialogue between Pantalone and various *zanni*, the bottom had to be hinged [see Plate 7] and was finally cut away altogether. As with other Commedia characters, the longer Zanni's nose, the more stupid he is.

Props. Temporary custodian of anything (especially bags, letters, valuables, food, etc.) that belongs to someone else.

Stance. Has a lowered centre of gravity; either because he comes from

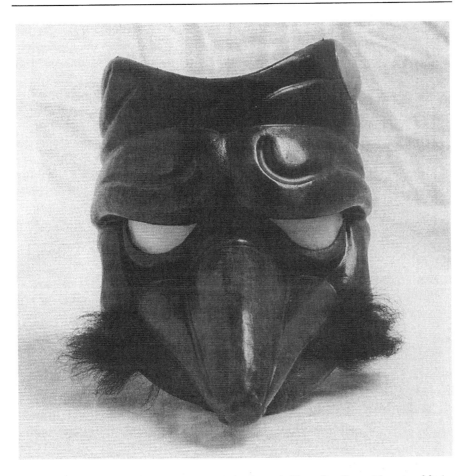

11 'Grande Zanni', long-nosed Zanni mask by Antonio Fava. Leather with natural hair. (See also illustration 30.)

the earth, or as a result of carrying heavy bags and sedan chairs. Zanni stands with an arched back, with his knees bent and apart and his feet splayed. The support knee is bent with the other leg extended, toe pointed. He changes feet repeatedly while talking or listening within the same position and without his head bobbing up and down. The elbows are bent and the arms half lifted. Vertical sleeping is done standing on one bent leg with the other foot crossed over to the knee. The support side arm crosses the waist to support the other elbow, the arm of which goes vertically up so the palm can provide a prop for the nodding head.

Walks.

1. Little Zanni walk: this is a development of the basic stance, foot-changing but taking a small step forward on each shift. The shoulders

down, elbows forward, feet pointed. The knees come high off the ground and to the side. Use a two-time rhythm in even beats with the head pecking like a chicken, but still without bobbing up and down. Zanni uses this walk when going somewhere, but with no great purpose.

2. Big Zanni walk: a curved lumbar is first achieved by sticking chest forward and the backside up (this is very demanding to sustain and should be complemented by a forward spinal release when out of character). With the feet in fourth extended, bend the support knee and lower the centre of gravity. Raise the front foot and turn the sole in, pointing the toes. The arms curve, alternately front and back, and make a scything motion when walking, with the hands also curving to meet the opposite foot. This walk is purposeful: for example slowly trying to cross the stage without being noticed or quickly escaping the consequences of an action without drawing attention to it.

3. Zanni running: a swift movement with legs kicked alternately to the front with pointed toes. Arms move with opposite legs.

4. Zanni jubilant: a skipping movement on the toes with centre of gravity shifting from side to side. Rest hands on belt, which is roughly at hip level. Head able to move independently, as always.

5. Vain Zanni: steps are a smaller version of the big walk, hands again resting on the belt. When the leg lifts, the chest is thrust forward and the arms brought back in chicken strut. Used when he has a new button or a feather in his cap.

6. Soldier Zanni: hold a stick cupped in one hand and inclined over shoulder like a rifle. In the march, shoulders move up and down in two-time but the feet do three beats. 'Trampety-tramp, trampety-tramp, tramp, tramp, tramp. . . .'

Movements. Dynamic, exaggerated, the head constantly moving independent of body. The quicker-thinking *zanni* are more agile and their shorter noses permit them to do acrobatics.

Gestures. Zanni's actions are always urgent. He appears nervous, talks a lot, his head moves constantly. The nose defines the rhythm of his body since it is the centre of his actions. The hands are very expressive and constantly used to illustrate what he is saying. All Zanni's bodily functions instantly and loudly make themselves known. He often sleeps by alternate farting and snoring. Sometimes his body becomes completely alien to him and different parts of it take on their own animation in order to act out an imaginary situation.

Speech. Loud, open-mouthed: the coarsened voice of a someone who makes an outdoor living by making themselves heard in a market or a busy street.

Characteristics. His survival instinct is strongest of all the Commedia archetypes. He suffers from the spasms of an ancestral hunger which is his basic, everyday condition; he is, as a result, insatiable, but capable of being spiritedly ironical about his plight. This great hunger leads to a vision of Utopia where *everything* is comestible, reminiscent of the followers of glut-tony in Carnival processions. His pre-Christian, animistic view of the world means he senses a spirit in everything: therefore it *could* be eaten. Hunger is a universal problem and, comedically at least, is capable of a universal solution. Zanni is ignorant and loutish, and has no self-awareness. The very act of thinking is alien to him – the very sight of Zanni straining to give birth to an idea is risible. But he is astute in knavery; a loafer, but willing and able to dish out heavy thwacks with his slapstick; intolerant of discipline and authority, but very faithful. He lives totally in the present: he never, for example, looks for somewhere to sleep, sleep just happens to him, often in totally unsuitable situations. All his reactions are emotional.

Relationships. A scenario must have two *zanni* (at least): the first is foxy and astute, the second more *stultus* – an ox, beast type, (*il furbo* and *il stupido*), but this distinction should not be absolute. Between them they might make up one person of less than average intelligence, in 60/40 pro-portions. Total cleverness is not funny, neither is total mental disability. Zanni often has the function of being addressed, particularly by Il Capitano, in order to prevent monologue. He is everyone's 'gofer'. The *facchini* were greatly disliked by the Venetians, but Zanni has frequent dialogues with Pantalone in a symbiosis of status and temperament.

Relationship to audience. He has the possibility of direct, four-square address to the audience, because he is the most sympathetic character. He treats the audience collectively.

Plot function. The principal contributor to any confusion.

Improvisation exercises

Enter, walk across stage, freeze on hearing 'Zanni' called. Standing on either foot, turn either in or outwards to face the other way and exit entrance-side using a different walk in response to the call. For example, enter slowly in the first walk, sad because of rejection from Colombina. She calls: freeze, register that you are forgiven, turn and exit using the fourth walk.

   Zanni, like *Pulcinella*, can be multiple rather than singular, a tribe rather than an individual. A group of *zanni* wake with cock crow. Hunger. They contemplate eating themselves, each other, the audience, anything – then realise that it is a cock that has woken them.

Zanni get the call to clear up the room – the master's coming! Flights of fancy are preferable to doing chores and chaos ensues (or this could be an exercise for Arlecchino on his own).

School for *zanni* – one teaches another how to pick pockets, etc. An exercise in precision in creating an imaginary situation.

Repertorio

'It is not easy to draw the line between the episodic "burle" and the more elaborate "lazzi" which stand to the Zanni instead of the speeches and conceits in the commonplace books of the other masks.'[4] It is not easy, either, to suggest a list of *lazzi* on which to base a *zanni repertorio*. Mel Gordon's book *Lazzi, the Comic Routines of the Commedia dell'arte* which attempts to catalogue all known sources, may give some authentic glimpses to the informed reader, but it is dull reading – hardly what you want when setting out to develop a personal store of funny business. I recommend watching Keaton, Laurel and Hardy, the Marx Brothers and Peter Sellers. It is significant that Hollywood employed Keaton as a gag writer in his declining years as a performer, gags being seen in the studios as being as separate from a screenplay as *lazzi* from a scenario.

Canovaccio

It would be misleading to give a *canovaccio* for Zanni since, although he features in everyone else's plots, his is, by definition, not a leading role.

Sample dialogue

The impoverished Zanni and his supposedly prosperous but tight-fisted master are the fundamental symbiotic relationship from which all others in Commedia grew. Pantalone is too mean to employ a better servant and Zanni has too much vitality to be oppressed by his lack of status. Within moments of the master/servant relationship being invoked, the roles have been reversed and instead of giving Zanni orders, Pantalone is begging him for his help:

> *Pantalone*: Come a little closer, my dear Zanni, I want to talk to you
>   about something, but you mustn't speak a word of it to anyone.
> *Zanni*: All right, boss, I won't say a word to anyone.
> *Pantalone*: I want you to know that I'm in love.
> *Zanni*: Love?
> *Pantalone*: Yes, love.
> *Zanni*: You, love! Ha! ha! ha!
> *Pantalone*: Why are you laughing, you donkey?
> *Zanni*: I'm laughing at you because you say that you're in love.

Pantalone: And why not? Don't I have a fine lover's physique?

Zanni: Yes, boss, a fine pig squeak.

Pantalone: You are a clot. I'm in love and the woman I love faints at the very sight of my handsome personage.

Zanni: And how do you know she loves you?

Pantalone: I know, because when she is at her balcony, I look at her and she looks at me. I smile at her, she smiles at me, I lick my lips at her, she licks her lips at me. What more do you want?

Zanni: She's making a monkey of you, boss!

Pantalone: You're the monkey.

Zanni: But who is this woman?

Pantalone: She lives here, that's her balcony. Ssh!

Zanni: Boss, you're dead and buried.

Pantalone: And why am I dead and buried?

Zanni: Because this woman has seven brothers who'd chop up a mountain as quick as a bale of straw.

Pantalone: But what have they got to do with me? They may already know about it!

Zanni: Boss, you're on the edge of a very dangerous precipice.

Pantalone: Zanni, you must help me.

Zanni: What do you want me to do?

Pantalone: I want you to go to her house, speak to her about me and take her this sonnet that I have made up for love of her.

Zanni: You want me to be the patsy? No way, boss. I don't want to get beaten up!

Pantalone: Zanni, I want you to earn yourself a sovereign.

Zanni: A sovereign?

Pantalone: A gold sovereign.

Zanni: Ah, right. *(He lies down and falls asleep)*

Pantalone: Zanni, wake up you animal and come here.

Zanni (rising): At your service, boss, as always.

Pantalone: Dear Zanni, take the sonnet.

Zanni: Give me the sovereign first.

Pantalone: I will give it to you.

Zanni: Where is it, then?

Pantalone: It's there.

Zanni: Show it to me.

Pantalone: There it is.

(Zanni tries to snatch the coin but Pantalone grabs it back at the last moment)

Zanni: Shit!

Pantalone: It's yours.

Zanni: How can it be mine since you've got it?

Pantalone: Trust me, my dear Zanni; take the sonnet and I will give it to you.

Zanni: Don't tell me your stories, boss, cheerio.

Pantalone: Where are you going?

Zanni: I'm just going.

Pantalone: Come here.

Zanni: I've got things to do.

Pantalone: Here's the sovereign.

(They repeat the previous business)

Zanni: Shit again.

Pantalone: It's yours, Zanni!

Zanni: Where?

Pantalone: Here!

Zanni: Where?

Pantalone: Here, but you must take the sonnet nicely. *(Gives it to him)*

Zanni: Right, boss, give me the sovereign and leave me to it.

Pantalone: Here is the sovereign.

Zanni: And here is the sonnet. *(Gives it to him and goes off)*

Pantalone: You're forgetting something.

Zanni (coming back): Ah, the sonnet. *(Takes it and pretends to read it)* You didn't write this.

Pantalone: Yes I did, with divine inspiration.

Zanni: With swine perspiration?

Pantalone: In true love of her.

Zanni: In blue rubber fur?

Pantalone: Zanni! Take the sonnet or give me back the sovereign.

Zanni: I'm going, I'm going.

Pantalone: Hey . . .!

Zanni: Yes.

Pantalone: Zanni, tell her I'm deeply in love.

Zanni: Deeply in love. I'm on my way.

Pantalone: Hey . . .!

Zanni: Yes, boss?

Pantalone: Deeply – in – love.

Zanni: I understand. I'm on my way.

Pantalone: Hey . . .!

Zanni: Whaaaaat?

Pantalone: Deee . . . *(He goes out)*

Zanni: . . . pleee in love.

(Zanni knocks on the door of Fiorinetta, the courtesan. She offers him a chicken, a sausage and a fish. He wraps the fish in the sonnet. Then she invites him in. Enter PANTALONE*)*

Pantalone: Zanni, Zanni! Where is the cretin. I've been waiting hours for a reply, and everyone knows how hard it is to wait:

especially where love is concerned.
(Zanni comes out of Fiorinetta's house completely drunk, singing)
Zanni: Show me the way to go home . . .
Pantalone: There he is, the reprobate.
Zanni: . . . I'm tired and I wanna go to bed.
Pantalone: Good heavens above, what is he singing?
Zanni: Uh oh, here's the boss.
Pantalone: Damn your hide! Where have you been all this time?
Zanni: I was over there.
Pantalone: Where, over there?
Zanni: With your beloved. Good news!
Pantalone: Reassure me, Zanni.
Zanni: I spoke to her with a lot of er . . . , come!
Pantalone: What?
Zanni: Er, come.
Pantalone: What?
Zanni: Accomplishment.
Pantalone: Ah, good!
Zanni: She listened to me with a lot of cont . . .
Pantalone: What?
Zanni: A lot of cont . . .
Pantalone: What?
Zanni: A lot of contentment.
Pantalone: This is killing me. But what did she say about me?
Zanni: She is very nice, absolutely charming!
Pantalone: I want to know what she said about me!
Zanni: She gave me a chicken.
Pantalone: What am I supposed to do with a chicken? *(Takes it and throws it into the wings)* Did you give her the sonnet?
Zanni: She gave me a sausage.
Pantalone: What am I supposed to do with a sausage? *(Takes it and throws it off)* Did you give her the sonnet?
Zanni: The sonnet? Good news!
Pantalone: Good news? You're going to tell me what she said about me.
Zanni: About you?
Pantalone: About me!
Zanni: About me? About you?
Pantalone: Yes, between you and me, what did she say?
Zanni: Between you and me, nothing.
Pantalone: What, she didn't say anything?
Zanni: No!
Pantalone: You gave her the sonnet?
Zanni: Oh, boss, I forgot.

Pantalone: But what did you do with it?
Zanni: Here it is.
(*Pantalone takes the sonnet and sees the fish inside*)
Pantalone: What on earth is that?
Zanni: It's lovely fish that I bought for my boss's birthday.
Pantalone: You've ruined everything!
Zanni: It's not too bad, you can scrape the sonnet clean with a knife.
Pantalone: Maybe, but that won't take the smell away.
Zanni: Yes, fish does smell rather!
Pantalone: Get back in the house. Get back in the house. You've
    ruined everything.
(*Zanni runs off, pursued by Pantalone*)[5]

Arlecchino

Name. Has an enduring, magical power, a testimony perhaps to the mystery of its origin. Theories include extreme suggestions, for example that he takes his name from a water-bird with irregular patches of diverse colour called 'harle' or 'herle'. But in Italian 'ino' is a diminutive and all Arlecchino's younger brothers have a similar ending to their name: Fritellino (= 'little brother' – *fratello* + *ino*); Trivellino (= 'little agile one'); Truffaldino (= 'little trougher' or 'truffler'), so it is likely his name means simply Hellecchino (= 'little devil'). Dante refers to a devil by the name of Ellechino.

Status. Servant, usually to Pantalone, but also frequently Il Capitano or Il Dottore. Second *zanni* if Brighella or Pasquariello is in the company, otherwise first. The later the piece, the more major the role: he has a minor function in Flaminio Scala's collection of scenarios, *Il teatro delle favole rappresentative* (1611), but is a central figure in Goldoni's Commedia-based plays written in the first half of the eighteenth century.

Origin. Probably created in France in the late sixteenth century by Tristano Martinelli from Mantua, a member of the Raccolti troupe. He seems to have crossed Zanni with a medieval figure from the French popular tradition, a kind of wild man covered in leaves.

Costume. A tight-fitting long jacket and trousers, sewn over with random, odd-shaped patches of green, yellow, red and brown – possibly remnants of the leaves mentioned above. The jacket is laced down the front with a thong and caught by a black belt worn very low on the hips. The shoes are flat and black. He wears a black beret or, later, a malleable felt hat with a narrow brim, with a feather or the tail of a fox, hare or rabbit fastened to it. Originally worn by some Bergamese peasants, apparently this was a sign of the wearer being a butt of ridicule. There is a sentimental French story of Arlequin's friends giving him the off-cuts from their *mardi gras* costumes for the poor boy to make one of his own, but the Italian Arlecchino has patches which are sewn on, rather than the sewn-together lozenges of the later French Arlequin and English Harlequin. A shape-shifter: he frequently adopts disguises and cross-dresses without demur.

Mask. A black stocking wound round the lower face and then up over the head is a vestige of the full Carnival mask, lending credence to the alternative African slave suggestion as to his origin. Low forehead with wart, small round eyes. The derivant Truffaldino has a less rounded mask, and longer, almond-shaped eyes. Martinelli is thought to have played him without a mask, in blackface with red and white squiggles.

Props. Always carries his *batocchio*, meaning in Italian 'clapper inside the bell', but also having an associated meaning which in English would come out as 'bats in the belfry'. The literal English etymology is 'bat' from the French *batte*, the usual translation, 'slapstick'. As a comedic device the *batocchio* was derived from the Bergamese peasant stick used for driving cattle. Two thin pieces of wood are kept apart at the handle and slap against each other when a blow is stopped at the moment of impact. It is stuck through the belt worn low on the hips. This belt often also has a pouch for carrying bits and pieces. In Antonio Fava's opinion, the bat *is* Arlecchino: he never puts it down, not even when somersaulting. It is a phallic symbol, but without menace – which is also true of its use as a weapon, usually against Pantalone, though often the tables are turned and it is Arlecchino who finds himself on the receiving end.

Stance. Continuously lowered position, caused originally by carrying bags or sedan chairs, leads to lordosis (excessive lumbar curvature). Yet this increased gravitational pull is compensated by an irrepressible upward energy in the torso: Caliban and Ariel united in the same body. The feet are in fourth extended, but always flat on the floor. Elbows are bent, arms in a jug-handle position, or hands on hips with thumb in belt.

Walk. All the Zanni walks, but more balletic in execution. In addition he has a three-time walk with little tiptoe steps. Begin with the left foot forward with the ball of the right coming to meet the heel of the left after which the left slides forward. The right foot then steps forward into the opposite starting position. There are thus four stages, although the walk is in three time.

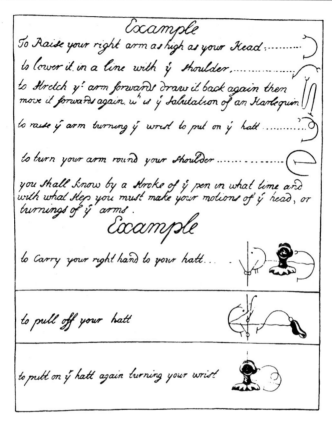

Example

To Raise your right arm as high as your Head ....

to lower it in a line with ỹ shoulder, ...

to stretch yͬ arm forwards draw it back again then
move it forwards again. wͨ is ỹ salutation of an Harlequin

to raise ỹ arm turning ỹ wrist to put on ỹ hatt ....

to turn your arm round your shoulder ....

you shall know by a stroke of ỹ pen in what time and
with what step you must make your motions of ỹ head, or
turnings of ỹ arms .

Example

to Carry your right hand to your hatt...

to pull off your hatt

to pull on ỹ hatt again turning your wrist

12 F. le Roussau's instructions for Arlecchino taking off and putting on his hat.

This is *not* waltz time, but even, i.e. one, two, three, not *one*-two-three. This walk shows alacrity; he also uses it to show off in front of Colombina. In the extended grand Zanni walk, the arms and legs circle as if in a mysterious cloak (which they often are!).

Movements. When Arlecchino spots someone or something, the mask moves first; he then hops round and into the gesture of greeting or whatever.

Gestures. He is quick physically and slow mentally, in contrast with Pulcinella and Brighella (who can, however, be fast physically when he needs to be). Gestures extend to the fingertips with each digit having a separate articulation; they should be developed to *imbroglio*, then clearly resolved. Arlecchino always describes precisely, both in word and gesture, even, in fact especially, when extemporising or fabricating. See Plate 12 for use of hat.

Speech. Guttural, Bergamese dialect, hoarse from street hawking. No pauses or silences for the sake of effect – he either speaks (continuously) or doesn't (silence).

Characteristics. Never pathetic, always *knows*: he is never the loser. Never just does something. For example, if, in the heat of the moment, his slapstick gets left on the ground, he somersaults to pick it up again. His paradox is that of having a dull mind in an agile body. Since, however, his body does not recognise the inadequacy of the mind which drives it, he is never short of a solution: the fact that he cannot read, for example, does not hinder him from divulging the contents of a letter. As developed into the French Arlequin in the mid-seventeenth century by Domenico Biancolelli (Dominique), he became more quick-witted. But even then he could only entertain one idea at a time, and never contemplated the consequences of an action or learned from the experience of it. He responds to everything – hunger, love, danger – in a way that is taken to apocalyptic proportions and then forgotten entirely – until the next time. A very Latin temperament . . . but never malicious. He is very likely to become disguised later in the action, for example as a priest in order to conduct a mock wedding, or as a Turk, a pilgrim, a rich benefactor, or cross-dressed in order to fulfil a rendezvous.

Animal. Cat/monkey, sometimes a fox.

Relationships. In love with Colombina, but his sexual appetite is immediate in terms of any passing woman (cf. Harpo Marx).

Relationship to audience. Occasionally aware they are there and can make asides during which he gives his full attention to the spectators before returning to complete absorption in the action.

Plot function. Distinguished from Zanni by having enough intelligence to hatch schemes, although they rarely work out as planned. But he is basically reactive rather than proactive. Complications of plot often derive from his mistakes or his refusal to admit shortcomings, illiteracy for example. He is possibly the world's worst messenger because something is bound to happen along the way which will be of more interest than delivering the message.

Improvisation exercises

Intention to commit suicide because Colombina no longer loves him. Makes to hang himself, but is afraid of heights. Pretends to tear himself to pieces which he eats, then realises how hungry he is and goes in search of food. As a variation, pretends Colombina is within earshot: 'I'm killing myself, now . . . I really am doing it.' Perhaps ends by frightening himself to death (faints).

The bored sentry who hears a bird (in fact he whistles himself) and pretends to become a hunter.

Repertorio

Lazzo of eating imaginary cherries and throwing pips with deadly accuracy.

Lay the tablecloth by jumping on the table, pulling the cloth over and then wriggling out from underneath.

Brains are knocked out by a blow from Pulcinella: immediately sets to and eats them with ceremony and gusto, then discovers he is even more stupid than before.

Taken short onstage, removes hat and uses it as a chamber pot, chucking the results into the audience.

Canovaccio

The street: PANTALONE instructs ARLECCHINO to guard his door and not let Colombina out. Exit PANTALONE – he is going to the fair. ARLECCHINO falls asleep (standing up). Enter COLOMBINA with a broom, sobbing; she crosses the stage and, pretending not to see Arlecchino, knocks him over. Exits other side. Returns, immediately, still crying, knocks him over again just as he is standing up. Exits and enters a third time – this time he cowers. She sees him, stops crying, and asks why he is crouching. He asks why she is crying. She says Pantalone won't allow her to go to the fair – she has to stay in and clean the house. Between sobs she lists all her favourite fairground amusements. To cheer her up, ARLECCHINO imitates them all (acrobats, rides, menageries, magicians, toffee apples, etc.). But she cries again each time and soon ARLECCHINO is sobbing in sympathy.

Sample monologue

> Ah, I'm so wretched! The Doctor is going to marry Colombina off to a farmer, and I'll have to live without her! No, I'd rather die! Oh, you stupid Doctor! Oh, you fickle Colombina! Oh, you naughty farmer! Oh you very unhappy Arlecchino! Let's make it a quick death. It will be written in ancient and modern History that Arlecchino died for love of Colombina. I will go to my room; I'll fix a rope to the ceiling, I'll kick the chair away, and there I'll be: hung. *(Mimes being a dangling corpse)* That's that, then, nothing can stop me, off we go to the gallows . . . *(Changes voice)* To the gallows? Don't be silly, mate, you mustn't even think of it. Killing

yourself over a woman, that would be a very silly thing to do . . .
Yes, Sir, but when a woman betrays an honest man, that's a
terrible, wicked thing . . . Indeed: but when you're hung, will you
be any the better off for it? . . . No, I'll be worse off for it . . . But I
want to be well off, I do: what have you got to say to that? . . . If
you want to share the benefits, you only need to come along . . .
Thanks, but no thanks; but you won't go anyway . . . Oh yes, I'm
going to go . . . Oh no, you won't . . . I'm going, I tell you. *(He takes
out his slapstick and hits himself with it)* Ah, that's got rid of the pest.
Now there's no-one to stop us, let's nip off and hang ourselves.
(He makes as if to go off, then stops suddenly) But, no. Hanging
oneself is a very commonplace sort of death, it wouldn't be
appropriate for someone like me. I need to find a more unusual
death, a more heroic death, a more Harlequinistic death. *(Goes into
a reverie)* I've got it. I'll block up my mouth and my nose, the air
won't be able to get out, and so I'll die. No sooner said than done.
*(He holds his mouth with one hand and his nose with the other and stays
in this position for some time)* No, that's no flaming good, the air's
coming out my bottom. Dear me, what a lot of trouble dying is!
(To the audience) Excuse me, if anyone would care to die so's I can
see how to do it, I'd be most obliged . . . Ah, blow me down, I've
got it. I've read somewhere that people have died laughing. If I
could die laughing, that would be a funny death. I'm very ticklish;
if someone tickled me long enough, then I would die laughing. I'll
tickle myself and then I'll die.

　　*(He tickles himself, starts laughing and falls on the floor. Pasquariello
arrives, finds him and thinks he is drunk. He calls his name, brings him
round, consoles him and carries him off.)*[6]

Sample dialogue

Although a written play, in French, of the late seventeenth century, this dialogue has many 'ur' sixteenth-century characteristics.

　　Arlecchino (shouting drunkenly into the wings): Don't give me that,
　　　　you stupid riffraff, I am not a drunkard. True enough, I have
　　　　been drinking; but when I get drunk it's not through dissolute-
　　　　ness, it's through habit. It's natural to have habits, and that
　　　　which comes from nature must be good: so, I am not to blame: if
　　　　I am drunk, it's because it's in my nature, and you're a stupid lot
　　　　of riffraff. And, anyway, why should one not refresh oneself? This
　　　　heat is intolerable. It's never been so hot. Like wearing a fur coat

while you're sitting in a frying pan. And then when winter starts we'll all freeze instead. But I don't care: I'm taking my medicine now to cool me down, and I'll take it then to warm me up. *(Sees Ottavio)* Ah, hah! There you are!

Ottavio (in a rage): At last you have arrived.

Arlecchino: A very nice boy, my life, very nice indeed.

Ottavio: What, you bounder!

Arlecchino: Very nice, I said, very nice. Two hours I've been waiting for you. Oh yes, very nice. Punctual, by heck, on the dot.

Ottavio: And where did you wait for me, since I've been here the last hour?

Arlecchino: Ah, very good! You've been here? Well then, stay here, I don't mind.

Ottavio: But didn't I say to you: 'Wait for me there with the food'?

Arlecchino: Yes, that's where I waited for you: there.

Ottavio: But where?

Arlecchino: In the bar.

Ottavio: Did I say in the bar, did I?

Arlecchino: No, but everyone has his own preferences. You like to wait in streets, I like to wait in bars.

Ottavio: Never mind, let's get to the point. Where's the food?

Arlecchino: It's here.

Ottavio: Where? I don't see it. Where's the basket?

Arlecchino: The basket? It's in the bar.

Ottavio: Give me patience! What, the food is here, but the basket is in the bar?

Arlecchino: Yes, Sir.

Ottavio: Let me see it then, now.

Arlecchino: It'll be a couple of hours before I can show it to you.

Ottavio: This is killing me! In two hours, you wretch! What about Angelica . . .

Arlecchino: Angelica can see it too, if she wants to, but no sooner.

Ottavio: But why not? Where have you put it?

Arlecchino: It's just that I've eaten it, and I'll have to digest it first. When I realised you weren't coming I was worried the cold meats might go off in the heat and . . .

Ottavio: What, those two roast chickens . . .

Arlecchino: I ate them.

Ottavio: And the six ortolans . . .

Arlecchino: Very good, those were: good grub!

Ottavio: And the six partridge . . .

Arlecchino: Six partridge? *(Goes into a reverie)* Ah, yes, yes, six partridge. I ate them: all six.

Ottavio: Heavens, no! And the whole ham?

Arlecchino: Oh, as for the whole ham ... that gave me quite a problem; I thought I'd never finish it, I was full to bursting.

Ottavio: Did you ever a see a more brazen scoundrel? You'll pay for this.

Arlecchino: There's thanks if you like! Blow me, boss, isn't it me who should be complaining? You get up a picnic for twelve people. Not one shows up. For fear that the meat might go off, I eat it for you, risking bursting my sides, and this is all the thanks I get? Tut-tut! Very naughty.

Ottavio: The cheek of the man! What about the rest? Where's the wine?

Arlecchino: Where's the wine? What a question? In your opinion, should good food be eaten without wine?

Ottavio: What? The six bottles of champagne?

Arlecchino: Them? I drank them first.

Ottavio: And the six bottles of burgundy?

Arlecchino: Without them, I'd never have finished the ham.

Ottavio: And the six bottles of port ...

Arlecchino: Oh, as for them, I drank them to help my digestion.

Ottavio: And the liqueurs?

Arlecchino: All gone. Thanks to your faithful Arlecchino! Because in the middle of all that good cheer, I didn't forget to cheer my master. Every new glassful I toasted the health of my worthy master Ottavio; my most esteemed master Ottavio; my most honoured master Ottavio; every good wish to my master Ottavio; my ...

Ottavio: Go to the Devil, and take your memories with you. *(Aside)* Let's keep our temper, at least until he's done the business that I thought up earlier. Very well, let's forget the food and come back to the matter in hand. You know what I said to you? Do you remember what it was, and can you carry it out?

Arlecchino: Leave it to me, I remember everything, and the meal that I've just eaten has really given me the stomach for it; don't you worry about a thing.

Ottavio: We must be ready for everything. Unless I'm very much mistaken, Angelica has arrived.

Arlecchino: Angelica has arrived? Blimey, that means Colombina will be with her. *(He takes his clothes off)* She will see me completely naked, the beauty of my body, the ... *(He places his clothes on the ground)* Look after my clothes, Sir.

Ottavio: The cheek of it! My patience is exhausted!

Arlecchino: Please look after them. They are yours, and if anyone takes them I won't be held responsible. *(He prepares to dive into the water)*[7]

Brighella

Name. According to Giacomo Oreglia his full name is Brighella Cavicchio from Val Brembana. 'Brighella from *briga* (trouble), *brigare* (to intrigue or wrangle) and also *imbrogliare* (to deceive, shuffle, confuse); *Cavicchio* or *cavillo* (quibble, pretext, chicane) because of his ability to find a solution for every difficulty.'[8]

Status. Whenever he appears he is always first *zanni* – he's the boss. In the social scale only a little boss, the keeper of an inn or the proprietor of a shop, but in the Commedia world, the very fact that he has managed to better himself to that extent gives him high status. Brighella can instruct someone of higher status than himself, for example he could teach a lover how to break into another lover's house in secret. In the dramatic situation he may, however, be required to rediscover the role of a mere Zanni, but will bring an extra dimension to it. More than a servant, he is thus a jack-of-all-trades who can be a recruiting sergeant, a hangman, a fortune-teller or anything that's required of him. He is never a victim and always maintains his status. In the late seventeenth and eighteenth centuries his status went down again and the role of Brighella became that of a mere valet.

Origin. From Val Brembana in Bergamo. Or he originates in the upper city of Bergamo itself whose inhabitants were supposed to be craftier and quicker in the uptake than those of the lower city (from where the second *zanni* originates). Others argue that he has a north African or Turkish derivation. He also may be the charlatan with assumed mysterious powers enhanced by sleight-of-hand.

Costume. White jacket and full trousers with green braid frogging down the side. White cap/hat with green border. 'The green and white uniform that I wear means: white because I have carte blanche to do or undo whatever I like; green, because I can always keep the desires of my clients green with the many tricks of my devising.' Belt with purse and dagger.

Mask.

> The bizarre, half-cynical, half-mawkish expression of his olive-tinted mask, once seen, is never forgotten. It is distinguished by a pair of sloe eyes, a hook nose, thick and sensual lips, a brutal chin bristling with a sparse beard and finally the moustache of a fop, thick and twirled up at the ends in such a fashion as to give him an offensive, swaggering air.[9]

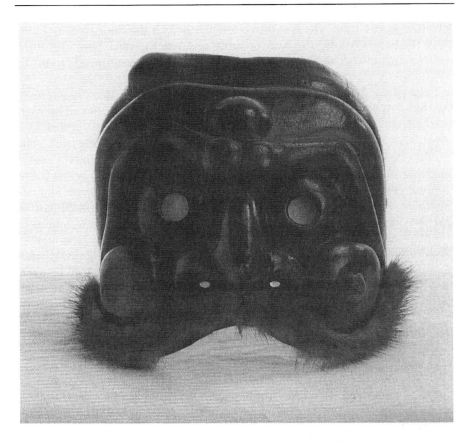

13 Brighella mask by Antonio Fava. Leather with animal hair moustache.

Fava's mask for him has larger, round eyes. He considers that 'There is something very human about his appearance. He first appears as a positive character, but underneath changes and he becomes devilish, mysterious and dishonest looking.' Goldoni, certain that he comes from Bergamo, said 'his swarthy mask is a caricature of the colour of the inhabitants of those high mountains, tanned by the heat of the sun'.[10]

Props. Apart from his dagger and mandolin/guitar, the props will change according to trade in any particular scenario – e.g. a napkin for a waiter.

Stance. Flat feet, ballet first position, knees slightly bent, belly forward. Or stand with weight on bent leg with the other extended, straight but flexible. The elbows up, the shoulders relaxed. Hands and fingers slightly spread. As with all *zanni*, the head is independent and can move in any direction at any time. The feet move constantly as if the floor were red hot. Place the hands behind the back or bring one arm forward, bent as if for a waiter's napkin. The lumbar curvature is less pronounced than in Arlecchino.

Walk. Brighella has all the *zanni* walks plus a characteristic one of his own in which the torso bends from side to side, but the head stays vertical. Use small steps with the shoulder going down as the hip goes up, i.e. a concertina effect of the shoulders and knees. The knees are thus obliged to open outwards in the step. The elbows bend to the same side as the knees (he is the only character in Commedia to walk so). The waist and hips move first, the shoulder and knee follow. Finally, the hands operate as if flicking flies from the knees.

Movements. Lithe, cat-like, without apparent muscular effort. Insinuates himself into nooks and corners and seems to disappear. Perfect balance comes from manoeuvring in tight situations with a tray held overhead on the fingers of one hand.

Speech. Melodious. Speaks his own special blend of Bergamese and Tuscan.

Animal. According to Dario Fo, half dog, half chicken. I think of him as a lazy cat combined with a rat. But he is less bestial than other *zanni*.

Relationships. None that are not exploitative, indiscriminately so. Will sell you his sister: his only redeeming feature is that he does not *have* a sister, but you won't find that out until it is too late to get your money back. He can even be Zanni's employer and profit from his labours – the mountebank and his assistant again.

Relationship to audience. Cynical.

Plot function.

His job is to guide the action of the comedy, to stir it up with intrigues and to give it movement. Therefore Brighella is indefatigable in weaving complicated intrigues; he breaks up some marriages and arranges others, insinuates suspicions, flatters vanity, prepares talismans, the philosopher's stone, the magnetic poultice, love potions . . .'[11]

Characteristics. Astute, ready (for anything), humorous, quick-witted: he is capable of intrigue, deceit, making a mockery of the entire world with his mordant, salacious wit. He likes a good time but is also a criminal. Despite his devilish origin, though, he is amoral rather than evil. He appears relaxed and calm with lateral movements behind the action until his schemes begin to hot up when he reverts to the urgency of Zanni. He is an observer, an amateur psychologist, a sometimes professional spy. Ingenious, making the most of every occasion. Cynical, a past master of cunning and deceit. Unscrupulous, always ready for a trick. Pitiless, never repenting of his crimes. Crafty, bold, a habitual liar who looks out only for himself. He thrives on quarrels, intrigues, secrets. Strong and lithe as a panther. Has flair and *savoir-faire*. Is always explicit about his own character.

> Brighella is always on hand if there is any intrigue afoot, or secret to be laid bare, or debauch to be organised, or dagger to be planted between the shoulders of a political rival; but it is best never to pay him until his work has been done and verified, for he owns not the slightest instinct of professional honour.[12]

Like Zanni he is always hungry and thirsty, but much more likely than his fellow servant to get food and drink through trickery or theft. Will go to enormous lengths just for one titbit.

As with food, will do anything to make money. However, the moment he has some he stops work and spends it on self-indulgence until it is all gone.

Attitude to women very similar to food, drink and money. Very persuasive and has a rakish attraction, especially as he sings, dances and plays the mandolin.

Improvisation exercises

Arlecchino has a rendezvous with Colombina. He has a present for her – a cake or a sweet. Brighella passes by and sees him. They greet as friends. Gradually, by pointing out a number of improbable symptoms, Brighella makes Arlecchino believe he is dead and therefore does not need the cake any more. (After he has gone Colombina enters and has the task of persuading Arlecchino that he is not dead any more.)

Brighella as head waiter in a busy restaurant, issuing orders to other waiters (*zanni*), staying imperturbable amidst chaos, rowing in the kitchen with the chef (Pulcinella), emerging to be all sweetness and light to an important customer (Pantalone).

Brighella instructs Arlecchino and Zanni in the art of picking pockets. They are very poor pupils, but because Brighella cannot lose status he must eventually succeed.

Repertorio

'Never mind if the house burns down so long as the flames keep me warm.'

On old age: 'Over and above the five normal senses, old men have another three: a sense of coughing, a sense of prattling and a sense of griping.'

'What's my age? I'm forty-seven years, six months, two weeks, four days, six hours and twenty-five minutes old.'

'My wife may be small, but at least that means there's nothing left over for anyone else.'

'No-one has ever complained about my work.' 'What is your job?' 'I'm a coffin-maker.'

On natural children: 'Banned books, published without licence from the censors.'

'A man who likes to keep a woman's company should grow his own lettuce, that way he doesn't have to go to market for it.'

'Keep it sweet: you can catch more flies with a spoonful of honey than a barrel of vinegar.'

'You can't disguise love, it's like a hole in a black stocking.'

'A man who talks to himself is like a mosquito in a bottle.'

'Don't be frightened of death, there's a wonderful contract you can make. When we're here, he isn't. When he's here, we're gone. That's how to avoid unpleasant encounters.'

'Capitano's sword is like an honest woman: ashamed to appear naked for the first time.'

'The best provisions are yesterday's bread, today's eggs, one-year-old meat, two-year-old wine, three-year-old fish and women less than twenty. For *(plays and sings)*

> That's the food to keep hunger away
> And even when you're old and lost your teeth
> You still need it every day.'

Colombina: 'Who's that knocking at the door?' Brighella: 'It's a cockerel seized with spasms that wants to cock-a-doodle-do in your love coop. It's a rat suffering from love hunger who wants to nibble a bit of matrimonial cheese.'

Canovaccio

The docks: BRIGHELLA, lounging around, sees PANTALONE come off a boat. He offers his services as a minder. PANTALONE refuses as he's too mean to pay for protection when he hears the price of it. BRIGHELLA goes off and returns disguised (several times in different characters, if necessary), pretending to look for the old merchant who his friend Brighella claims is ripe for mugging. Graphic descriptions of what Pantalone can expect to happen to him. BRIGHELLA returns and PANTALONE begs him to become his employee. BRIGHELLA plays hard to get and puts the price up.

Sample dialogue

Brighella is a recruiting sergeant.

> *Brighella*: If you become a Captain of the Dragoons, it'll be the good life wherever you go. No troubles, no sorrows, nothing but pleasure. What happiness! You receive an order to join your company. Immediately you take a coach; the whole journey long you get to eat partridges, quails and hummingbirds' wings as your staple diet. Waiters come up and say 'Just taste this wine, Sir . . .' *(Mimes,* ARLECCHINO *reacts)* 'To your liking, Sir?' And that's nothing compared to some of the vintages they'll offer you. Then you arrive in camp. Your apartment is on the ground floor . . .

> *Arlecchino*: That's good: I don't like going up stairs too much.

> *Brighella*: You'll get plenty of fellow officers coming to visit you. You play cards, smoke cigars, sing songs, drink as much as you like.

> *Arlecchino*: Blimey, that's the way politicians live. I thought war was supposed to be hell.

> *Brighella*: It's only those who have never tried that speak badly of it. Meanwhile, the enemy advances, and the Captain of the Dragoons is ordered to go and reconnoitre – that is to ascertain the whereabouts of the enemy camp, what their manoeuvres are, and what their concentration is. There's nothing to it. First of all you march smartly at the head of your company. No, no: I see you on horseback, a heroic figure . . . Why are you shaking your head?

> *Arlecchino*: I'll never stay on: I can't even ride a donkey. Can't we leave the horse out of it?

> *Brighella*: Certainly not, you're a ranking officer. So, you advance on the enemy position. As soon as they see you, they open up with an artillery battery. Bang! Bang! Zap!

> *Arlecchino*: Aaaaaaaaagh!

> *Brighella*: It's nothing, you've only lost an arm.

> *Arlecchino*: You call that nothing?

> *Brighella*: A mere trifle. When the top General gets the report of your action he promotes you to Colonel and you get posted to another regiment. Your orders are to attack. The enemy fights back like mad: Crack! Bang! Bang! Yeeeeeeowbam! Zap!

> *Arlecchino*: Another zap!

> *Brighella*: A grenade shot has taken off one of the Colonel's legs, but it's only a trifle.

> *Arlecchino*: The Devil if I didn't suspect as much when I heard that zap!

> *Brighella*: What do you expect? That's war for you. You'll get

treatment for your wound, your name published in the *Gazette* and you'll get made a Brigadier.

Arlecchino: Is that bigger than Colonel?

Brighella: I should say so! All your fellow officers will come and compliment you on your promotion. Meanwhile the enemy have rallied: they're on the counter-attack. The Brigadier has to run everywhere, issuing orders left, right and centre. It's a hard battle, with no quarter given. Finally the enemy is routed and the shout goes up 'Victory is ours!' At that moment a twelve-gun battery which the enemy has mounted on a little hill opens up: Whummmmph! Whummmmph! Zap! Zap!

Arlecchino: Uh oh, there were two zaps!

Brighella: What a shame! How unfortunate can you get? The poor Brigadier has had his remaining arm and leg blown off.

Arlecchino: I'm not surprised: I've never had much luck with zaps. *(By now he is kneeling with both arms behind him)* Look what I'm down to!

Brighella: Be brave, my friend. These missing limbs of yours are tokens of your courage. Your name will again appear in the *Gazette*, and you'll be made a top-ranking General.

Arlecchino: That's something I've noticed: the higher my rank, the fewer limbs I've got left.

Brighella: As soon as you're made a General, you always appear on horseback.

Arlecchino: Excuse me: how do I mount a horse with no arms or legs?

Brighella: You'll manage somehow because this is a new opportunity to cover yourself with glory. The enemy are weakened, you've got them surrounded, you gallop and prance all over the place, issuing orders, giving the men your encouragement.

Arlecchino: And what do I do for courage when I've given it all away?

Brighella: Whichever way you turn, you see nothing but carnage: bomb-holes, bodies and cannon balls: Pow! Pow! Crack! Bang! Yeeeeeeeowbam! Whummmmph! Zap!

Arlecchino: I knew it. It's that one again!

Brighella: A bullet has taken off the General's head.

Arlecchino: Another trifle, eh?

Brighella: Exactly.

Arlecchino: I can't wait to know what rank I'm going to get now. Can't you just pin a medal on my basket and send me home: I don't want to be in the Dragoons after all.

The old men

From the Greek comedies down to our own modern vaudeville, from the old satyr besmeared with grape-juice down to Cassandre besmeared with snuff, at the hands of Aristophanes, Plautus, Terence, Macchiavelli, Beolco, Molière and Goldoni, the old man of the comedy, like the old man of the farce, has been always more or less niggardly, credulous, libertine, duped and mocked, afflicted with rheum and coughs, and, above all, unhappy.[1]

MAURICE SAND

 Pantalone

Name.

Pantalone's name has given a good deal of trouble to students; he was quite certainly not christened after St. Pantaleone. . . . A modern derivant from the Greek, *pantos-elemon* seems still less likely. . . . The name Pantalone was semi-proverbial by 1658, whatever its derivation.[2]

Winifred Smith also denies that he was named after Piantaleone, meaning to plant the standard of the lion of Venice on, for example, the islands of the Mediterranean and in the Levant. But it should be noted that the lion was also the merchant's stamp on goods which were traded through Venice, thus providing Pantalone, 'Il Magnifico' stay-at-home, his power-base. In the fifteenth and sixteenth centuries, Venice was the richest and most commercially minded city-state in Italy, controlling all trade on the Adriatic and with north Africa and the Near East: the magnificent lion. However, it may be that Magnifico does not mean the Magnificent but the Munificent (from Latin *munifice*, bountiful, charitable), and the name is thus an ironical reference to Pantalone's miserliness. Sometimes he is Pantalone de Bisognosi, literally 'of the needy', presumably meaning that you have to be pretty hard up to regard him as well-off.

Status. Top of the pecking order. Pantalone *is* money: he controls all the finance available within the world of *commedia dell'arte* and therefore his orders have, ultimately, to be obeyed. He is the employer, giving orders to his servants, and the father, dictating to his children, controlling the social structure which obtains before the events of the scenario take place. However, Dario Fo considers:

> The Magnifico is a character satirised by the bourgeoisie of the sixteenth century. He's been overtaken by the great merchants, like Shakespeare's Merchant of Venice, so he's a defeated character, a landed gentleman cut off from commerce, from the economy of the banking world, letters of credit, etc. Not only in France, but also in Germany and Constantinople. This new society satirises the old one . . . and this old prince wants to hold on to his property.[3]

Inherent in this attempt to hold on to an old order is Pantalone's influence as a stabilising figure, limiting the world view of Commedia, and thus enabling it to endure while bursting at the seams as the young (the Lovers) and the dispossessed (the *zanni*) eternally attempt a take-over.

Origin. God of the dying year at Carnival (the Lovers are spring to Pantalone's winter).

Physical appearance. Lean and scrawny, often short in stature. Early form often has a phallic codpiece.

Costume. Goldoni:

> He has always preserved the ancient Venetian costume; the black dress and woollen bonnet are still worn in Venice; and the red underwaist and breeches, cut out like drawers, with red stockings and slippers, are a most exact representation of the equipment of the first inhabitants of the Adriatic marshes.[4]

Tight-fitting long red trousers or red breeches and stockings, a short, tight-fitting jacket, a loose long black cloak with plain sleeves, red woollen skull-cap, and yellow Turkish slippers. Supposedly, he changed the colour of his tights and/or cloak to black as a sign of mourning when Negroponte was captured by the Turks from the Venetians.

Mask. Long, hooked nose with bushy eyebrows, sometimes also a moustache. Pointed beard juts forward as if to meet the nose coming down, thus giving a very dynamic profile. 'The mask of the early Magnifico, on the other hand, has a quite different physiognomy – it is highly stylised, with prominent features, deep rings circling the eye sockets and two round holes for the eyes.'[5]

Props. Gold chain round the neck with a large medallion. Dagger.

Stance. His back bends the other way to the *zannis*, giving him an old man's stoop, protecting his purse and his penis and effectively restricting the motion of his legs. The feet are together, toes apart, knees well bent and facing apart creating a focus on the crutch. However, early illustrations show a much more vertical basic posture, complemented by an erect phallus nestling next to his dagger. The legs are also much more muscled

14 A sixteenth-century Pantalone (from the Recueil Fossard).

with the possibility of sustaining extreme forward positions of the torso or making large strides. The Pantalone of the *zannata*. A genuinely magnificent figure, but there is no inheritance of how to play Pantalone in this way, although Dario Fo has made a reconstruction:

> Bullying, aggressive, mean-minded, all trace of his forebears had vanished, leaving only a pauper who had squandered his dignity along with his cash. Always on the prowl, he could be termed a Beelzebub of sex. Any woman who happens to cross his path becomes at once an object of winks, leers and nudges. . . . *Puts on the mask and parades up and down in a series of showily self-important struts, trips, trots and sudden halts.*[6]

Little by little he seems to have lost his puissance and retained power only in his purse, which is, appropriately, the way Nico Pepe played him in Goldoni's *The Servant of Two Masters* for the Piccolo Teatro.[7]

Walk. The same as for little *zanni*, but smaller steps. He can only walk at one pace: whatever his feet do his legs cannot go any faster, whatever the motive or stimulus.

Movements. Can mimic those of any other character, but only in a form diminished by age. Sometimes falls flat on his back on hearing bad news (usually financial). Like a beetle he cannot then right himself.

Gestures. Old in body, but his head, feet and hands are still active. The hands (which he can't keep to himself) flutter continuously, gesticulating each thought as it comes into his head. The only way he can stop this is to hold them behind his back, underneath his cloak.

Speech. A high-pitched chicken squawk:

> His youthful hose, well sav'd, a world too wide
> For his shrunk shank, and his big manly voice,
> Turning again toward childish treble, pipes
> And whistles in his sound.[8]

Characteristics. Two only: avarice and trouble with his prostate gland. Pantalone operates on the assumption that everything can be bought and sold, and this turns out to be true, with the exception of loyalty (and love). But he also loves money for its own sake and will therefore only part with it when there is no other option. He always wants to marry his daughter to a wealthy man – and avoid giving her a dowry. When things do not go his way he quickly slips into emotional extremes, particularly enraged petty tyranny. He has a long memory and never forgets or forgives the slightest past transgression. Pantalone is action, not words – in contrast with Il Dottore.

Animal.   Chicken or turkey.

Relationships.   Mean to his servants, narrow-mindedly proscriptive to his children, fawning to Il Dottore, scheming with Il Capitano, lecherous with Colombina and indulgent to himself.

Relationship to audience.   Too self-interested to be aware of spectators.Yet his main, perhaps only, virtue is that of transparency: his motives are so obvious that he almost emerges as an honest man – again unlike Il Dottore.

Plot function.   An impediment to the action. For example, he typically wants to marry the same woman as his son Flavio, or is too mean to provide a dowry for his daughter, Isabella.

Improvisation exercises

Pantalone is alone in his house, having sent eveyone else away. Finally he can have a party, since it will cost as little as possible. To be played slowly, lingering over choice of food, drink, etc. Gradually slips into a trance of second childhood, finds himself in a dusty room full of objects of reminiscent significance.

Meets someone and they ask: 'How are you?' (he's never well); 'How is your daughter/financial affairs etc.' (all bad); then: 'Can you lend me some money?' (exit in great frenzy).

Two Pantalones meet. There is a purse lying on the floor. There are three phases to their encounter: 1) Greeting – each thinks the other has not seen it and attempts to get rid of him; 2) Recognition of the fact that it is there and statement of claims and counter-claims; 3) Contest: a race for the prize.

Pantalone is pressed for money by other Masks – debtors (e.g. Pulcinella, Brighella) and servants wanting their wages (e.g. Colombina, Arlecchino). He faints. Il Dottore arrives and pronounces him dead. The others improvise a wake. As they eat and drink, Panatalone comes to and hears what they are saying about him. He rises like a ghost and scares them all away.

Repertorio

Ah, love, love, it's a widespread affliction and there are very few who escape it. I've been unfortunate enough to catch it myself:

it started when I was a young man. Since then my outward behaviour has changed, but not the inner man. From the ages of 10 to 17 I was like a pigeon, the way I fluttered around young women, looking for a crumb here or a grain there, and occasionally getting my beak in for a little peck. Between 17 and 24 I was at it like a tomcat. At the age of 24 I got married and did it like a post-horse, flat out for an hour, followed by a day of rest. And now, now I'm like a dog, one little sniff and then off I go.

Canovaccio

The street. BRIGHELLA watches an unknown woman, FIORINETTA, enter a house. Enter PANTALONE: he has decided to remarry (see dialogue below) and enlists BRIGHELLA's help. BRIGHELLA says he knows just the person: she's young, beautiful, faithful and going cheap – an illegal immigrant, perhaps. But money 'up front' will be necessary. PANTALONE refuses to part with a penny until he has seen the goods. BRIGHELLA takes him to the door of the house and they peer through the keyhole at FIORINETTA. PANTALONE beomes sexually excited, and for each peep, BRIGHELLA charges an increasingly exorbitant price. A rendezvous is promised for tomorrow. Exit PANTALONE. BRIGHELLA knocks at the door and tells FIORINETTA that he is collecting old clothes for charity.

A room in Pantalone's house. BRIGHELLA dresses ARLECCHINO in FIORINETTA's clothes. He conceals himself as PANTALONE arrives for the rendezvous. ARLECCHINO asks him for more money, which he refuses until he has sampled the goods. ARLECCHINO pretends to be shy and makes PANTALONE close his eyes, then gets him into a compromising position, beats him with his slapstick and runs off.

Sample monologue

Oh son (I almost said of a randy old goat) how have you repaid all that I have done for you, the sleepless nights you have caused me, the bezants I have paid out for you, the labours I have undertaken for you. With what ingratitude you repay a father who has done so much for you! . . .

But since you want to live like a beast, may all the beasts of the world be against you: may the cocks disturb your sleep, the dogs gnaw at your bones, the cats scratch your hands, the crows peck out your eyes, the lice eat your flesh and shame you in your clothes, may the fleas, bugs and horseflies give you no rest with their bites, their stings and their puncturings. When you go out into the country may you be bitten by snakes, stung by wasps,

ripped open by oxen, gored by bulls; when you are in the city
may you be jostled by oxen and trampled on by horses; if you
voyage by sea may the dogfish poison you and the dolphins
signal tempests; if you travel by land may the litters and carriages
break your bones and, finally, may all the animals created for the
service of man become for you nothing but toads, serpents,
dragons, panthers, basilisks, hydras and Spanish flies.[9]

Sample dialogue

A good example of how the highest-status character can be the lowest in
esteem. After being made fun of by Arlecchino to the point of irascibility, he
turns his excitement on his daughter. However, although Isabella may
reveal something of her father's temperamental instability when in a frenzy
of love, in a domestic situation she takes his crustiness (and lustiness) in her
stride:

Pantalone: Arlecchino, Arlecchino.
Arlecchino (off): Calm down, I'm coming.
Pantalone: Will you come here? *(Aside)* I want him to go and fetch
    my daughter. Well, are you coming?
Arlecchino: Wait a minute, can't you, she's just about to boil.
Pantalone: Who, my daughter?
Arlecchino: No, Sir, my kettle.
Pantalone: If I have to come after you, you'll know all about it.
    (Enter ARLECCHINO*)* Come here: I thought you were talking about
    my Isabella.
Arlecchino: No, no, Sir, I was just pouring.
Pantalone: Pawing? Who, my daughter?
Arlecchino: No, Sir, the kettle.
Pantalone: Shut up about your kettle when I'm talking about my
    daughter.
Arlecchino: Yes, Sir, I just didn't want her to get her bottom burned.
Pantalone: Isabella?
Arlecchino: No, no, no, for Pete's sake, the kettle, the kettle.
Pantalone: You rapscallion scamp of a gallows-bird, if you don't stop
    going on about your kettle I'll pull both your ears off.
Arlecchino: Yes Sir, well, as far as your daughter's concerned . . .
    she's too hot to handle – the kettle that is.
Pantalone: Just for once stop making jokes and go and fetch my
    daughter.
Arlecchino: That's a useless task – here she is.
(Enter ISABELLA*, carrying her embroidery)*

Pantalone: Good morning daughter.

Isabella: Good morning father.

Pantalone: What are you making there, young lady?

Isabella: It's a coverlet for my bed. But I'm afraid I'm making it too small: two people will never get under it.

Pantalone: When, might I ask, do you think there might be any reason for sharing your bed with someone?

Isabella: Well, if I were to have the good fortune to get married, for example . . .

Pantalone (enraged): If by good fortune or bad, you came to be married, you'd soon find a way. Oh yes, I know your little games. You don't always need to have a needle and cloth in your hand to do some fancywork. But that isn't why we are here. Put your work down and listen to me. The question of marriage . . . Oh, so you're laughing already! Tcha! Don't jump the gun . . . Marriage, I say, being a state as old as the world itself, since people were married before you and will be after . . .

Isabella: I know, father. I was told so a long time ago.

Pantalone: I have decided, in order to perpetuate the Pantalone family name . . . You see what I'm driving at? I have therefore decided to get married again.

Isabella: Oh! Father!

Pantalone: Oh! Daughter! Why are you so astonished! Don't I still cut a fine figure? Look at my distinguished appearance, my trim physique, my lightness of foot! (*He makes a leap and stumbles*)

Isabella: Then you're going to get married, father?

Pantalone: Yes, if you think it's all right, daughter.

Isabella: To a woman?

Pantalone: No, to an organ pipe . . . I ask you, what a question!

Isabella: You're going to marry a woman?

Pantalone: Are your brains in a sling? Is it that you think I'm too old to carry on my ancestral line? One is never as old as one looks, you know! The chemist was only saying to me this morning, when I dropped by for my prescription, that I didn't look a day over forty . . . five.

Arlecchino: Sir, that's because he couldn't see your face!

Pantalone: I know how old I am, but I'm sure that what I need is a woman. I'm bursting with health and I've found a girl who's just right for me: beautiful, young, clever, rich. A golden opportunity.

Isabella: Another daughter, who didn't know how to behave, would tell you, Father, that you were taking a big risk in getting married. But I, fully aware of the respect that I owe you and seeing you bursting with health, say that you are quite right to take a wife.

Pantalone: Oh! Oh! You're taking it very well! Since you're being so reasonable, come with me right away so that I can introduce you to your future mother-in-law. *(They go off)*[10]

 Il Dottore

Name. Il Dottore Gratiano, later called Balanzone, Scarpazon, Forbizone, Boloardo.

> The origin of Gratiano's name is no clearer than that of Pantalone's. The creator of the Mask, according to the older scholars, was Luzio Burchiello who subscribed himself *Lus Burchiello Gratià* and who imitated an old barber, Gratiano delle Celtiche. . . . Ancona, commenting on this, prefers to agree with the derivation of the Doctor from the 'canonist Graziano'. If Gratian were indeed the learned original of all the foolish clowns who caricatured under his name the pretentious scholar, until 'a Gratiano' became a synonym for fool, the distortion would be no more curious than that of Duns Scotus' unfortunate first name into our English dunce.[11]

Boloardo means dolt, a *balanzone* is a balance scale, presumably an ironical suggestion that he is balanced in his head or a reference to his inability to make any proposition without also giving voice to its antithesis.

Status. Bachelor or widower. When he does marry he is immediately cuckolded. Often father to one of the Lovers.

Origin. A gross Carnival figure, who also appears in folk plays, for example the English Mummers' plays. These invariably contain a section usually called the cure, consisting of the mock Doctor's boast in which he brags of his travels and his powers, followed by a haggle over the fees, the administration of the cure and the resurrection of the fallen hero.

> The doctor is only second in importance to the combatants themselves, and like them he appears to be a survival of the ritual; he is the medicine man of primitive races, and in origin an unusually gifted savage who assumed control of the ceremonies. This theory of the doctor's origin might at first seem to be untenable because

as a rule it is the doctor himself, or the doctor in conjunction with his servant, who provides most of the rude comedy that enlivens the Mummers' Play. But the reason for the comic aspect of the doctor is not far to seek. The medicine man of savage races is hated so long as he is feared, and his natural or inevitable fate is to become a target for witticisms as soon as that fear is no longer felt.[12]

Il Dottore is a close relation to the mountebank quack. Lodovico de'Bianchi, the Gratiano of the Gelosi, had himself been a mountebank and published a book of 'conceits' for the role that probably represents his mountebank's stock speeches.

Physical appearance. He is *grande*, even *grandissimo*: his huge size comes directly from Carnival and contrasts with Pantalone. Later French types became lean pedants, reptilian like Molière's Tartuffe.

Costume. Black academic dress satirising Bolognese scholars. Long jacket with black coat over-reaching to his heels, black shoes, stockings and breeches, and a black skull-cap. Lolli, in mid-seventeenth century, added a wide ruff round the neck and a very wide-brimmed black felt hat.

Mask. Covers the nose and forehead only. The actor's cheeks are thus revealed and often reddened to show Il Dottore's fondness for the bottle. According to Goldoni the mask itself has a bibulous origin: 'the idea of the singular mask which covers his face and nose, was taken from a wine stain which disfigured the countenance of a jurist-consult of those times'.[13]

Props. White handkerchief.

Stance. Weight back on heels, belly forward, hands gesturing in front. The later French pedant is more dapper and leans forward from the waist.

Walk. Walks peripatetically in figures of eight, using tiny, mincing steps. His walking posture descends while he thinks (out loud, of course) and rises up again on the solution of the problem. The later French version walks like a lizard, leaning forward, using his head.

Movements. Relatively static in front of the audience.

Gestures. Needs all the space to himself and gains it by gesturing out from the body as if sowing seed.

Speech. 'Parps' like a trombone. Pronounces 'S' as 'Sh'. Speaks a mixture

15 Il Dottore Graziano, mask by Antonio Fava: arguably the hardest mask to make since there is so little of it. The bridge of the nose is inherently weak in construction. Leather with lambswool.

of Bolognese dialect, Italian and Latin, known as minestrone. Later French types fussy in their elocution.

Characteristics. From Bologna, the home city of Italy's oldest University, not that he ever went to it. Specialises in *everything*, and can talk a load of old boloney about it. Very oral, both in and out: he also eats a lot (Bologna is the home of lasagne). He is essentially belly, not intellect-centred. Il Dottore is inclined, like Pantalone, to be stingy, but in his case it is because he doesn't have any money. He is never put off his stroke by parody, interruption, or even physical abuse. Makes crude sexual jokes and has a weakness for pornography.

Animal.   Pig. Later a lizard.

Relationships.   Neighbour and friend or rival of Pantalone (either way they are inseparable), and, since he is a natural parasite, sees the advantage of being patronised by him. Often the master of Pedrolino, whom he treats badly since he is envious of true creativity and natural understanding.

Relationship to audience.   Needs a context in order to make a direct address – the giving of a lecture for example.

Plot function.   Gives the other characters a break from physical exertion by his prolixity – sometimes to the point where he has to be carried off by them, still talking. For this reason he stays a relatively long time onstage. A survivor, not a target figure like Pantalone.

Improvisation exercises

Il Dottore's perverse monologues (see below) are called *sproloquio*. Practise doing 'just a minute' on topics suggested by other characters.

Give favourite recipe while thinking of own gastronomic satisfaction to the point of orgasm (while Zanni, in attendance, slavers in anticipation). Melt with the butter, sizzle with the chips, finally 'coming' in epicurean delight.

Il Dottore is fond of giving the etymology of words. (Soldano Aniello, one of the earliest interpreters of the role, wrote a book of *Fantastic and Ridiculous Etymologies*.) Have another character read a newspaper article and interrupt with fantastic definitions, syllable by syllable, of any long words.

Trio: two doctors (of law) appear for the defence and prosecution in the trial of Zanni. Their alternate speeches become a competition in legalistic jargon, gradually losing sight of the actual case, despite Zanni's protestations.

Repertorio
More than any other role, the key to this Mask is present-day observation, rather than reliance on traditional technique:

> To play this so attractive role, he who is disposed to act it on the stage should first of all form a good idea of such a man. He should seek to be modern with a contempt for antiquity, and must at the proper moment emit sentences appropriate in content but disjointed in expression. These should be seasoned with the dialect of Bologna as it is used by one who believes that there is no finer way of speaking; then, from time to time he should with

some gravity let fall from his lips those words he considers most elegant but which are in truth the most ridiculous ever heard. . . . Sometimes, too, the actor should seize upon some silly, trivial, and very well-known fact and then demonstrate or pretend to believe that it is the newest, most curious, and most mysterious thing in the world. Then, without giving even a hint of a smile, he should behave as if he had caused a sensation.

This character, poorly described by my pen, should be played by one who would light a great torch by the tiny light of a taper which I have illumined merely as a guide, since I am certain that the aim of anyone wishing to play Graziano will be to play the part in his own way.[14]

A personal notebook is therefore crucial since Il Dottore is essentially unoriginal in everything he says – an anthologist of scraps of seeming significance: 'He who is always wrong is less right than anyone else.' 'A ship in mid-ocean is far from port.' 'Anyone who is sleeping has not yet been awakened.' 'A person who is ill may well say that he is unwell.'

Cure for toothache: 'Hold a ripe apple in your mouth and put your head in the oven; before the apple is cooked your toothache will be gone.'

Sample monologue

You have seen that I have slipped up: indeed, I might have fallen. Had I fallen and hurt myself I would have put myself to bed: a doctor would have been called. He would have prescribed a remedy: such prescriptions are composed of various ingredients: such ingredients come from the Levant, whence, according to Aristotle, emanate the winds. Aristotle was tutor to Alexander the Great. Alexander the Great was master of the world, and the world is held up by Atlas. Atlas is, necessarily, a man of considerable strength: it is such strength which supports columns, and columns support palaces. Palaces are built by masons, masons are instructed by architects, architects make drawings, drawing is the basis of painting, painting is a fine art of which there are seven, seven also were the wise men of ancient Greece who studied eloquence, the Goddess of which is Minerva, Minerva . . . (*et cetera, et cetera*).

Sample dialogue

Since the Doctor is essentially a monologuist, there is little recorded dialogue; the following, although something of a curiosity, does show a balance in his relationship with Pantalone. The latter, not noted for his perspicacity, clearly sees through him and is, for once, in collusion with Zanni:

Pantalone: So, my dear Doctor, you have been to hell?

Dottore: Yes, friend Pantalone, and there I saw many things.

Pantalone: And you, Zanni, you've been as well?

Zanni: Oh yes! Pantalone, Sir, and I've seen things no-one would believe.

Pantalone: And exactly what did you see?

Dottore: Let me do the talking, if you don't mind.

Pantalone: You speak first, then.

Dottore: I walked for a long time through the countryside until one could no longer see anything except the earth and the sky and then, as destiny would have it, I fell into a black river, the which river was saturated with water.

Pantalone: What a beautiful, learned discourse, you talk like a donkey eats straw.

Dottore: On the other side there was an immense crowd, throngs of young lovers singing songs about love going wrong amongst lovers in love. Ah! Love! Ah! Unhappiness! Ah! The burning sun! Oh! The stars have gone out! I am inflamed, I'm kissing myself, I am consumed with passion!

Pantalone: Such beautiful words!

Zanni: And me, I'd like to tell you my story too.

Dottore: Let me speak.

Pantalone: No, it's Zanni's turn.

Dottore: Why should he do all the talking?

Zanni: Me too, I've been where the Doctor's been, except he was on his side and I was on mine. I saw a river of ice and I saw a river on fire.

    In the river of ice I saw all those who raise the price of coal when the temperature drops, and all the innkeepers who put water in their wine.

    In the river of fire, I saw all the cooks who burn their meat on the outside without getting the inside cooked.

    I saw a few parasitical servants who had fawned on their masters being beaten forty times every quarter of an hour with a cudgel with plenty of nails through it.

    I saw all the shoemakers who say that a pair of shoes that are too small will stretch with use, being pulled apart by ropes tied to their arms and legs . . .

Pantalone: I wish you'd have told me sooner, Zanni.

Zanni: . . . by fifty devils, fifty thousand times a day . . .

Pantalone: An excellent remedy! Very good for the circulation!

Dottore: Shut up, I want to talk as well.

Pantalone: Go on then, tell your story: it'll be interminable as usual, no doubt!

Dottore: I saw an ignorant pedant naked on all fours like a horse, and fifty times a day they tanned his hide with a red-hot poker and a hundred times a day they bombarded him with copies of every book in the world.

Pantalone: That'll be your destiny, Doctor: being bombarded like that, ignoramus that you are.

Dottore: And that was nothing . . .

Pantalone: Go on, then, since you've got the floor.

Dottore: I saw surgeons, the ones who cut people up unnecessarily, being stoned to death with glowing embers, hot stones and burning coals.

I saw pathologists pierced all over with nails, knives, swords, then chopped into little bits like fine parsley to be put in soup.

I saw bankrupt apothecaries, the ones who put hot water in enemas whilst swearing that it's oil. They have to empty their bowels every fifteen minutes, and, afterwards they have to eat it all up again.

Pantalone: And whilst you were passing, Doctor, did you try a spoonful?

Zanni: It's time the Doctor shut up!

Pantalone: Yes, well past time!

Dottore: Let him talk, let him talk! For as the proverb says:
The man that talks well dines well. The man that doesn't talk, takes the biscuit.

Pantalone: Beautifully put!

Dottore: If I put my mind to it, I could do worse.

Pantalone: I believe you, I believe you.[15]

The Lovers

If then true lovers have ever been crossed
It stands as an edict in destiny.
Then let us teach our trial patience,
Because it is a customary cross,
As due to love as thoughts, and dreams, and sighs,
Wishes, and tears – poor fancy's followers.[1]

SHAKESPEARE

Names.   In Italian, the Lovers (of whom four – two would-be pairs – are usually needed for a full scenario) are called *innamorati*. The males have names such as Silvio, Fabrizio, Aurelio, Orazio, Ottavio, Ortensio, Lelio, Leandro, Cinzio, Florindo, Lindoro, etc.; the females: Isabella, Angelica, Eularia, Flaminia, Vittoria, Silvia, Lavinia, Ortensia, Aurelia, etc.

Status.   High, but brought low by the hopelessness of their infatuation.

Origin.   The aristocracy of the Italian Renaissance courts amused them-selves with a form they called *commedia erudita* based on the plays of Terence and Plautus, for example *Calandria* by Cardinal Bibbiena which, like Shakespeare's later *Comedy of Errors*, is based on Plautus' *Menaechmi*. As the professional improvised comedy looked to extend its range it seems to have borrowed the Lovers from the amateur form.

Physical appearance.   Young, attractive.

Costume.   In the latest fashion. Males sometimes dressed as young sol-diers or cadets. Wigs. Actresses would show off their wardrobe in the better companies by changing costume several times during the course of the action.

Mask.   No actual mask, but heavy make-up. Mascara and beauty spots for both sexes. The make-up in fact becomes a mask enabling performers to play

16 Lelio as drawn by Maurice Sand.

the role well into middle age, or even beyond – Giovan Battista Andreini, son of Francesco, played Lelio until he was 73. Vizard or *loup* could be worn for disguise, usually made of black velvet. This was a normal accoutrement for society ladies when walking to a rendezvous and could be half- or full-face. But since it has no expression it does not count as a mask in the Commedia sense, although it does provide plenty of plot potential, enabling, for example, Colombina to attend rendezvous in her mistress's place.

Props.   Handkerchief. Posy. Fan for women.

Stance.   They lack firm contact with the earth. Feet invariably in ballet positions, creating an inverted cone. Chest and heart heavy. They are full of breath, but then take little pants on top. Sometimes when situations become too much for them, they deflate totally.

Walk. They do not walk so much as teeter, due to the instability of their base. First the head leans the other way to the body sway. Then the arms have to be used, one above the other, as a counterweight.

Movements. Actors would use the same dancing masters as the well-to-do whom they were parodying in order to point up the ridiculousness of exaggerated deportment. Movement comes at the point of overbalance leading to a sideways rush towards a new focus, with the arms left trailing behind. Stop at the new point (usually the beloved or some token thereof) before (almost) touching it. The Lovers have little or no physical contact. When there is any, the minimum has maximum effect.

Gestures. Often while holding a handkerchief or flower etc. in the leading hand. The arms never make identical shapes. Because of their vanity, they frequently look in a hand-mirror, only to become upset by any minor imperfection which is discovered. Even in extremis they are always looking to see if a ribbon or a sequin is out of place. A button found on the floor or a blemish in the coiffure equals disaster.

Speech. Language: Tuscan, making great display of courtly words and baroque metaphors. Well read, knowing large extracts of poems by heart (especially Petrarch). They speak softly in musical sentences – in contrast with the *zanni*. Their sentences are often flamboyant, hyperbolical, full of amorous rhetoric. By the end of the seventeenth-century in Paris, the Lovers spoke in French.

Relationships. They relate exclusively to themselves – they are in love with themselves being in love. The last person they actually relate to in the course of the action is often the beloved. When they do meet they have great difficulty in communicating with each other (usually because of nerves). And they relate to their servants only in terms of pleading for help. The Lovers love each other, yet are more preoccupied with being seen as lovers, undergoing all the hardships of being in such a plight, than with actual fulfilment. Consequently they frequently scorn each other and feign mild hatred; they rebut, despair, reconcile, but eventually end up marrying in the way of true love when the game is up and they know they cannot play any more. After a quarrel the male may try a serenade to win back favour. This will often be (dis)organised by Zanni: he employs musicians who are drunk or spends the money on something else and has to use tramps off the street. The result is total chaos, but in the end the serenade is beautifully played and sung because everyone miraculously turns out to be good at their job after all.

Relationship to audience. Extremely aware of being watched, playing to the audience for sympathy in their plight, occasionally giving themselves away by flirting with a spectator.

Plot function. Indispensable. Without them and their inability to resolve their own problems, there would be no function for the *zanni*, no struggle between the ineffectuality of youth and the implacability of age. The Lovers are never alone on stage – they always have someone with them or spying on them.

Characteristics. Three, like primary colours: fidelity, jealousy and fickleness. They are vain, petulant, spoilt, full of doubt and have very little patience. They have a masochistic enjoyment of enforced separation because it enables them to dramatise their situation, lament, moan, send messages, etc. When the Lovers do meet they are almost always tongue-tied and need interpreters (i.e. a *zanni* and/or a *servetta*) who proceed to misinterpret their statements, either through stupidity (Zanni), malicious desire for revenge (Brighella) or calculated self-interest (Colombina). Their attention span is short like young children's. The fear that they might be nobodies keeps them hyper-animated. Their element is water: they are very wet creatures indeed. The females are more passion-wrought and energetic than their male counterparts.

The Lovers exist very much in their own world – and in their own world within that world. Self-obsessed and very selfish, they are more interested in what they are saying themselves and how it sounds than in what the beloved is saying. They are primarily in love with themselves, secondarily in love with love, and only consequentially in love with the beloved. What they learn, if anything, from the tribulations of the scenario is the need to reverse these priorities.

They do, however, come off better than most other Commedia characters: there is no viciousness in them, and less to be reproached for – except vanity and vapidness, which, given their parents, they can hardly be blamed for. They represent the human potential for happiness.

Improvisation exercises

Dialogue throwing ball back and forth. He sets up a conceit, she returns it (see dialogue below).

Extremes of emotion. Blowing on a dandelion – he loves me, he loves me not. Followed by the arrival of contradictory messages: 'Assignation for tonight' . . . 'She can't come, she's ill' . . . 'She's feeling better' . . . 'But her father is making her marry another man' . . . 'But it's you she loves!' . . . 'Heartbreak is making her really ill' . . . 'She's dead' . . . 'No, it was only a rumour'.

A garden bench meeting: mutual flattery almost followed by the declaration of love. But . . . she takes against him for some minor reason. He now has to make a massive declaration of his love. Finally she gives in.

A double scene: both enter their dressing rooms, each rehearsing a speech to the beloved. Audience hear both monologues, which thus constitute a dialogue.

Both enter from opposite sides, lamenting that they cannot see the other today. Teeter and swoop from side to side just missing each other, oblivious to all but their own presence. Handkerchiefs etc. can be swapped.

Reaction to false reports of beloved's behaviour/circumstances.

Wrong letter delivered, causing despair.

Inability to speak when rendezvous finally made.

Cooee in the dark: a botched-up rendezvous, usually at night in a park or a graveyard, with *zanni* in disguise and further complications from a randy Capitano, Pantalone, etc.

Rushing up to the wrong person, on the point of blurting out passionate feelings, find a way of extracting yourself without breach of etiquette.

Repertorio

Cecchini insists that

> those who delight in playing the difficult part of the lover should enrich their minds with a fair stock of elegant discourses covering the variety of topics that can come up on the stage. But they must be careful that the words immediately following the insertion of such speeches fit uniformly with what was premeditated so that the borrowing may appear natural and not theft. To accomplish this, I would suggest that they should be continually reading literature to acquire a habit of pleasing expression which is capable of deceiving the hearer into supposing that it springs from the natural wit of the speaker.[2]

And reading is not enough: selected passages have to be learned by heart and then only used as appropriate, avoiding, for example, addressing 'a stupid servant or a common wench with forms and sentiments that are only appropriate to men of rank and education'. A daunting task; the actor who used to play the second Lover with the Confidenti is reputed to have been too lazy to undertake the constant study required and changed to playing a Capitano.

Perrucci gives a miscellany of the sort of speeches an actor should have 'conned' for ready introduction on suitable occasions. As a basis for a commonplace book for an actor playing *innamorati* roles he suggests collecting material under such headings as 'Love: reciprocal, rejected, importuning, disdainful; or Jealousy, Friendship, Reconciliation, Reward,

Leave-taking'.[3] He gives conceits, soliloquies, dialogues and rhymed couplets intended to signal the end of a speech.

Conceits (*concetti*) are defined by Perrucci as brief speeches containing some witty paradox or metaphor. But they also show how vague soppiness is not the key to successful portrayal: the passions are generalised but distinct and always taken to a similitudinous extreme. For example, on reciprocated love (*amor corrisposto*):

> Precipitate yourself, my heart, totally into my eyes, where the sight of your beloved will overcome you with joy, and, my soul, if it is true that you exist more truly in the love of another than of yourself, be happy, rejoice and shine, for see, here comes that which gives you feeling and life.

Rejection (*scaccia*):

> My heart is like the anvil that resists the hammer-stroke of your obstinacy: my breast is marble, nay agate, to withstand your fire; my bosom is ice, but ice so hard that your flames cannot melt it, and you are a fury for my torment in the realm of love.

Disdain (*sdegno*):

> Who would have thought it from her appearance? She showed a face in springtime, but there were vipers entwined in her flowers; a heavenly vision but harbouring furies; a calmness of temperament, but when she murmured tempests sprang up. Cursèd be these flowers which entrance only to betray; cursèd be this heaven which hides such furies, this ocean of serenity which entices in order to engulf.

Jealousy (*gelosia*):

> I am jealous because I am in love. O strange mutual revulsion! The fire of love is so conjoined with congealing jealousy that they slay me simultaneously, and my passion by reason of these two torments is a suffering by which I am frozen without while within a burning fever consumes my vitals.

Reconciliation (*pace*):

> Who then could save my heart, bitten as it is by the venomous serpents of jealousy, if it were not the balm of reciprocated love? And the restoration of health is even dearer to me than the stings

were mortal; that is why I will hang the votive offering of my heart in the temple of fidelity, as thanks for rescuing me from the jaws of death.

Parting (*partenza*):

I am leaving, beloved, but what heart I am taking with me, Cupid alone knows, for if one tears a plant from the earth which bore it, the petals drop off, the leaves wilt, and it dries up. Thus my heart, torn from the bosom whence it drew the sustenance of love and of life, loses its petals of delight, its leaves of longing, and becomes as dry as dust.

Canovaccio

The street. FLAVIO and ARLECCHINO rehearse what he is going to say to SYLVIA (ARLECCHINO pretends to be SYLVIA).

Sylvia's house: SYLVIA prepares for Flavio's visit. Enter FLAVIO and ARLECCHINO. Despite earlier rehearsal FLAVIO becomes tongue-tied. Since he cannot manage to speak above a whisper, ARLECCHINO has to speak for him. Like Chinese whispers, the words come out all wrong and finally a row ensues at the climax of which FLAVIO discovers he is speaking for himself and even making a passionate declaration of his love.

Monologue

In any given situation the Lovers would rather soliloquise about the problem than do anything about it, for example when entering an unknown town or climbing a ladder at night.

Dialogue

Lines are frequently short, alternated stichomythically, and spoken fast. Breaths should always be taken in mid-sentence.

A trifle like a ring, a flower, a ribbon, or a tobacco pouch, or one of the favourite academic problems such as, 'Who loves the better, man or woman?', 'Which gives more delight, the mouth or the eye?' might afford a suitable occasion for the introduction of premeditated dialogue either plain or ornate. Perrucci implies that the brisker style was more popular than the *stile asiatico* which depended on conceits and sustained metaphors. The retort of the *stile laconico* was appropriate for scenes of disdain, reproach, and peace-making.[4]

Or, indeed, for one incorporating all three as in this oft-quoted dialogue of scorn and reconciliation in which they feed off each other, often using and adapting each other's sentences, not so much in *contrasto* dialogue, more in the form of an operetta duet:

He: Go away!
She: Disappear!
He: . . . from my eyes.
She: . . . from my sight.
He: Fury with a heavenly face!
She: Demon with a mask of love.
He: How I curse . . .
She: How I detest . . .
He: . . . the day I set eyes on you.
She: . . . the moment that I adored you.
He: How can you dare . . .
She: Do you have the audacity . . .
He: . . . even to look at me?
She: . . . to remain in my presence?
He: Do you not realise . . .
She: Do you not consider . . .
He: . . . your shortcomings,
She: . . . your transgressions,
He: . . . so that you believe . . .
She: . . . so that you think . . .
He: . . . that I am staying here just to look at you?
She: . . . that I remain here just to gaze lovingly at you?
He: I cannot deny that you are beautiful . . .
She: I must confess that you have great charm . . .
He: . . . but of what worth is beauty . . .
She: . . . but of what use is charm . . .
He: . . . if it is defaced by falsehood?
She: . . . if it is accompanied by deceit?
He: I could never have imagined . . .
She: I could never have been persuaded . . .
He: . . . that heaven could become hell!
She: . . . that Cupid could become Lucifer!
He: And yet have I had such an experience!
She: And that, however, is what I have discovered!
He: Get away, disappear!
She: Get out of my sight!

He: I do not want to!
She: I cannot!
He: I do not know what holds me back.
She: An unknown force prevents me.
He: But, believe me, it is not love.
She: You can be sure it is not affection.
He: What then is stopping you?
She: What then keeps you here?
He: I do not want to give you the satisfaction . . .
She: I do not want to give you the pleasure . . .
He: . . . of hearing me say . . .
She: . . . of me saying to you . . .
He: . . . that I still love you.
She: . . . that I cannot forget you.
He: Oh! Never will I say it!
She: You will be dead before you hear it!
He: I would still love you . . .
She: I would still adore you . . .
He: . . . if you had been faithful.
She: . . . if you had been constant.
He: So you would be as sincere . . .
She: So you would remain as pure . . .
He: . . . as my Faith?
She: . . . as my Love?
He: You deceived me!
She: You betrayed me!
He: So leave at once!
She: So be off with you!
He: Yet when I try to go . . .
She: Yet when I make to go home . . .
He: . . . what spell holds me back?
She: . . . what unknown force prevents me?
He: Your sorcery is too strong for me!
She: Your hypnotic power is too great for me!
He: Fickle hope deludes me . . .
She: Your handsomeness persuades me . . .
He: . . . to find you faithful.
She: . . . not to find you guilty.
He: You lie, for I never was!
She: You are wrong, for I protest I always was.
He: And your love of other men?
She: And your penchant for other women?
He: You have been deceived!
She: You have been misled!

He: I do like you.
She: I do find you pleasing.
He: I adore you.
She: I idolise you.
He: My hope.
She: My love.
He: My life.
She: My blessing.
He: My light.
She: Breath of my life.
He: My goddess.
She: My idol.
He: All other thoughts . . .
She: All other affections . . .
He: . . . I hereby renounce,
She: . . . I find repulsive,
He: they are odious.
She: and abhorrent.
He: Peace, dearest eyes.
She: Peace, sweetest lips.
He: No more wars, only loving touches!
She: No more scorn, only melting glances.
He: When you alone I love . . .
She: When my soul adores but you . . .
He: . . . Cupid lives once more.
She: . . . and disdain it is that dies.[5]

One of the Lovers deserves special mention, being virtually a Mask in its own right, arguably the only one to have been created by a woman out of personal resource rather than circumstance.

Isabella

Name. There was a sixteenth-century *innamorata* Vittoria degli Amoevoli who took the name Isabella, but the name has become permanently associated with Isabella Andreini (1562–1604), who joined the troupe of the Gelosi and married Franceso Andreini (Capitano Spavento). Well versed in Latin, a prolific writer of poems and songs and a member of the Paduan Academy of Letters, she was fêted, honoured and admired throughout France and Italy by all classes, including royalty. Accepted in courts in her own right, she was also a poet, writing a pastorale as well as many sonnets and songs.

When she died in childbirth in Lyon, the city went into official mourning.

Status. Prima donna *innamorata*, therefore usually the daughter of Pantalone.

Origin. Developed from *innamorata*, but less dilettante, more perspicacious.

Speech. Refined, lacking the pretentiousness of other Lovers, never lost for the correct phrase.

Characteristics. Flirtatious, provocative and stubborn in turn, so headstrong she usually gets her own way, even over her father. Men continually fall in love with her and she continually teases and tests their veracity. Can be something of a prude. As in the fine arts,[6] the patronage of Commedia, whether through the 'bottle' for trestle-stage performances in streets and piazzas or princely commission, was in the hands of men. As the grip of the church on live performance loosened, male audiences wanted to see women onstage. Women like Isabella Andreini made the most of their comedic opportunity. She was also able to introduce a level of dramatic intensity, perhaps as a result of her knowledge of classical tragedy: feigned madness due to love in her passionate (*pazzia*) scenes was common. At such moments Isabella may rush off and snatch a phial of poison or produce a convenient dagger.

Plot function. Less at the mercy of events than the *innamorati*: initiates solutions on her own account. Isabella Andreini sustained the role into later life, the character often becoming a marriageable widow or proprietress of an establishment, thus having a central plot function.

17 The young Isabella, as imagined by Sand.

Il Cavaliere

There is an unmasked Capitano, Il Cavaliere, who is not an impostor, but a real soldier. He is usually after revenge and/or Isabella. Laughs and sneers and is above everyone, including the audience. Constantly unfaithful and flatters any woman who happens to be present.

18 Il Cavaliere, engraving by Jacques Callot. The moustaches become the mask, betraying hubristic self-esteem.

Il Capitano

Name. Self-appointed: if (and it's a big if) he ever held the rank of captain, he was long since stripped of it. Various names:

Giangurgulo:
Spanish/Calabrese. Long phallic prick of a nose, long pointed felt hat, rapier rather than sword, scarlet doublet and hose with yellow sleeves. Name means Jack Glutton or John Gargler. Obsessed with women, but also terrified of them. All usual Capitano traits, but is also impoverished and famished (hence his name). Often resorts to theft in order to eat. Vain, stupid and sneering.

Coccodrillo:
A crocodile who never bites, he is all *fanfarone* and easily deflated.

Fanfarone:
Calabrese. An impostor, pretending to be Spanish when he is in fact a trumped-up Zanni.

Matamoros:
The original Spanish mercenary – name means killer of Moors – created by Francesco Andreini. Powerfully built, very lavishly dressed, clothes of his servants supposedly made from the turbans of his victims. Has a hedgehog on his coat of arms, the result of his exploits at the battle of Trebizonde where he claims to have fought his way into the tent of the Sultan himself and dragged him through the camp while fighting off the entire enemy army with the other hand. There were so many arrows stuck in him by the time he fought free that he resembled a hedgehog.

Spavento:
Has the shortest nose and therefore the most to prove (*spaurire* = to terrify).

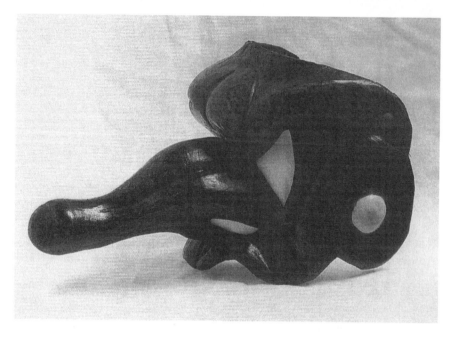

19 Mask for Capitano Coccodrillo by Antonio Fava.

Meo Squasquara:
A 'little shit', a parvenu who wants to become a Capitano.

And many more:
One of an actor's first duties as a Capitano is to invent a new name and lineage, preferably several lines long.

Status. A loner. Il Capitano is never indigenous to the town where the scenario is set and is able to pretend to high status as a result. His downfall to the level of his actual social standing is an essential part of the denouement.

Origin. Has a twofold origin: 1) literary: as in Plautus' *Miles Gloriosus* and Trasone in Terence's *Eunuchus*; 2) fake Spanish mercenary.

> Superimposed as it were on to the Italian comedy was the type of the military adventurer, of the Spanish hildago,[1] violent, tyrannical, overbearing and rapacious; a mixture of Don Juan, Pizarro and Don Quixote; at first rather terrible than ridiculous, and growing into a bona fide comic figure, into a threadbare and hungry adventurer, a cowardly sonorous fire eater, a Captain

Fracassa or Matamoros, only in proportion as the redoubtable kingdom of Philip II, odious but dignified, turned into the tattered Spain of the seventeenth century, execrable, but ludicrous.

Riccoboni [in his *Histoire du théâtre italien*, Paris, 1728] gives us two distinct figures of Captains: the Italian and the Spanish. The former is in the act of posing in all the pride of his tall figure, his stupendous pair of moustaches, the hilt of his long sword; the latter in the attitude of one who, in insolent manner, wards off a blow.[2]

Costume. Satire on military profession, therefore dress follows period changes of uniform. Feathered helmet or hat (*mon panache*). Huge boots (not necessarily a matching pair) with exaggerated garters. Spanish varieties have exaggerated ruff. Costume sometimes diagonally striped or slashed in the style of François I. But whatever the style, close scrutiny reveals the truth: 'Magnificent in words, but his purse always empty and under his beautiful richly damascened cuirass he wears but a frayed and tattered leather jerkin.' Il Capitano himself, however, always claims that his tattered undergarments are caused by the amazing virility of his bodily hair bursting through whenever he gets angry. Indeed, for this reason he used to wear no shirt at all 'but now that I have calmed down I wear linen like any other man'.[3]

Mask. Long nose, often unambiguously phallic.

Props. Long sword. Use of his weapon is part of his personality, a gestural extension like *zanni*'s slapstick, not an accessory.

Stance. Feet planted apart in order to occupy maximum space, chest pushed forward, back straight, hips wide.

Walk. Mountain walk: the heels of his high boots come down first, then the foot rolls on to the ball. Straight back, unlike *zanni*. Big strides. Step off on ball of foot giving lift and bounce to step. Feet on ground, head in clouds. (Rises up with each step so head comes above clouds in order to see!) The actual steps are small (he is in no hurry to get to war, but wants to do so with maximum effect).
Promenade walk: toes down first, strutting and preening with the head.
Chest walk: a side-to-side movement of the trunk, the shoulder commences. Used in confined spaces.

Run. When he hears a frightening noise he drops everything, but only succeeds in running on the spot, head thrown back, arms in the air, kicking his feet forward and howling piteously. When he hears a wolf (or a small dog) he shrinks little by little until he has made himself as unnoticeable as possible, then scurries away in a crouch. When fleeing from a mouse he adopts a kind of leaping promenade walk in order to prevent it running up his legs. When not scared witless he occasionally runs to be seen, to show off his legs, etc.

Gestures.   Extravagant and sustained.

Speech.   Loud basso profundo, turning to castrato squeak when frightened. When Spanish, the accent is Castilian.

Characteristics.   Four types:

1. Politic – if the Turks invade, he becomes a Turk.
2. Total coward – shits himself and plays dead.
3. Really courageous, but a danger only to himself and his own side when he fights.
4. Non-masked, Il Cavaliere – thinks he's good-looking and God's gift to women. (See under Lovers.)

Whichever type, there's only one thing he ever does: pretend. Thinks he's: (a) strong; (b) handsome; (c) brave and (d) a hell of a good guy. In Italian one speaks of the *bravura* of Il Capitano, in French of his *panache*. But he lives in an infantile, make-believe world, full of famous mythological and historical battles into which his imagination projects him as the hero of the day. He would be the last to arrive at the scene of any real battle – and the first to retreat. His element is air, not to say wind.

Animal.   Fo suggests he is a cross between a hunting dog and a Neapolitan mastiff.[4] I think of him as a peacock who has moulted all but one of his tail feathers, but does not know it.

Relationships.   Originally employed by Pantalone to do his dirty work for him. They worked well together as lechers with financial aspirations: Il Capitano to get rich, Pantalone to remain so. Pantalone would often congratulate Il Capitano on his efforts, then betray him to others. Since he saw him as a contemptible mercenary there was no reason to protect him. Later Il Capitano developed status in his own right and would arrive, however impoverished, with a Zanni, often half-starved. Il Dottore is no threat to him because he recognises his intellectual pretension as being as hollow as his own boasts. 'Doctor' and 'Captain' are both self-appointed honorary titles. He is threatened, however, by Pedrolino's genuine knowledge and understanding of life and by Colombina's plain speaking, especially in matters of sexual conquest. She sometimes uses him to humiliate Arlecchino, of whom Il Capitano is also wary because of his ability to outwit him.

Relationship to audience. The whole world is an audience. Stops whenever he sees the actual audience and makes a salutation so that he can be admired. Initially his *bravura* may take in the other characters, but never the audience: something in his very first entrance (a trip for example) should give him away.

Plot function. Exists to be 'de-masked' by the plot. Always a complete final transformation from pride to humility, confidence to panic.

Improvisation exercises

Man-eating woman passes five Capitanos. Il Capitano passes five man-eating women.

    Several Capitanos march off to war full of pomp, waving to the crowd as they pass. Shortly followed by a bedraggled retreat back across the stage, too embarrassed even to acknowledge the existence of the audience.

Repertorio
'I, when I was born, was already clad in a suit of armour, roaring like an impatient lion and hissing like an enraged servant.'
    'Italy trembles at my name, Spain reveres me and I terrify France.'
    'In peace all love me, in war all fear me.'
    'I'd crunch a Turk between my teeth as easily as an onion.'
    'I am the Prince of Cavaliers, the bravest of the brave, master of the universe, son of the thunder, nephew of the lightning, near-related to Death and Suzerain and close personal friend of the Great Devil of hell.'

Canovaccio
The street. IL CAPITANO boasts to ARLECCHINO of his prowess with women. Makes ARLECCHINO pretend to be Isabella and demonstrates how he would make love to her. Exit. Enter FLAVIO with a message for Arlecchino to take to Isabella. ARLECCHINO says she won't want it since she's in love with the Captain now – demonstrates how he reacted to Il Capitano's advances. Enter IL CAPITANO. FLAVIO challenges him to a duel, there and then, on the spot. IL CAPITANO thinks up as many reasons as possible why that is impossible while striving to maintain as much 'face' as he can, e.g. because he is wearing the wrong sword or 'The Duke of Bologna has decreed there is to be absolutely no duelling during the truffle season, which, as you know, began today, but if you insist we must repair at once to Mantua where I will slay you until your honour is satisfied.'

Sample monologue

While I am fighting there comes a cannon ball and strikes me in the mouth, knocking out, as you see, two teeth, but without doing me any further harm. I turn this ball round in my hands and hurl it back against the enemy, and, striking a tower in which there are fifteen hundred men, knock it down, killing all the soldiers and reducing the whole to dust so that there remains no trace of it whatsoever.

Cleofila, seeing my valour, comes against me sword in hand to slay me; I parry her blow and with mine take off her arm and fling it on to the ground together with the sword. Then I take her by the hair and fling her with such fury against the sky that, on reaching the central point of the hemisphere, she breaks through it and enters into the fifth heaven, finds Mars playing at chess with Venus and breaks his head.

Venus begins to cry out 'help! help!' and all the gods and goddesses of Olympus, terrified, call on Jove to help them.

Jove, seeing Mars lying on the ground, and being frightened by the whole affair, comes to his window, and, while I brandish my sword against the enemy till it flashes like the fire rising from some new Mongibello, says: 'Be silent, all of you, for he who has slain Mars is Captain Coccodrillo, and now he is so enraged he might come into heaven and slay us all.[5]

Sample dialogue

A very lightweight Capitano, Capitano Saltafossa, renowned for his ability in leaping ditches (when running from the enemy), is no match for Colombina:

Capitano (singing): The Captain on his prancing steed
Returns to the land of his sweetheart.
Colombina (mimicking): The Captain my old lover, sticks like old fish skin
And plagues me with his stories.
Capitano: Salutations to you . . . You're very haughty . . . I'm not a dog, even though I am poor . . . You're wrong not to want me any more.
Colombina: What are you talking about, you wretch: do you want me to begin making a list of your defects? . . . Oh! I'd better be quiet before I say anything too gross.

Capitano: You are wrong, Colombina, to speak like that, for you know very well what I'm capable of when I'm angry. Even if you have gone up in the world, have you forgotten one who gave you pleasure once and knows how to do so still?

Colombina: Pleasure, you say? Is that the pleasure of seeing you come here every day to give me the once over, look at what's cooking in the pot, give the barrel a shake and say 'Yesterday evening I saw off four muggers at once', and tell me your yarns about your daring deeds. I'm fed up with your stories, I don't want anything more to do with you.

Capitano: Poohah! If I weren't so badly disembowelled by your words, I'd kill you. Grr! I'm going to blow your house sky high! My God, look how my arm is shaking: I'm going to cut your moustache off!

Colombina: I know you: you couldn't even cut off a lump of butter. You might as well take your weapon and scour the sea with it.

Capitano: If I had my breastplate and my gloves here, I might get very nasty.

Colombina: Ah, good grief, how ugly he is, on my mother's life, I'll have to squeeze his head flat and pull his sardine off. Ah, good grief, here he comes now: look at that menacing look. How many weapons do you need to deal with one girl? I'm stronger than you, I'll mash your head in and scramble your brains.

Capitano: Lust of the flesh!

Colombina: Blarney of the stone!

Capitano: Cheerio charwoman!

Colombina: Bye-bye boaster!

Capitano: May I be eaten by a moth if I don't chop you into little pieces, flesh and bone.

Colombina: Slavering animal!

Capitano: Beast of hell!

Colombina: Tinpot tyrant!

Capitano: Monstrous manipulator!

Colombina: Look at this cur that's been beaten by every stick in the world.

Capitano: Pestilential appurtenance!

Colombina: Hypocritical hyena!

Capitano: Hotbed of iniquity!

Colombina: Fake trouser bulge!

Capitano: You're lying, you maggot-eater, you know very well that I make the world tremble at my feet.

Colombina: Hold it, don't come till I'm ready. I know that when you drink it makes the bottom of your glass tremble.

Capitano: Ah, if I only had my father's blunderbuss, that'd soon make you shut your mouth.

Colombina: Off you go, it's getting dark, you wouldn't want to bump into anyone nasty. Off you go to the hen-house.

Capitano: You can say what you like. You no longer exist. Tell your boyfriend he can consider himself dead and buried.

Colombina: What are you saying about my boyfriend? Listen, imbecile, if he was here, I swear by all that's holy, you wouldn't be giving yourself so many airs.

Capitano: I'd wring his neck like a chicken, by God, and a hundred like him.

Zanni (entering): What's that you're saying?

Colombina: Zanni, he's threatening me and he says he wants to settle scores with you.

Zanni: What! Draw your sword, if you dare.

Capitano: It's just women's talk: in fact I'm very fond of you. As heaven is my witness, I don't want to pick a fight with you.

Colombina: Oh, look how he's melted, but he was threatening me just now.

Capitano: It was your fault, Colombina. But I would like to eat the heart and liver of anyone who harmed a hair on your head, for I consider myself yours to command.

Zanni: Let's sort this out here and now.

Capitano: Put your sword away, for I would like to settle this in the old-fashioned way – let's have a drink on it.

Colombina: Zanni, I want him to beg my pardon, and then I want you to crush him like an insect.

Capitano: I humbly beg your pardon, both to you Sir, and to you, Madam, and to the whole household.

Zanni: Then hop it, you: I order you never to set foot here again.

Capitano: In order to oblige you, Sir, I'm on my way; I commend myself to you. *(Exit)*

Colombina: Zanni, do you love me?

Zanni: I love you . . . I love you as much as I love sausages and bacon.[6]

Colombina

Name. Generically, the female of *zanni*: *zagne*. The role was first called *sobretta* (*soubrette* in French), later known as *fantesca* (maid) or *servetta* (female servant). Although Colombina became the dominant name, especially as Colombine in France and England, she was originally also called Franceschina, Smeraldina, Oliva, Nespola, Spinetta, Ricciolina, Corallina, Diamantina, Lisetta, etc.

Status. Personal maid to the prima donna *innamorata*.

Origin. *Le ballerine* (French *danseuses*) and/or *le cantarine* (French *chanteuses*) with a tambourine provided *entr'acte* entertainment before women were allowed into the stage action proper. Here, for once, there is an indisputable link with Roman theatre. Its relatively late development meant that the role, unlike the male Masks derived from Carnival, was much more dependent on the character of the performer herself and on the taste of the audience. The early street performers (who were more often called Franceschina, Smeraldina, etc.), were older, lustier and more buxom than the later seventeenth- and eighteenth-century Colombinas who, as well as being younger and more graceful and engaging, were less overtly sexual. In borrowing from the *commedia erudita* which had a tradition of the maid appearing in place of her mistress, the *servetta* would have had a lot to do. But once the Lovers actually appeared, she was reduced to the role of confidante and message carrier. It seems that was too small a part to be afforded by a travelling *commedia dell'arte* troupe, who would need their third actress to carry an equal share. 'A new part was worked out in which the "fantesca" became the counterpart of Zanni in function and the reflection of her mistress in manner and mood.'[1]

A history of the role can therefore be glimpsed from a roll-call of its principal interpreters:

20 Colombina holding up the mask of Comedy by Maurice Sand. A conventional frontispiece which typifies Sand's tendency to over-authenticate his Commedia drawings which has trapped some of the Masks in his idealisation of them. The position, however, is identical to a pose with tambourine on a Herculaneum vase painting. (See also Plate 1.)

c. 1570	Franceschina – Silvia Roncagli.
1593–1659	Ricciolina – Antonazzoni.
c. 1653	Diamantina – Patricia Adami played first in Italy, later in France. 'Slight of stature and rather brown of skin, but extremely pretty.'[2] Took over the role from Beatrice of whom no more is known than Foret's quatrain:

> Maid pour enchanter les oreilles,
> Pâmer, pleurer, faire merveilles,
> Mademoiselle *Béatrix*
> Emporta, ce jour-là, le prix.

c. 1675	Olivetta – V. Teodora Archiari.
c. 1683	Colombina – Caterina Biancolelli, daughter of Dominique-Arlequin. Inherited name from great-grandmother (Teresa) and later passed it on to her daughter (also Teresa). Well-educated, speaking several languages and dialects. 'She was small and brunette, but of a very comely countenance. She had more than beauty; she had physiognomy, a fine air, easy gesture and a sweet pleasant voice.'[3]
c. 1697	Spinetta – sister-in-law of Constantini-Mezzetino.
c. 1716	Violetta – Margherita Rusca.
c. 1744	Corallina – Anna Véronèse, daughter of Véronèse-Pantalone
c. 1745–69	Smeraldina.

Physical appearance. Initially strong and attractive, like a circus artiste, later petite and pretty.

Costume. Better dressed than male servants since she is a lady's maid. Mob cap and apron, wearing a 'folly' dress underneath. Skirts fell usually just below the knee. Neckline of bodice low and often frilled. Several colours of material.

Mask. Unmasked, but the eyes wide and well made-up. Can wear domino for special excursions.

Props. Often carries a basket.

Stance. One knee bent, the other leg extended. Slight forward tilt from the hips to show best features. Tiny waist and wide hips.

Walk. Little flick of foot at end of grand *zanni* walk.

Movements. All *zanni* movements, in any combination. Movement continues during speaking, shifting balance from one foot to the other and moving the head sharply as if searching for someone other than the person being addressed. Fast and nimble in order to escape unwanted attentions or butt in, then escape from a situation.

Gestures. Hands either on hips, holding apron or making significant gestures. When excited she throws her hands up as if still dancing with the tambourine. A good mimic.

Speech. Sharp, gossipy, with frequent variations of pitch. Originally Tuscan, but could be any other dialect.

Animal. Dove.

Relationships. Loves Arlecchino, but sees through him. Feels a need to look after him, educate him in the hope that he too can break the bounds of being a fixed type. She therefore scolds him, punishes him, deserts him, takes him back, but in the end he does not change and she has to accept him for what he is, which is still more lovable than Il Dottore, Pantalone, Il Capitano, etc. She can be very affectionate to other characters as well, and her affections seem to flow through her physically, but she always holds something back. As a result she is pestered by other men, especially Il Capitano and Pantalone. She is always ready to help the Lovers, perhaps through natural sympathy with their plight.

Relationship to audience. Collusive – she is a spectator herself. Very strong relationship with the audience, almost confidential in the sense that she too can see what fools the rest of them are. Flirts with spectators, moving closer so they can see her eyes, but not too close.

Plot function. The still centre of the turning wheel, in on everything that is going on, she exerts a benevolent influence on the outcome.

Characteristics. The only lucid, rational person in *commedia dell'arte*, analogous to Maria in *Twelfth Night*. Autonomous and self-sufficient, she has no negative attributes; she has enough to eat, decent clothes and no ambition to be rich. She can read and write: in fact she is very fond of books and owns several. She sings, dances, captivates, but has gone beyond her *entremetteuse* origins to become a self-educated woman:

> during the Renaissance a learned woman was known as a *virago*. Which meant that this was a woman who by 'courage and under-standing' and by her natural attainments, 'raised herself above the masses of her sex.' It is curious that the word *virago* should have taken on an entirely different and opposite meaning.[4]

In this respect she is influenced by contact with Isabella, indeed it is difficult to see how the latter could confide in anyone who did not share her outlook on life. The main difference between *servette* and *zanni* is that whereas Arlecchino thinks on his feet, Colombina uses her brain and thinks things through. Like Il Capitano she is a lone figure, capable of appearing *solus*. Often, in fact, the prologue is entrusted to her. Although capricious and coquettish she is good at her job, careful with money, and will, with great reluctance, make an excellent housekeeper one day . . . cf. Susanna in *The Marriage of Figaro*. Although she seems sexually very knowing she is sometimes a virgin, when it suits her.

Improvisation exercise

Together with a Zanni, mimic a love scene by standing behind two Lovers, then parody them by standing at the side.

Canovaccio

The street. PANTALONE tells IL DOTTORE of his desire for Colombina. His manhood is, however, letting him down. IL DOTTORE prescribes his patent Consummation Pills. Sends Arlecchino for them. ARLECCHINO (mishearing?) brings Constipation Pills. Exit PANTALONE in search of Colombina. The mistake is realised and ARLECCHINO goes after him with the right medicine.

A room in Panatalone's house. PANTALONE tries to seduce COLOMBINA but is increasingly troubled with his bowels until he has to leave. ARLECCHINO arrives and COLOMBINA, laughing, hears his story. She makes him take the pills and they wait for them to take effect.

Sample prologue

Yes, yes, yes and yes again, I am getting angry!

I am a serving maid, it's true! But the status of servant does not condemn me to working like a slave: cleaning rooms, killing myself in the kitchen, carrying wood, drawing water, doing the shopping, washing shirts, starching collars, mending clothes, etc.

Do you know, ladies and gentlemen, that the people back there even want me to deliver the prologue!

No, no and no again!

My misfortune was to become serving maid to a company of actors. They led me to believe that their profession was paved with delights, full of joy, covered in contentment and sprinkled with sweetness. No way!

They had me believe that the greatest pleasure you can have is to travel the world: to see one day a great city, the next hillsides covered with fruit trees. To perceive distant summits or traverse countryside as far as the eye can see. Or again, to hug the coast of enormous seas.

To listen to them you'd think I was about to strike it rich!

All these promises turned out to be lies! In reality, the pleasure of seeing the world, if you want to know, is rain, ice, snow, lousy hotels, dreadful horses, broken wheels, hoteliers who won't keep their hands off you and other little pleasures of a similar kind.

And in the mornings, ladies and gentlemen, it is the name

of Colombina which resounds to the four points of the compass. Like this, listen: 'Hey, Colombina, bring me Fiammela's book on love, I want to study it'; old Pantalone: 'Hey, Colombina, bring me the Magnifico's book of melancholy sayings'; the Captain: 'Hey, Colombina, *bella mia*, bring me *il libro* which relates the brave deeds of my great friend Capitano Spavento'; Arlecchino: 'Colombina, Colombina, quick, quick, I want you to read me *Turlupino's Tricks*'; Doctor Boloardo: 'Little Colombina, since you are aware that Hippocrates is my master and since you wish to be appraised of the fundamentals of his profound thinking, let it be your hands which place in mine the works of his which, bla, bla, bla, bla'; Leandro, the Lover: 'Colombina, Colombina, may the work of the learned Plato which you are about to bring me nourish my innermost thoughts.'

Colombina here, Colombina there, Colombina, Colombina, Colombina. Enough is enough. All these works are going on the fire and I hope they are all hissed when they get on this stage where they've sent me to do the prologue.

If they come after me, I put myself at your mercy, ladies and gentlemen. If they hurt me, I beg you to tear me from their hands. And if the person who comes to my aid wants me for a serving maid, then I am at your service.[5]

Sample monologue

Men! They are all cruel to us, some more, some less. They demand the most absolute fidelity, and on the least shadow of suspicion they bully us, ill-treat us, and are likely to murder us. And what about their fidelity? They say they don't like to eat one kind of cheese all their lives! And why should men have more privileges than women do? Because it's the law! Pooh! Who made the law? If I were a queen, I'd make every man who was unfaithful carry a branch of a tree in his hand, and I know all the towns would look like forests.

Well, if you have got to marry one or another of them some day, you must take marriage like you take medicine when you're ill. And like medicine, it sometimes makes you feel better! For myself, if my husband samples another kind of cheese, I'll lose no time in showing him what's sauce for the goose is sauce for the gander![6]

Sample dialogue

Colombina: My dear friend! Tell me truly, do you love me?

Arlecchino: Oh yes, of course I love you. I love you as much as old men love money.

Colombina: I love you as much as cabbies love bad weather.

Arlecchino: And I, as much as pawnbrokers love hard times.

Colombina: And I, as much as dancing masters love beautiful clothes.

Arlecchino: And I, as much as doctors love an epidemic.

Colombina: And I, as much as boys love lying.

Arlecchino: And I, as much as women love looking beautiful.

Colombina: And I, as much as the young love spending money, short skirts, long trousers and big ties.

Arlecchino: And I, as much as pickpockets love big crowds.

Colombina: And I, as much as playwrights love applause.

Arlecchino: And I, as much as musicians love to drink.

Colombina: And I, as much as arms dealers love a war.

Arlecchino: Ah! Hold it there; I can't think of anything stronger than that.[7]

Other Masks

Pedrolino

Name. Athough there is a record of a Piero in 1547, throughout the rest of the sixteenth century the character was obscure until re-emerging as Pagliaccio (1570), then Gian-Farina (1598), becoming Pedrolino as the creation of Giovanni Pellesini who played first with a company known simply as Pedrolino's (1576), then with the Gelosi, then with the Uniti, and finally the Confidenti. The name Pedrolino was used throughout the seventeenth century, finally being adapted in France from a minor variant, Pierrotto, into Pierrot in 1665.

Status. Most Commedia troupes were family-based. Pedrolino, being the role given to the youngest son, is therefore bottom of the pecking order, the one who has to sleep in the straw with the animals: *Pagliaccio*, (from *pagliaio*, a pile of straw). He is often the butt of jokes, especially concerning his cowardice, but he never loses his dignity.

Costume. His baggy white clothes are hand-me-downs and too big for him, sometimes even with sleeves too long for his hands to be visible. In early illustrations he can easily be confused with Pulcinella. Tunic has pockets to keep a variety of small objects, usually only of sentimental value. Pointed white hat.

Mask. White face, originally floured (Gian-Farina). He thus has a range of emotional expressions denied to other Masks.

Stance. Feet in third position, not too much movement in the knees. Elbows bent, hands kept up and active.

21 The development of Pierrot, reconstructed from drawings by Maurice Sand: from left to right, Pagliaccio (c. 1600), Pedrolino (c. 1670), Peppe-Nappa (c. 1770), Pierrot (c. 1850).

Walk.   Direct, in straight lines. Head moves like a chicken, elbows up.

Speech.   His voice is light and lilting, in contrast to Arlecchino. It is very easy to make his inflections 'camp', but this is not correct and can create wrong assumptions in the spectator.

Characteristics.   Stoicism in the face of misery, survived his oppression by pretending to be simple. Anaesthetised his sensitivity by pretending to have no feelings. Gives vent to feelings only when alone. Totally honest. Aways tired due to his poor accommodation: frequently falls asleep, especially when ordered to watch over something. Conscientious and full of remorse at the slightest harm to another.

Animal.   His job is to look after the animals – the pack mule, perhaps a performing bear or some monkeys. He has a special affinity with dogs since he shares their abused, half-starved lives. Although an animal-lover, he remains intensely human, a human animal, not a hybrid like the other Masks.

Relationships.   A loner, an observer of the follies of others, but unhesitatingly faithful to his master and to Colombina for whom he suffers eternally unrequited love. If she deceives him he blames himself for not being adequate as a lover.

Plot function.   Initially the warmer-up or barker for the show, later grew, especially in the scenarios of the Flaminio Scala troupe, to be the linchpin. He takes a child-like delight in practical jokes and pranks, but otherwise his intrigues are on behalf of his master – he is too honest and self-effacing to do otherwise. At times, however, the best he can scheme for is to escape the punishment others have in store for him.

Improvisation exercises

Canovaccio

The street. PEDROLINO has been trying to help his master, Pantalone, but one of his tricks has backfired. PANTALONE is furious with him. Struck dumb by his master's ingratitude, PEDROLINO remains motionless and silent in the middle of the stage. One after another several characters enter and address him: he does not make any acknowledgement. Irritated by his seeming dumb insolence, IL CAPITANO starts to beat him. Suddenly PEDROLINO screams and leaps in the air. IL CAPITANO and the others are terrified while PEDROLINO walks calmly away.

Sample dialogue

The longer the Italian companies stayed in Paris, the more bilingual their performances became. Here Il Dottore interpolates gobbets of Italian and Pedrolino's ability to understand him when he does so is greater than that of most of the spectators would have been. He refuses to be patronised by the Doctor's supposedly superior knowledge of the universe – he has his own reality, which is based on natural and sympathetic understanding, not spurious learning:

Dottore: *E possibile, Pedrolino, che tu non voglia chetarti?* Be quiet, I beg you.

Pedrolino: But, Sir, how can you want me to shut up? I don't get a moment's rest. The whole day long I have to run after your daughter, your niece and your maidservant; then as soon as it is dusk I have to run after you. As soon as I go to bed you start your alarm call: 'Pedrolino, Pedrolino, get up quickly, light the candle, and give me my telescope, I want to go and observe the stars.' And you would have me believe that the moon is a world like our own. The moon! Holy cow! Don't make me mad.

Dottore: Pedrolino, ancor una volta, taci. Ti bastonarò.

Pedrolino: Blow me then, Sir, before you kill me, I must pour out what is in my heart. I am not so stupid as to believe that the moon is a world; the moon, the moon, good Lord, it's no bigger than an eight-egg omelette.

Dottore: Don't be impertinent! If you had the slightest ability to understand I would explain it to you. *Ma tu sei una Bestia, un ignorante Animale che non sa doue s'habbia la testa se non se la tocca; e però chiudi la bocca,* and for the last time shut up, if you know what's good for you.

Pedrolino (becoming annoyed): I'll chop it into pieces, by God!

Dottore: *La mia patienza fa miracoli.* Nevertheless, let us see if we cannot extract ourselves from this contretemps. *Ascolta, animale,* have you ever remarked on those clouds that are to be seen around the moon, those . . .

Pedrolino: I know, you mean the garnish round the omelette.

Dottore: Devil take you. Shut up *in malhora,* and stop dreaming about omelettes. These clouds, therefore, that one observes around the moon, are known as crepuscules. Or so the argument goes.

Pedrolino: Let me see.

Dottore: If there are crepuscules in the moon, *bisogna ch'a vi sia una Generation, & una Corrution; e s'al ghé una corrution, & una generation, bisogna ch'a ve nasca dei Animali, e dei Vegetabili; e s'al ghe nasce dei animali, e dei vegetabili, ergo la Luna è un Mondo abitabile com'al nostro.*

Pedrolino: *Ergo* whatever you like. For my part, *Nego*; and here's how I can prove it to you. You say that in the Moon there are three ... pus ... threepus ..., Threepus-stools.

Dottore: *Crepuscoli*, and not pustules, cretin.

Pedrolino: Anyway, these three ... are you listening to me? And if there are these three crapstools, then there has to be a generation and a corruption?

Dottore: *Certissimo.*

Pedrolino: Right then, here's what Pedrolino says.

Dottore: *Vedremo.*

Pedrolino: If there is regeneration and corruption in the moon, then there must be lettuce: how else could the moon be green? Hey? Do you get me? There's no answer to that!

Dottore: *Al credo ben. Orsu, Pedrolino, lassem andar la Luna, e parlem d'altre cose.*

Pedrolino: That's a good idea, because the way you go on about your blessed moon, I'm worried that one day you'll end up just the same, having phases.[1]

▥ Pulcinella

Name. Means little chicken. (*Pulcino* = day-old chick in Italian). His full name is Pulcinella Cetrulo (*citrulo* = stupid). He became Polichinelle in France, Hanswurst (Germany), Toneelgek (Holland), Kasperle (Austria), Petrushka (Russia), Karagöz (Turkey), and Mr Punch in England.

Status. Can either be employer or employee: no respecter of persons either way, e.g. magistrate, baker, schoolmaster, spy, even poet.

Origin. Of all *commedia dell'arte* characters Pulcinella is the one most likely to have derived from the Atellenae. 'This mask is the last stand of those who believe in the classical origins of the commedia dell'arte.'[2] George Sand was their foremother, writing in 1852 that, 'the most ancient of all the types is the Neapolitan Polichinello. He descends in direct line from the Maccus of the Campagna, or rather, he is the same character.' In her opinion, a statue found in Rome in 1727 shows the former equipped like his descendants with two enormous humps, a nose hooked like the beak of a bird of prey, and heavy shoes, tied about the ankle, which are not unlike our modern sabots. . . . The ancient type must have been somewhat baser and more hateful than the modern Pulcinella; provoking laughter chiefly by his deformities . . . I am confirmed in this opinion by the fact that in the Neapolitan farces two Pulcinellas are to be found: one is base and doltish, the veritable son of Maccus [Pulcinello]: the other is daring, thieving, quarrelsome, Bohemian and more of a modern creation [Pulcinella].[3]

Others hold that he is descended from Pulcinella dalle Carceri, a grotesque patriot of the thirteenth century, and others that his creator was a sixteenth-century peasant, Puccio D'Aniello, who lived in Acerra, a town near Naples not far from Atella. A company of strolling comedians is said to have visited a field where peasants were harvesting, and found themselves subjected to a steady flow of humorous and cutting interruptions. Getting tired of it they returned sally for sally, and concentrated their fire on Puccio, who, besides being one of their wittiest interrupters, had a comic face and a long nose which offered a target for their wit. The peasant gave better than he got and finally they returned to town defeated and red-faced. It then struck them that he would make a good addition to the company; they returned and proposed he join them.

What is certain is that Pulcinella was introduced into *commedia dell'arte* proper in 1620 through the efforts of Silvio Fiorillo, the celebrated Captain Matamoros, who played him as a white-smocked peasant up from the country (cf. the origin of Zanni) who gradually became the burlesque representative of the working class of Naples.

Pulcinella has taken root and undergone separate development in other countries. This is because he is the product of local social and cultural circumstances – Antonio Fava (who has inherited the mask from his father) thinks he cannot be translated into another language without complete transformation. In one of his one-man shows he plays him as an Italian migrant worker coming to terms with life in the south of France. 'The stranger is converted into a national type to be the mouthpiece of all that is unique and untranslatable in the humour of a race.'[4] The character still grows in Italy, with numerous solo performers having their own version, whereas other Commedia characters have reached a 'final' stage of development or decay.

Physical appearance. Hump-backed (sometimes with even two humps, indicating his split personality) and pot-bellied. By the end of the seventeenth century the humps disappeared.

22 Antonio Fava as Pulcinella.

Costume. Long baggy white blouse, tied around the waist with a leather belt which carries his stick and his purse. No collar. Wide (pleated?) trousers. Grey felt hat replaced by the end of the seventeenth century by a white sugar-loaf (*coppolone*).

Mask. Brown or black with long, beaked nose. Furrowed with wrinkles with large wart or carbuncle on forehead. Bristling black beard and moustaches, abandoned during the seventeenth century.

Props. A cudgel, which he calls his staff of credit, because it is the money with which he pays off his debts.

Stance. Weight is basically on one leg as if compensating for his hump, even in later renditions where deformity has been dispensed with. Centre of gravity high.

Walk. Small jerky steps, sometimes very fast and agile in a skipping walk or half run.

Movements. Slow and top-heavy, contrasting with the speed of his thought and speech. But can also be acrobatic and perform on trapeze or slack wire.

Gestures. Broad and sparing. An excellent mimic, anticipates twentieth-century corporeal mime in that he will impersonate birds and animals, and even inanimate objects such as trees and houses.

Speech. A chicken squawk, very like the result of the 'swazzle' used by Punch and Judy Professors. A chatterbox who never knows when to shut up. He speaks Roman, Neapolitan or Calabrese, or the dialect of his adopted region.

Characteristics. He can be played as either stupid pretending to be clever, or clever pretending to be stupid. Either way he is the complete egotist. His good-humoured exterior conceals a ferocious interior and he cares no more for human life than for that of a flea. He delights in quarrels, makes a point of seeking them, and takes great pleasure in bloodshed. He is not, however, a boaster, and does not speak of his dastardly deeds. His chief predilections are women, drink and food (he is very fond indeed of macaroni – the Neapolitan pasta – and gnocchi). A chameleon, despite the distinctiveness of his appearance, he can be any type by turns: 'faithful, revengeful, sly, gullible, nervy, audacious, jealous, cowardly, bullying, sentimental, lazy . . . yet behind all these there is an essential quality which we recognise as Pulcinella, just as we are aware of his nose and accent [whatever his disguise].'[5] He has a fatalistic philosophy – nothing gets to him. He sees all nature in his own image: brutal, ugly and destructive. Since he has no capacity to receive human kindness, he has no concept of how to extend it to others.

Pulcinella has a secret: he cannot help telling everyone everything.

Animal. Cockerel.

Relationships. Zanni usually has a sweetheart, but rarely a wife: Pulcinella is the opposite. He is very domesticated and quite capable of impersonating a wife and mother if no other is available.

Relationship to audience. Direct, quarrelsome. Always signs off:

> I am Prince of everything,
> Lord of land and main
> Except for my public
> Whose faithful servant I remain.

The stage is his natural home, so he often forgets he is on it, for example when answering the call of nature. But he is, above all, a popular figure in his own right and one with whom the audience (Neapolitan or wherever) identifies since, despite his deformity and inhumanity, he is

> popular in the struggle with the oppression of slavery and ugliness. Pulcinella personifies the accomplished revolt; he is hideous but he is terrible, severe and vengeful; neither god nor devil can make him tremble when he wields his great cudgel. By means of this weapon, which he freely lays about the shoulders of his master and the heads of public officers, he exercises a sort of summary and individual justice which avenges the weak.[6]

Plot function. A loner, if he does not fit into a northern scenario structure he becomes second Zanni.

> Comparing the repertories of the first, with those of the second half of the seventeenth century, it is clear that the popularity of Pulcinella hastened the disintegration of the *commedia dell'arte* by increasing the output of ill-constructed farces. Why labour with the implications of a neo-classical intrigue when the appearance of a Pulcinella in one disguise after another, turning off practical jokes or quarrelling with Rosetta, is what the audience enjoys? He is given a free hand, *lazzi a son gusto* . . . as the ivy the tree, so he first kills the *commedia dell'arte*, then supports it when the sap, the *vis comica*, is dried up.[7]

Improvisation exercise

Repertorio

> I have no illusions on the score of my physical appearance and I shall not disclose to you the secret of my success with women, because I do not know it; on the other hand, can you explain women to me? He who pleases them does so because he pleases them; there are no other reasons. Woman is a bizarre and mysterious being: she is the only good thing in this world after wine and hard knocks.[8]

The *lazzo* of the goodness of Pulcinella is that he, having heard from Il Capitano or from others that they want to kill him, and not being known to them, freely praises himself with the words: 'Pulcinella is a man of infinite wit, a humble man, a good man.'

Pulcinella, having been left by his master to guard the house, on being asked if there is anyone inside, replies that there isn't even a fly. The master discovers three men there and reproaches Pulcinella, who replies: 'You didn't find any flies, you only found men.' When his master is talking Pulcinella is continually interrupting. Three times his master tells him to shut up. Then when he calls for Pulcinella, the latter pays him back in the same coin and says 'shut up!'

Coviello asks Pulcinella what the name of his wife is. Pulcinella says it begins with an O and that he must guess. Coviello tries various names beginning with O, then gives up. Pulcinella says her name is Rosetta. Coviello protests that that begins with an R, not an O. Pulcinella replies 'So what – she's my wife, if I want to begin her name with an O it's no business of yours!'

When being taken away to prison he says he must first tie his shoe laces. Then he bends down, grabs the legs of his two guards, up-ends them and runs away.[9]

Canovaccio

> In *Le Ruine di Pompeia*, Pulcinella, who is in love with one of the daughters of the custodian of the place, has attached himself to a group of foreign visitors, whom he amuses with his sallies, and at whose expense he regales himself, stealing the best bits of their dinner, and forever juggling away the coin which they place in the custodian's hand. The visitors end by seeing through his game, are displeased with it and seek to seize him by the collar. Pulcinella grows angry; he raises his voice indignantly to protest that anyone should suspect an honourable man such as he, a person of his importance. He pretends to be, by turns, an English Lord and a French officer. Soon, however, being convicted of imposture, and closely pressed, he plies his cudgel, takes to flight through the ruins and suddenly disappears at the very moment in which his pursuers believe they have captured him. He is found at last in one of the newly discovered caves, lying amid a litter of empty amphorae in company with the custodian's daughter. Everything is arranged, and the piece concludes with a marriage which appears to be extremely necessary.[10]

Sample monologue

> 'You should assist yourself with your legs when it is not practicable to do so with your hands', says a fencing-master in a footnote to the thirtieth chapter of the *Treatise on Valour*, which I would

translate into normal language as: 'He who doesn't trust his hands takes to his feet', as do, mostly, the *spadaccini* from my country, what you would call hit-men, who, when the chips are down, turn out to be excellent sprinters who can show you a clean pair of heels.

Yes, my God, didn't I do well to escape, to avoid getting eliminated, and let's hope it turns out that it was just a nasty moment, when things were beginning to get a bit hot, and today's another day.

Listen, here's the whole sad story: you'll die of shock when you hear it. A few days ago, after I'd eaten my bellyful, I got this notion to go and make love with that bit of stuff that lives round the corner; and since it was that time of night when the police stay indoors, I put in my pocket, for the defence of my poor little life, a worn-out old clasp-knife. And, whilst I'm whistling under my bird's window, I hear some dick-head coming up behind me; he says 'Who goes there?' – Uh-oh, says I, this is a Spaniard from Spain: I'm done for. But I plucked up courage and I said to him: 'Listen, you'd better go because there's a man here having a crap and he's about to dump.' The Spaniard said: 'You're drunk: get out of my way.' 'What I'd like to offer you,' I replied, 'is the chance of going to the Devil and hanging yourself.' You should have seen this Spanish bozo then: he looked like he wanted to swallow his tongue – and wash it down with wine. Then me, I said: 'You and whose army?', feeling a bit tasty, I said 'Bog off, old man, or I'll give you a hundred whacks where it hurts.' Fish-face says to me: 'You drunkard, I'm going to kill you with my pistol.' 'Stick your gun,' says I, 'and keep still, because I'm going to have your guts', and I stood en garde. And then this pig-dog shoots an enema syringe full of cold water from under his coat and I get it right in the face. I'm terrified: we're off, me in front and fish-face after me; I'm running like mad with this blighter on my heels, and the water was so cold, that for a week after I was shitting sorbet all over town. And if you don't believe me, take a walk down to the shops with your tongue like this: there's a few tasty ones down there.[11]

Sample dialogue

A powerful *contrasto* between Pulcinella and the strongest of the Capitanos, Matamoros, the Spanish mercenary. Written by the originator of both characters, there is no record of which he would have played:

Capitano: Italian!
Pulcinella: Spaniard!
Capitano: Italian spaghetti!
Pulcinella: Spanish paella!
Capitano: Pedlar of blasphemies!
Pulcinella: Donkey-dropping!
Capitano: Pox on you!
Pulcinella: Snivelling drunkard!
Capitano: Gutless dog!
Pulcinella: Get stuffed! Go and take a running jump. You're getting
 on my tits!
Capitano: Milksop! You're spraying like a bitch on heat!
Pulcinella: You brothel-bred shithead, you and your brother and your
 sister!
Capitano: Pig-gob, parrot-chops!
Pulcinella: Cocksucker, crablouse!
Capitano: I won't endure your insults any longer: I'll scrape them up
 in a sick-bag and chuck 'em in your ugly mug.
Pulcinella: And I'll throw them back in your grog-blossom face,
 Spanish dog, bad-luck charm, walking plague-sore.
Capitano and *Pulcinella* (*together*): Syphilitic strumpet's brat sired
 by a thousand fathers, wart-faced son of a worn-out trollop . . .
 [etc.]
Capitano: Silly little girl, pile of rotten straw! How dare you say *tan-
 tas de mauves palabres* to me!
Pulcinella: I haven't started yet! One more insult from you and you'll
 get it back ten billion times over. I warn you, I'll get you with my
 knife and my stick and put the boot in. *(To the audience)* Hold
 me back or I'll scrag him!
Capitano: Let him go, so that I can squash him!
Pulcinella: Hold me back or I'll have his guts for garters!
Capitano: Let him go so that I can assassinate him!
Pulcinella (*to the audience*): I'll beat him to a pulp for you.
Capitano: You can keep him, he's all yours.
Pulcinella: I kill him. *(He takes out his stick)*
Capitano: Try this fart for size! *(Lazzo of Pulcinella being knocked
 flat)* I'm the prettiest, I'm the greatest, I'm Beelzebub, the busi-
 ness, that's what I am.
Pulcinella: Now do you understand? You're so proud, you're so smart,
 you're a poet, you sing, you play the guitar.
Capitano: *Que quieres decir por este, cabron?*
Pulcinella: Listen and split yourself. Here is the sonnet written by
 the great Marino, son of Apollo and nephew of the Muses, it could
 have been made for you.

The bleating sheep goes: baa, baa . . .
The snorting pig goes: snort, snort . . .
The neighing horse goes: neigh, neigh . . .
The chirping cricket goes: chirp, chirp . . .
The hooting owl goes: toowit-toowoo . . .
The crowing cock goes: a doodle-doo . . .
The clucking hen goes: cluck, cluck . . .
The quacking duck goes: quack, quack . . .
The miaowing cat goes: miaow, miaow . . .
The crowing crow goes: croak, croak . . .
And the braying donkey goes: ee-aw, ee-aw, and you,
you pork-pie seller, tell us the truth for once: you are
the king of the donkeys so let's hear you bray.

Capitano: Ah, Pulcinella, I've had enough of this: since you want to make something of it, since you want to fight with 'migo', with me, cross naked steel or with tassels on if you prefer, or . . .

Pulcinella: I'm fed up with your blathering, I don't want to play any more.

Capitano: I want to fight, I want to fight.

Pulcinella: What do you want?

Capitano: I want to fight.

Pulcinella: Ah, you want to fight! No!

Capitano: No? Why not?

Pulcinella: The eagle does not fight with a slug.

Capitano: Don't worry about that! You are of such humble extraction and I am so nobly born that I can easily arrange matters! *(He dubs him)* Thus you become my equal.

Pulcinella: And now that I am a noble, what name shall I take?

Capitano: Milord scapegoat.

Pulcinella: Scapegoat yourself, since you get slaps by day and smacks by night. I accept the challenge and before dawn breaks, I will amuse myself with you with weapons of my choice.

Capitano: Pulcinella, at last my honour is satisfied. But do you realise you have just agreed to fight a duel?

Pulcinella: Of course I realise. But now I want some grub, for if you've got to die, it's best to do it on a stomach full of minestrone. *(Exit)*[12]

▥ Scapino

Name. Derives from *scappare*, 'to flee', which gives us the English slang word, 'scarper'.

Status. First Zanni.

Origin. Created by Franceso Gabrielli (1588–1636), famous for his ability to play a great number of instruments and, according to Barbieri, the best Zanni of his era. The best-known interpreter of the role was Giovanni Bissoni (1666–1723) from Bologna. Scapino (or Scappino) was derived from

23 Scapino is never still: in this engraving Maurice Sand captures a sense of the Mask in movement as well as its criminal propensities.

Brighella, as a valet-cicerone and handyman. He is, however, more of a coward – as his name would suggest.

Physical appearance.   Wiry.

Costume.   A basic baggy white *zanni* top and trousers, but with more cut. Shovel hat with long, rakish feathers.

Props.   Slapstick and a *zanni*-style porter's sack, a sort of swagbag which he carries at all times in case of opportunity.

Walk.   Light-footed: his speciality, as name suggests, is running (away).

Animal.   A bird. 'In temperament Scapino is very like a starling. He skims away, swoops back, twitters and warbles, pilfers right and left, flies off, but never fails to return.'[13]

Relationships.

> He is as amorous as birds in spring, and for him it is spring the whole year round. He deserves some credit for his modesty, for he is not an amorous Don Juan in his amours: he invariably prefers to make off with a servant-girl rather than a king's daughter. He falls in love for the sheer joy of it, and, like a bird, flits from one love to another, never becoming deeply involved and always obeying every impulse that enters his flighty head.[14]

Plot function.   Schemes against old men for the sake of money, revenge or both.

Characteristics.   'Scapino is bereft of all sense of logic; he makes confusion of everything he undertakes, and forgets everything except to hold his hand out for a gratuity.'[15] He is a liar by instinct, but his lies, like himself, are of slight importance. Molière's Scapin in *Les Fourberies de Scapin* is perhaps slightly too 'heavy', predominantly Brighella. The latter, however, was losing his force at the time and gradually becoming more of an obsequious valet.

Sample dialogue

The famous 'Que diable allait-il faire dans cet galère?' scene from *Les Fourberies de Scapin*. The San Francisco Mime Troupe substituted Il Dottore for Molière's Géronte; I have preferred Pantalone and restored Scapin to Scapino.

> *Scapino (pretending not to notice Pantalone's entry)*: Oh, Lord! What a disgraceful thing to happen! It's the father I feel sorry for! Poor old Pantalone, what will he do?
>
> *Pantalone (aside)*: What's he saying about me with a face as long as a fiddle?
>
> *Scapino*: Can't anyone tell me where Mister Pantalone is?
>
> *Pantalone*: What's the matter, Scapino?
>
> *Scapino (going off, pretending not to hear him)*: I must find him to tell him about this disaster.
>
> *Pantalone (running after him)*: What's the matter, then?
>
> *Scapino*: I've looked everywhere for him, but not a chance.
>
> *Pantalone*: Here I am.
>
> *Scapino (still pretending)*: He must have hidden himself somewhere no-one would ever think of looking.
>
> *Pantalone*: Hey! Are you blind? I'm here.
>
> *Scapino*: Oh, Sir, I couldn't find you anywhere.
>
> *Pantalone*: I've been standing under your nose for the last hour. What's the matter, then?
>
> *Scapino*: Sir . . .
>
> *Pantalone*: What?
>
> *Scapino*: Sir, your son . . .
>
> *Pantalone*: My son what?
>
> *Scapino*: Has had the most incredible bad luck imaginable.
>
> *Pantalone*: How?
>
> *Scapino*: I came across him a little while back terribly upset by something, I don't know what, that you had said to him. We went for a walk down to the harbour, to try and cheer him up. There, among other things, we noticed a Ruritanian yacht – beautifully equipped. A handsome young Ruritanian invited us on board and it was handshakes all round. Once we were aboard he was kindness itself – gave us a buffet lunch with excellent fruit and choice wines.
>
> *Pantalone*: What's so terrible about that?
>
> *Scapino*: Wait a minute, Sir, we're coming to it. While we were eating, the yacht put to sea, and, once outside territorial waters, the Ruritanian has me put in the tender and sends me to tell you that if you don't send me back at once with five hundred guineas he'll make your son work his passage to Africa.
>
> *Pantalone*: What the devil! Five hundred guineas!
>
> *Scapino*: Yes, Sir, and what's more he only gave me two hours.
>
> *Pantalone*: Grrr . . . Ruddy Ruritanian! He's trying to bleed me white!

Scapino: It's up to you, Sir, quick, think of some way of saving your son. I know how deep your affection is for him.

Pantalone: What the devil was he doing on the yacht?

Scapino: He had no idea what would happen.

Pantalone: Off you go, Scapino, and tell this Ruritanian I'll have the police on him.

Scapino: The police on the high seas? You must be joking.

Pantalone: What the devil was he doing on the yacht?

Scapino: It must have been his unlucky day.

Pantalone: Scapino, the situation demands that you act like a loyal servant.

Scapino: What, Sir?

Pantalone: Go and tell this Ruritanian to send my son back, and you stay in his place until I've got the ransom money together.

Scapino: Eh? Do you realise what you're saying? Do you think this Ruritanian is so daft as to take a miserable wretch like me in place of your son?

Pantalone: What the devil was he doing on the yacht?

Scapino: He couldn't guess what was going to happen. Remember, Sir, he's only given me two hours.

Pantalone: You say he wants . . .

Scapino: Five hundred guineas.

Pantalone: Five hundred guineas! Has he no moral standards?

Scapino: Yes Sir, his morals are standard – for a Ruritanian.

Pantalone: Does he know how much five hundred guineas is?

Scapino: Yes, Sir: he knows it's five hundred pounds plus five hundred shillings.

Pantalone: Does this cheapskate think five hundred guineas can be found just like that?

Scapino: These people don't listen to reason.

Pantalone: But what the devil was he doing on the yacht?

Scapino: It's unfortunate, but there you are! You can't foresee these things. Please, Sir, hurry up.

Pantalone: Here, take the key to my desk.

Scapino: Right.

Pantalone: Open it.

Scapino: Fine.

Pantalone: In the left-hand drawer you'll find a big key which opens the attic door.

Scapino: Yes.

Pantalone: Take all the old clothes in the big trunk and sell them to the pawnbroker to ransom my son.

Scapino (giving back the key): Eh? Are you crazy, Sir? I wouldn't get five pounds for that lot, and what's more you know how little time they've given me.

Pantalone: What the devil was he doing on the yacht?

Scapino: Oh, save your breath! Forget about the yacht and remember that time's short and that you're in danger of losing your son. Oh, poor young master, I may never see you again, even as I speak you're being carried off to Africa! But God is my witness that I did all I could for you, and if you don't get ransomed you've only a hardhearted father to blame!

Pantalone: Wait, Scapino, I'll go and fetch the money.

Scapino: Hurry then, Sir, I'm terrified in case the clock sounds the hour.

Pantalone: Four hundred, did you say?

Scapino: No, five hundred.

Pantalone: Five hundred pounds?

Scapino: No, guineas.

Pantalone: What the devil was he doing on the yacht?

Scapino: Yes, indeed, but hurry.

Pantalone: Why didn't he go for a walk somewhere else?

Scapino: That's true, but be quick!

Pantalone: Oh, that confounded yacht!

Scapino (aside): The yacht's got him, good and proper.

Pantalone: Here, Scapino, I've just remembered that I was on my way to the bank with exactly that sum. *(Holding out his wallet)* Here, go and ransom my son.

Scapino (holding out his hand): Very good, Sir.[16]

 # Scaramuccia

Name. Means 'little fighter' or 'skirmisher'. His nickname is 'bumble-bee'.

Status. Servant to an impoverished gentleman, often employed as a go-between.

Origin. A primitive southern Italian type developed by the Neapolitan actor Tiberio Fiorilli (1602–94), probably the son of Silvio Fiorillo, Capitano Matamoros and developer of Pulcinella.

> Towards 1680 the Spanish Captains came to an end in Italy, and the old Italian Captains having been long forgotten, it

> became necessary to find in the companies of Neapolitan comedi-
> ans an actor to replace the Spanish Captain; thus Scaramuccia
> was created. In Italy this personage has never had any character
> other than that of the Captain; he is at once a boaster and a
> coward.[17]

The type of the Neapolitan adventurer, Scaramuccia is boastful and cowardly, more supple, less definite and more solemn than the Spanish
Capitano.

Physical appearance.

> As to Scaramouch's physical constitution he was, as I have said
> already, short-sighted, deaf in one ear, and had one shoulder
> entirely withered. He was tall and very upright and remained so
> until extreme old age, and even then stooped but little. . . . One of
> the most agile players ever seen.[18]

Costume. Black throughout with the exception of a very wide white
floppy collar and white cuffs. Floppy black hat falling back over neck, even
below shoulder level. Skirted, buttoned-through jacket with tightly fitting
sleeves and epaulettes on the shoulders, large black cape, sometimes to
ground level: 'in point of cut it is an imitation of the Spanish dress, which
in the court of Naples, had long been the dress of courtiers, of magistrates
and of men of war'.[19]

Mask. Originally masked, but Fiorilli discarded it. He powdered his face
white with blackened-in arched eyebrows, a drooping Zapata moustache
and a pointed Imperial beard.

Props. Beribboned mandolin.

Movements. Very agile: when Fiorilli was over 80 he could still deliver
a kick to head height.

Gestures.

> He was not content merely to let the spectator hear what he
> wished to say, he even made his words take shape before his
> eyes, so great was his talent for uniting speech to gesture. It
> may be said that every part of him had a tongue, his feet, his
> hands, his head, and that his least gesture was the fruit of
> meditation.[20]

Speech.

He had a lively imagination but rarely spoke, having great difficulty in expressing in words what he wished to say but, in return,
nature had endowed him with a wonderful talent which enabled
him to explain by the postures of his body and the grimaces of his
face, all that he desired; and that in so original a manner that the
celebrated Molière, who studied him for a long while, confessed
frankly that he owed to him all the beauty of his gestures.[21]

Characteristics.   He boasts not so much of his physical prowess as that
he is a marquis or a prince of several countries which exist, however, only
in his own imagination. He loves women but they will not have anything to
do with him, so he brags of imaginary conquests and pretends to have
rebuffed those who have jilted him. A sly thief. Sand says that 'like the bow-
man of Bagnolet, he fears nothing but danger'. He thus combines qualities
of Il Capitano and Zanni.

Animal.   As an invented character, he does not have origins in animal
mimicry.

Relationships.   Has a sense of perfect honour among thieves when with
Pulcinella, and likes to go on the town with him. He then slips away when
Pulcinella gets drunk and loses his temper.

Plot function.   A stirrer.

Improvisation exercise

Canovaccio

Ottavio, having given Angélique an assignation in the Tuileries,
desires that a gallant collation shall be prepared to afford her a
pleasant surprise. He begs Scaramouche to attend to it and
departs. Scaramouche, left on the stage, falls into a reverie.
Arlequin enters and Scaramouche begs of him to think of a way
but without telling him what is the subject. Thereupon the two of
them walk up and down the stage, their heads in their hands, and
from time to time one of them turns to the other exclaiming:
'Faith, I have it!' [only] to add afterwards: 'No, that idea is worth
nothing,' and to recommence their goings and comings in silence.
Suddenly they meet and Scaramouche exclaims: 'Ah, this is sure

to succeed!' Whereupon they depart without any further explanations.[22]

(How many mangled and unfunny attempts one has seen at that. It is clearly crucial to the humour of the situation that Arlecchino does not know what he is trying to have an idea *about*.)

Tartaglia

Name. From the Italian verb for 'to stammer'.

Origin. Seems to have been created by Beltrani from Verona around 1630, probably in Paris in order to compensate for the lack of enthusiasm among French audiences for Pantalone and Il Dottore.

Status. A utility figure. Frequently a lawyer, but can be a retainer or minor official, apothecary, coachman, policeman.

Physical appearance. Corpulent and pot-bellied, no facial hair and completely bald (the only *commedia dell'arte* character to be so).

Costume. Grey cloth cap, ample calico collar, cloak and tunic in green with yellow stripes, white stockings and yellow or brown leather shoes.

Mask. Huge thick round green or light blue spectacles covering half his face.

Stance. Weight on heels, belly forward.

Walk. A waddle.

Animal. I would suggest a cross between a duck and an owl, but as with Scaramuccia, there is no primitive origin to point to.

Relationships. As an older man, can be a friend of Il Dottore.

Plot function. Rarely has more than one scene in a scenario, thus giving extra emphasis to, say, a trial. Often has no function other than as additional comic opportunity. In late scenarios sometimes took over the duties of Il Dottore, with Pulcinella usurping the role of Pantalone.

Characteristics. A stammerer. Liable to get stuck on the most obscene syllable in any given phrase. The comedy does not lie only in the stutter but in the nature of the words he tries as alternatives in order to get past the block. For this reason Perrucci's description is untranslatable:

> L'artificio farà intoppare quelli che facciano un qualche equivoco con altre parole; volendo dire è buono, dica: è bu-bu-bu, dove non si sa se voglia terminare in bue, bucefalco o buffone, e così co-co-co, non si sa se termina in contento, consolato, conforto o cornuto o altro, dal che la parte ridicola può cavarne con l'equivoco la risata.

Tartaglia flies into perpetual rages with himself and others when thus failing to communicate. As always in Commedia, there is a social reality behind a comical shortcoming: 'He represents the southerner worn out by the climate, suffering from chronic ophthalmia, and in a condition bordering on cretinism.[23]

Improvisation exercises

Wants to read a tragedy to his friend (and fellow southerner) Pulcinella. He gets ready to inform him of the title, which is *Coriolanus*, but after the initial 'Co' follows an immediate plurality of diverse syllables, eventually mutating 'Coriolanus' into 'Cor, 'e laid into us'.

Sample dialogue

Arlecchino, disguised as a marquis, imagines he is dying. He has sent Il Dottore for Tartaglia, a notary, to make his will:

> *Tartaglia*: Your illustri . . .tri . . .tri . . .tri. . .
> *Arlecchino*: This notary is from Tripoli.
> *Tartaglia (sits down, draws pen and paper and begins to write)*: Dated . . . in the yea . . .yea . . .yea . . .
> *Arlecchino*: Will someone put this donkey in the stable?
> *Tartaglia*: I . . . I . . . I . . . I am . . . I am . . . am ready.
> *Arlecchino*: Good! I leave this house to the Doctor.
> *Dottore*: But the house is mine!
> *Arlecchino*: I know, that is why I am leaving it to you: if it were not yours I should not leave it to you. I leave my cabinet to my aunt.
> *Tartaglia (writing)*: My ca . . .ca . . . ca . . . ca . . .
> *Arlecchino*: Get rid of this notary at once, before he soils the furniture.

Tartaglia: ... binet to my a ... a ...

Arlecchino: I leave sixty-five acres of broadcloth to pool amongst my relatives to make them mourning clothes.

Dottore: You are making a mistake. Cloth is not measured by the acre.

Arlecchino: It seems to me that a man may measure his own property as best he pleases.

Tartaglia: Poo . . .poo . . .poo . . . amongst relatives in the morning.

[And so on until:]

Arlecchino: Lastly, I leave to the notary here, a pig's tongue with which to replace his own.

Tartaglia: Pi . . .pi . . .pi . . .pig yourself!

(Arlecchino gives him a kick which sends him flying, together with his pens, paper, portfolio and inkhorns. Tartaglia gets up, his face covered with ink and goes off in such a rage that he is unable to articulate intelligible sounds.)[24]

Minor Masks

AMARILLI: Female Lover. A pastoral figure: the lonely wife of a shepherd.

BERTOLINO: Zanni. A friend of Coviello.

BRANDINO: Zanni.

BRIGANTE: Old man. Mutton dressed as lamb.

BURATTINO: Zanni. A flat-nosed idiot, always in search of food.

CASSANDRO: Old man. A friend of Pantalone from Sienna or Florence. More level-headed. When he appears, he takes the place of Il Dottore in a scenario. Pantalone was rebaptised Cassandre in France at the end of the eighteenth century.

COLA: Zanni or old man. A ridiculous, acrobatic character from Naples.

COVIELLO: Zanni/Capitano from Naples. Jumped up Zanni or low-life Captain. His personality is such that he has the musical and acrobatic talents of Arlecchino and the happy-go-lucky pomposity of the Doctor. Wears a white costume with bells and a large-nosed tan mask. During the Rome Carnival of 1636 Salvator Rosa made him a success. Speaks Calabrese. Perrucci complained:

> At appropriate moments [the first Zanni] should introduce sharp and witty phrases, without making them just absurdities, and he should not step out of role by incorporating the second Zanni's ridiculous buffoonery, an error often made by the Neapolitan *Covielli* who, because they over-step the line between wit and stupidity, produce an unacceptable concoction – for *zanni* should

be always witty or always stupid, and when first *zanni* are stupid they transgress their role, the proper business of which is to draw out the intrigue by ingenuity and guile.

A character akin to that of Pulcinella: he favours all that is grotesque, obscene and mischievous.

FEDELINDO: Lover. Son of Tartaglia.

FICHETTO: Zanni. A pedantic but clumsy and restless servant.

FIORINETTA: The Signora, the type of the great courtesan. Derived from Isabella, but separated off in order to allow the latter to be irreproachable in her morals. Overdressed, wore too many jewels, coiffure too elaborate, dress too modish in cut and covered with too much trimming, flowers, feathers and ribbons. Attractive but flashy.

GABBA: Servant. Valet to the miser, Roberto.

GIANDUJA: Born in the puppet booths of Piedmont. A robust Piedmontese peasant with huge shoes and a keen mind. Open, florid face, loves pleasantry, wine and big women, although forever in love with Giacometta with whom he has an indefinite number of children known as Giandujotti.

LA RUFFIANA: Old Neapolitan woman based on well-known type of garrulous old peasant wife, obstinate, limited, narrow, primitive in all her reactions, yet withal good-hearted and generous in spirit, if not in purse. In other parts of Italy appeared as La Guarassa, and in France as L'Entremetteuse or La Commère. Wore Neapolitan peasant costume and role was generally that of the mother of Fiorinetta.

LATTANZIO: Zanni. Friend of Coviello.

MENENGHINO: Milanese, who as Pulcinella for Naples, represents the entire character of the Milanese people. An honest man, prudent and resourceful, has balanced judgements and a generous disposition. Costume originally white, tunic down to the knees with belt, green socks and huge clogs. Later turned into a brown jacket edged with red, multicoloured undergarment, short trousers and striped socks, a brown tricorned hat and a wig tied back with a red ribbon.

MEZZETINO: Brighella derivant, softened during the eighteenth century. Elegant valet who combines wise and foolish characteristics. Sensitive young man. Wears red-striped costume. No mask.

PASQUARIELLO: Old man or servant. A variation of Pulcinella, became the garrulous Polichinelle in France. A schemer who carries a sword. Wears a long-nosed mask.

PEPPE-NAPPA: Zanni. A Sicilian valet who dresses like Pierrot, only in blue. Performs with swift double-jointed movements. No mask.

ROBERTO: A Pantalone type, reduced to one characteristic, miserliness.

ROSAURA: Usually wife to Pantalone. An older, sexually experienced Colombina. Man-eater, takes lovers, particularly Il Capitano.

ROSETTA: Servant. A maid or the wife of Pulcinella. Wore an Arlecchino-style patched dress.

STENTERELLO: Florentine. Also known as Menenghino, Gianduja, Zacometo, Jeannot and Jocrisse, a master of all trades, a character actor. Filler-in of incidental action where the plot goes beyond what the basic Masks can supply. Admires Arlecchino and his defects are shadows of his: lazy, fidgety, greedy and a rascal. Dresses in extremely gaudy colours which do not match, wears a black cravat and odd stockings. Wig with pigtail. No mask, but heavily made-up eyebrows, eyes and lips on a pale base with traces of red. Enjoys misusing words and making up neologisms. Gives illogical tirades, as much an acrobat with words as Arlecchino is with his body.

TRAPPOLA: Zanni. The Captain's valet.

TRISTITIA: Servant. An assistant to the miser, Roberto.

TRIVELINO: Zanni. A rival or companion to Arlecchino.

UBALDO: A general-purpose old man.

ZANOBIO: From Piombino. Similar to Cassandro.

Part III

The twentieth century

What follows, in the third part of this book, is a collection of essays which investigate the practice of some of those who have attempted to reconstruct or renovate the *commedia dell'arte* in the twentieth century. It is a selection based on occasional, adventitious personal research, not a comprehensive account — and I apologise unreservedly to those left out. The arrangement is loosely chronological, though there are thematic connections, such as that between Meyerhold and TNT (a later company basing their work on his early ideas), or between Copeau and Lecoq and in turn between Lecoq and Strehler, Fo and Mnouchkine. The final essay recounts some of my own experiences as a teacher and practitioner and attempts to articulate the persistent quandary between restoration and renovation.

Craig at the Arena Goldoni

At the beginning of the century Edward Gordon Craig, as he edited (and largely wrote under some sixty or so pseudonyms) his periodical *The Mask*, stated his hopes for the study of Commedia:

> In the present number of *The Mask* we proceed with the story of the *commedia dell'arte* and of those men of genius, the great Improvisators, who brought it to its perfection. . . .
>
> The general reader must remember that what we are introducing to him was a phase of the dramatic art almost without parallel; that it appealed not only to the people but to the aristocracy; in short that it captured and held the Public . . . not merely a public . . . for three centuries.
>
> The specialising reader will want to know the reason for this. . . . To us it seems quite evident that when that reason shall be clearly demonstrated to the actors and the artists of the theatre a new form of Acting and a new form of Drama will come into existence.[1]

Craig was in voluntary exile, setting up his school in the Arena Goldoni in Florence. From 1907 until 1914 he made his base there, although various enterprises took him at times to Germany, France, Russia and back to England. At first he had thought to create his school in London, but despite his exhibitions being crowded, his editions sold out and his productions mounted with the express purpose of raising support, no-one there would offer the means by which his project for training for the theatre of the future could be carried out. This was perhaps hardly surprising since he was known to refer to London theatres as 'counting houses' and hold English actors in impatient opprobrium:

> There was a cleverish young actor in London whom I first met

163

some nine years ago in a theatre. I think he was playing the part of a cook. He looked well, he seemed interesting; he seemed out of the usual run. Then only last year I met him again in London. He said that one of the three famous playwrights had promised to write a part. He was worrying about that part; it didn't hurry up enough for him; he was out of work . . . he was one of ten thousand others . . . and was waiting for Barrie or Shaw or Pinero, I forget which, to write him a part. A nice fellow, too; but, great Jupiter, Apollo, Dionysus, the young fellow was *waiting*!

He'll wait right enough. Patience . . . . what a vice it has become, what a blanket to put out the fire, what a cloak under which to hide the ashes of incapacity. And that's what thousands of English actors are doing . . . waiting for what they call 'their chance'.[2]

Such actors, Craig felt, were not only under the yoke of literature (in the hands of the playwrights), but also in the thrall of realism (subjugated to the designer's brush) and, worst of all, slaves to their own egoism (which prevented them from becoming artists in their own right, true collaborators in the creation of theatrical artworks).

The second issue of *The Mask* contained his essay on 'The Actor and the Über-marionette' which was to be made notorious through misinterpretation. In it he did not advocate, as was generally supposed, the abolition of actors and their replacement with giant puppets, but a symbolical style of acting, based on the creative imagination: 'Today [actors] *impersonate* and interpret; tomorrow they must *represent* and interpret; and the third day they must create. By this means style may return.'[3]

One of Craig's intentions in founding a school was to 'open wide the larger doors of the future to the actor so that he may with self-reliance know that all parts are ready for the comedian who cares to undergo the training which gives the power to improvise'.[4] Improvisation would free the actor from reliance on text and personality-based casting and perhaps ultimately place the control of performance in the hands of the performer – a far cry from being manipulated by some despotic puppeteer. But he was realist enough to perceive that such control would not easily be gained, for as he later wrote, 'No-one believes improvisation to be the invention of the last minute.'[5] Training was to be essential. In 1911 he offered in a letter to Stanislavsky, attempting to enlist his support in founding the school in Florence, that he would demonstrate within a year

(1) the principles of movement of the human body
(2) within two years I will give you and demonstrate to you the principles of movement on the scene of single figures and of massed groups of figures –

(3) and within three years I will give you the whole principle governing action, scene and voice;
(4) after that I will give you the principles of improvisation or spontaneous acting with and without words.[6]

Undoubtedly one of the bases of that improvisation training (which was clearly going to take longer than three years) was to be the *commedia dell'arte*. As a preliminary he conducted extensive research in the libraries of Florence, aided by his collaborator Dorothy Nevile Lees, which they published in *The Mask* under the *nom-de-plume* of Dr Michele Scherillo. Nevile Lees also translated the introduction to Gherardi's *Le Théâtre italien*.

As an actor-centred form, Commedia offered Craig two further advantages: open-air playing and the use of mask. If theatre were reduced to essentials he considered

> We are left with the daylight and the open air . . .; with a covering for the body called costume, and a background known as scenery. . . . We already have costume and scenery, and we can, if we will, turn on the light of day; it is cheap enough. But we cannot. To turn the light of day on to our modern scenery, costume, actors and dramas would be to cheapen them at the same time. Daylight is only for works of art; humbug works by artificial light.[7]

And it was reliance on facial acting, aided and abetted by artificial light, that in his view was preventing the actor from transcending personal emotional tics and participating fully as a plastic entity in the Art of the Scene. Performing in daylight, as the Greeks and the Commedia actors had done, implied the use of the mask in order to simplify and intensify the expression of the features, thus rendering the performance simultaneously both more artistic and more real:

> Drama which is not trivial, takes us *beyond* reality and yet asks a human face, the reallest of things, to express all that. It is unfair. . . .
> Masks carry conviction when he who carries them is an artist, for the artist limits the statements which he places upon these masks. The face of the actor carries no such conviction; it is over-full of fleeting expression – frail, restless, disturbed and disturbing.[8]

Craig's advice to the actor who was 'waiting', had he met him again, might thus have been quite simple:

> To rise up from such a depth as that in which the Theatre is today

> sunken will demand no little disinterestedness. . . . Get to your
> masks quickly. *When you learn their use and their invincible power
> you will be better fitted to ascend.*[9]

Outdoor performance, mask work and, ultimately, improvisation were to
be the cornerstones of the training offered. All three might have found a
common denominator in the study of *commedia dell'arte*.

The School for the Art of Theatre finally opened in March 1913 (though
the Arena Goldoni had been used as the headquarters for publishing *The
Mask* since 1908). Thirty students were enrolled and work had hardly begun
when war broke out. Funding ceased and the school had to be shut. By 1916
the buildings had become a barracks and were later destroyed. In 1921 Craig
wrote:

> It came in 1913; it went in 1914 . . . for the war swept it away, and
> my supporter did not see the value of keeping the engine fires
> 'banked'. So the fires went out. It is a rare business, as you know,
> to relight the fires once they are allowed to go out.[10]

Meyerhold *Dappertutto*

The first known visit of *comici dell'arte* to Russia was in 1733 when an Italian troupe (in between tours of Poland), played in front of the Empress Anna Joannavna. From the mid-eighteenth century, when French was adopted as the Court language, until 1787, and again in the nineteenth, the Russian nobility never allowed St Petersburg to become too distant from Paris, especially in matters artistic and theatrical.

In the 1920s, after another revolution, Meyerhold and other Russian theatre directors such as Vakhtangov and Foregger sought a new popular form with which to sweep away the cultural leavings of oligarchy. The overt theatricality of the *commedia dell'arte* had a strong influence on their quest for a new Soviet theatre, presaged by Meyerhold's experimental work in the previous decade. But the example available to them to work from was not the Italian root form as had played at Court, or even as developed in Paris in the eighteenth century, but the inheritance of a nineteenth-century sensibility founded in the *fiabe* of Gozzi, the fantastical romances of E.T.A. Hoffmann and the popular pantomimics of the Harlequinade.

In order to understand the strength of those influences it is necessary to know something of Meyerhold's experiments in the years immediately preceding the 1917 revolution. Around 1910 many Russian artists had been undecided in direction: realism was passé and the initial enthusiasm for symbolism was waning. It was in 1910 that Meyerhold danced Pierrot in Mikhail Fokine's production of the ballet *Carnival* at a ball (the part of Florestan was danced by Nijinsky). A growing preoccupation with Commedia thus became intertwined from the outset with the development of his fascination with rhythmical movement to music. Fokine later wrote:

> I believe this was his first contact with the art of rhythmic gesture
> set to music . . . he was a man from a different world at the first
> two rehearsals. His gestures lagged behind the music. Many times
> he 'showed up' at the wrong time, and 'took off' from the stage

167

24 Meyerhold as Pierrot in Blok's *The Fairground Booth*.

without reference to the music. But by the third rehearsal our new mime had matured, and in the performance gave a marvellous image of the melancholy dreamer Pierrot.[1]

Meyerhold had previously acted a Commedia character in 1903, in Franz von Shönthan's *The Acrobats*, but the passionate phase of development in his acquaintance with Commedia dates from his own production of Alexander Blok's *The Fairground Booth* (1906). From then on he began a search for a theatrical style that was not derived from literary sources, but from investigation of the plasticity of the actor. His 'official' productions for the Imperial Theatre up to 1917 included Molière, Calderon, Gozzi and Blok, but he also directed experimental productions privately under the Commedia *nom-de-théâtre* Doctor Dappertutto – 'Doctor Everywhere', a Mask from Hoffmann's tale, *Adventure on New Year's Eve* – perhaps an ominous image for a director, since Dappertutto is a magician who steals people's shadows and souls. It was, however, an itinerant omnipresence of the actor, not the director, which he sought; in his 1912 essay 'The Fairground Booth' (deliberately eponymous with Blok's play), he wrote:

> Surely the art of man on the stage consists in shedding all traces of environment, carefully choosing a mask, donning a decorative costume, and showing off one's brilliant tricks to the public – now as a dancer, now as the intrigant at some masquerade, now as the fool of old Italian comedy, now a juggler. . . .
>
> The theatre of the mask has always been a fairground show, and the idea of acting is based on the apotheosis of the mask, gesture and movement is indivisible from the idea of the travelling show.[2]

And in 1914 he began an essay, the title of which translates cumbersomely into English as 'The Fairground Theatre-wagon', with a quotation from Blok:

> On the dark and muddy road
> The fog does not lift.
> A creaking wagon transports
> My faded old show, my theatre.

> Two sorry old nags pull a worn-out theatre-wagon, but the actor . . . see with what conviction and pride he says: my faded old show.
>
> 'And in a corner Colombina arranges a motley of rags and patches.' She murmurs joyously as she arranges them: my motley rags.
>
> My wagon. My motley, made from rags and patches. My sorry old nags. My songs from other times.
>
> What has he become now, this actor who speaks of the joys of his kingdom?
>
> He is amongst the actors of yesteryear whose faded portraits seem to speak to us today of their stage, their wings, their favourite poets.
>
> With his light step he will come, the one for whom we are waiting. Two mirrors facing each other and, from one side and the other candles, like an evening Epiphany, will create an endless corridor, and their gilded frames will define the succession of many theatrical epochs.
>
> And we already know that, crossing threshold after threshold of each section of the corridor of reflections, carrying on him the mark of each of those epochs, he will arrive, the promised one. . . .

Even before crossing the sacred threshold, the new actor already knows that his technical mastery must give birth to an artistic oeuvre in which his personality will rise up through a mask which dissimulates through him the traits of another mask that other people, in other circumstances, have already seen in times past.

It is for this reason that the actor, so obstinately, aspires to plunge into the study of fabulous techniques from epochs when the theatre was theatrical.

And, almost immediately, the new actor asks: what then should my theatre be? The passionate manner in which he has pronounced the word 'my' is enough: we know already that, in the paradise of his songs from other times, overgrown paths will be re-opened.[3]

The experimental productions mounted in quest of this fairground booth style - *Colombine's Scarf, The Adoration of the Cross, Harlequin, the Marriage Broker, The Unknown Woman* and *The Fairground Booth* itself – were performed literally *dappertutto*, sometimes even in friends' apartments. They were supported by and interacted with two other activities: the short-lived journal, *Love of Three Oranges*,[4] in which Meyerhold began expounding his views on the retheatricalisation of theatre; and the Meyerhold Studio, a school of acting opened in the autumn of 1913 in a large apartment in St Petersburg. The latter lasted until the 1917 revolution, although in the last year its activities understandably fell off. The primary emphasis was on the concepts and methodology of *commedia dell'arte*. Meyerhold was no longer turning to symbolism or impressionism in search for an anti-naturalistic theatre – popularisation, not mystification, was now seen as the answer. In terms of an actor-training alternative to that of Stanislavsky, he posited the redevelopment of the cabotin, the strolling player, 'a kinsman to the mime, the histrion and the juggler; the cabotin can work miracles with his technical mastery; the cabotin keeps alive the tradition of the true art of acting'.[5]

The chief scholar, historian and theorist in the school was Vladimir Solovyev who took a course entitled 'Methods of Staging Commedia dell'arte Performances'. The stated intention of these studies was not to attempt faithful historical reproduction but to serve an apprenticeship through the reconstruction of a form: '*Commedia dell'arte* was an aide of considerable richness in terms of ideas, of theatrical tradition, means of studying the purpose of theatre, and in the practical area of stage techniques.'[6] The syllabus for Solovyev's course was as follows:

Dramatic techniques of the actors of the *commedia dell'arte*. Setting out of the basic movements necessary for each of the characters of the Italian comedy. Bergamask dances and other educational preparations required to be able to tackle the difficulties to follow.

Using the harlequinade *Harlequin, the Marriage-broker* by Volmar Liutsinius [a pseudonym for Solovyev himself], familiarisation with the gestures and movements of the principal Masks: Arlecchino, Smeraldina, the Doctor and Pantalone (the old men), Aurelio and Sylvia (the Lovers). Brighella, Truffaldino, Tartaglia and the secondary Masks of the Italian comedy: Eularia, Celio etc. . . .

Determining of the geometry of scenes involving a group of masks. Assimilation and reconstruction of traditional productions from surviving manuscripts of *scenari*. Reconstitution of the following scenes: 'the night', 'the duel', 'the harem', as forming principles for independent study in the deciphering of fundamental systems.

Principles of the parade. The stage assistants and their role in the production. The significance of the grotesque, which Carlo Gozzi calls 'a mode of extravagant parody'.

Mise en scène of the second intermezzo of the divertissement *The Love of Three Oranges*.

Determination of the moment of dramatic tension, and principles of verbal improvisation.

Application of scenic techniques from the *commedia dell'arte* to the following plays: *Arlequin poli par l'Amour* by Marivaux, and *La Grotte de Salamandre* by Cervantes.[7]

These classes were theoretical, intended as a preparation for Meyerhold's practical course which

> began with the techniques of stage movement and gesture with controlled examples on stage. Exercises were transformed into études, and from études arose the pantomimes. Thus, from the exercise 'shooting a bow' arose the étude 'The Hunt', and subsequently a pantomime in which all 'generations' of the Studio were involved. Several of the exercises and études became 'classics' and later entered into the teaching of biomechanics.[8]

The concept with which Meyerhold intended to unify Solovyev's historical research into Commedia with the contemporary acting experiments in his movement class was his vision of the grotesque which he took from Ernst von Wolzogen, the founder of the first literary cabaret in Germany in 1901. His manifesto, according to Meyerhold, was in essence an apologia for the principles of the fairground booth and its favourite device – the grotesque:

> Grotesque (Italian – *grottesca*) is the title of a genre of low comedy in literature, music and the plastic arts. Grotesque usually implies something hideous and strange, a humorous work which with no apparent logic combines the most dissimilar elements by ignoring their details and relying on its own originality, borrowing from every source anything which satisfies its joie de vivre and its capricious, mocking attitude to life.[9]

The experimental productions which stemmed from the work in the Studio were practical essays in the quest for a grotesque style. For example, here is a contemporary description of *Colombine's Scarf* (1910, at the Interlude House):

> The frivolous Colombine, betrothed to Harlequin, spends a last evening with her devoted Pierrot. As usual she deceives him, swearing she loves him. Pierrot proposes a suicide pact and himself drinks the poison. Colombine lacks the courage to follow him and flees in terror to the wedding ball where the guests await her impatiently. The ball begins, then, whilst an old-fashioned quadrille is playing, Pierrot's flapping white sleeve is glimpsed first through the windows, then through the doors. The dances, now fast, now slow, turn into an awful nightmare, with strange Hoffmannesque characters whirling to the time of a huge-headed Kappellmeister, who sits on a high stool and conducts four weird musicians.
>
> Colombine's terror reaches such a pitch that she can hide it no longer and she rushes back to Pierrot. Harlequin follows her and when she sees Pierrot's corpse he is convinced of his bride's infidelity. He forces her to dine before the corpse of the love-stricken Pierrot. Then he leaves, bolting the door fast. In vain Colombine tries to escape from her prison, from the ghastly dead body. Gradually she succumbs to madness; she whirls in a frenzied dance, then finally drains the deadly cup and falls lifeless beside Pierrot.[10]

The play was freely adapted from Arthur Schnitzler's *The Veil of Pierrette* and mimed to music by Dohnany. The three scenes were broken down into fourteen brief episodes with constant, grotesque, switches of mood. Such directed aesthetics took Meyerhold a long way from the intentions later stated in the essays quoted above: the creativity of the actor was in fact effectively denied in favour of that of the choreographer.

The following year, Meyerhold's production of *Harlequin, the Marriage Broker* (written and used for teaching by Solovyev) was first performed at the Assembly Rooms of the Nobility. Meyerhold himself gives the following description:

This harlequinade, written with the specific aim of reviving the theatre of masks, was staged according to traditional principles and based on our studies of the scenarios of the *commedia dell'arte*. Rehearsals were conducted jointly by the author and the director; the author, in accordance with his aim of reviving the traditional theatre, would outline the *mise en scène*, moves, poses and gestures as he had found them described in the scenarios of improvised comedies; the director would add new tricks in the style of these traditional devices, blending the traditional with the new to produce a coherent whole. The harlequinade was written in the form of a pantomime because, more than any dramatic form, the pantomime is conducive to the revival of the art of improvisation. In the pantomime the actor is given the general outline of the plot and in the intervals between the various key moments he is free to act *ex improvviso*. However, the actor's freedom is only relative because he is subject to the discipline of the musical score. The actor in a harlequinade needs to possess an acute sense of rhythm plus great agility and self-control. He must develop the equilibrist skills of an acrobat, because only an acrobat can master the problems posed by the grotesque style inherent in the fundamental conception of the harlequinade.[11]

Thus, whereas *Colombine's Scarf* had subordinated its masks to a dance rhythm in a Hoffmannesque key, in rehearsing *Harlequin, the Marriage-Broker*, Meyerhold considered he was trying to resurrect the basic traditions of Commedia; yet the *mise en scène* was still without dialogue, meticulously choreographed in a light, whimsical style, with occasional breaks for mimed *lazzi*, most of which (although intended, by way of contrast, to be improvised coarse buffoonery) seem also to have been prearranged.

Meyerhold's mimes treated each other to shoves and blows, they fought, cavorted, then suddenly jumped from the stage into the auditorium. Silvius chopped Pantalone's paper nose off with a wooden sword, whereupon the Doctor immediately attached a new nose.[12]

Why, after studying in supposed depth the origins of Commedia, and devoting part of a course to improvised dialogue, did Meyerhold and Solovyev develop such a whimsical, mute variant with paper masks to music by Spiess von Eschenbruch? A possible answer is that at this early stage Meyerhold's quest for a new supremacy of the cabotin was so anti-literary as to mistrust dialogue altogether. A subsequent performance in the home of the writer Fyodor Sologub attempted contemporary relevance by retaining the masks but dressing the actors in tuxedos. A second production (by the Teryoki Cooperative Theatre of Actors, Musicians, Writers and Painters at a summer school in 1912) reinstated verbal language via the addition of the role of Author, who read the prologue and participated in the action as interlocutor. A contemporary review reveals:

> The movements of the actors, their mime, gestures, were precise, airy, minted as it were . . . the movements of the author mannered and extreme, his reading [of the prologue] with cries and pauses was typical of the Harlequinades. The connection between the viewer and the action on stage was emphasised – by the Author's address to the public at the start and the end, and by the joint scene where the Author and Harlequin run into the auditorium.[13]

There was a new set, too, replacing the traditional house-either-side staging of the first production with a backdrop painted by Kulbin consisting of

> a sky with a purposely crudely painted portion of roof, along whose narrow peak the flour-covered Harlequin either creeps or stops in order to throw handfuls of stars. Lower, at the very edge of the roof, could be seen the bent figure of another Harlequin, flying head down, while against a background of blue sky, there was a distinct yellow stupid disk of the Moon on the left, a mask on the right.[14]

And again there was a score to move to, this time by de Bourg, based on adaptations of Haydn and Araja.

It seems then, that despite the soi-disant reconstruction of Commedia developed from the courses given in the Studio, Dr Dappertutto's productions remained more responsive to Meyerhold's movement classes and his need for trained bodies moving silently to given impulses with which to develop biomechanical choreography, than to Solovyev's researches into *commedia dell'arte* and improvised dialogue. Meyerhold's perception of Commedia in this pre-revolutionary period seems also to have been distorted by his quest for the grotesque. His characters were not the original types as researched by Solovyev, but the sentimentalised figures of the late eighteenth century trapped in a nineteenth century world of Gothic fantasy. Over that world loomed the solitary, silent, sublunary figure of Pierrot, Meyerhold's true *doppelgänger*. In his urgency to create a physical theatre capable of dealing with the metaphysical, Dr Dappertutto stole the pale shadow of Commedia when what he had really craved was its original soul.

In the post-revolutionary period Meyerhold made no further experiments with Commedia *per se*, but much of the method of non-naturalistic characterisation which he developed did embody the essence of the Masks without being limited by inadequate understanding of their form. His production of Ostrovsky's *A Lucrative Post* (1923), for example, marked a return to the mode of theatrical characterisation he had been developing before the revolution. This did not mean he was capitulating to socialist realism or reverting to Stanislavskian psychological acting, but looking for means of portraying social types on the principles of Commedia.

> While completely preserving the passion for innovation . . .
> Meyerhold proceeded in the present case not by way of external
> forms of innovation, but by way of delving deeply into the
> material of the dramatist and boldly revealing the content in all
> its richness. . . . Instead of showing psychological characters,
> Meyerhold at this time sought to reveal typical psychological traits
> as a sharp and effective means of social exposure.[15]

The production of *Lucrative Post* was not well documented, unlike Crommelynck's *The Magnificent Cuckold*, which opened the previous April, and 'for all its modernist exterior, was a revival of the spirit, and in good measure the letter, too, of the *commedia dell'arte*. It was fitting that Meyerhold should choose this production to commemorate the tercentenary of Molière.'[16]

The theme of marital jealousy is brought to total, farcical and absurd extremes: a young mill owner, Bruno, suspects his virtuous wife Stella of infidelity and in order to prove her guilt invites every male in the village to pass through her bed, thinking that whoever refuses will be the guilty party. 'What I need is to recognise amongst all those who come to her, the one who will not come.' As he drives himself further and further into paroxysms of suspicion he becomes a Brighella to his own Pantalone, Iago to his own Othello.

Igor Ilinsky playing Bruno exemplified Meyerhold's concept of the new actor's function, embodying both the idea of suffering and his own parody of it in biomechanical demonstration rather than a realistic living out. All the actors wore blue overalls, but his had red clown pom-poms dangling round the neck, a last vestige of Pierrot, which accentuated the grotesqueness of the character's jealous madness by extending his gesture into frenzied biomechanic semaphore. Although not masked, his face contorted into a series of extreme expressions.

But the interpretation of the leading role of Hlestakov in *The Government Inspector* (1926) by Erast Garin was perhaps Meyerhold's most successful creation of a new Commedia type, even down to the attribution of a regional origin:

> He appears on stage, a character from some tale by Hoffmann,
> slender, clad in black with a stiff mannered gait, strange

spectacles, a sinister old-fashioned tall hat, a rug and a cane, apparently tormented by some private vision. He is a flaneur from the Nevsky Prospect, a native of Gogol's own Petersburg.[17]

And Mikhail Chekhov described him as a man 'driven mad by his own falsehoods, one who has lost his sense of time, who would seemingly lie *forever*'.[18] In other words, a Mask existing outside as well as inside the context of the production. Paradoxically, Meyerhold had told his actors to 'avoid everything that is strictly comedy, everything that is buffoonery. Nothing must be taken from the *commedia dell'arte* and everything is to be presented as tragi-comedy.'[19] But what they were to portray was a deadly satire on the social realities of an atrophied society: barring the front door to the distorted Commedia of his earlier work enabled it to make an authentic appearance through the back.

Copeau's new improvised comedy

In the watershed years of the decade before Russian revolution and the Great War, a parallel experiment to those in Florence and Moscow was taking place in Paris. Jacques Copeau, who had admired Craig's writings for some years, read Alexander Bakshy's *The Path of the Modern Russian Stage* in 1916. Unaware of Meyerhold's work till then, he noted in his diary his sense of amazement in finding:

> all my own ideas, my central and most insistent preoccupation (the pre-eminence of the actor and of the actor's role) in Meyerhold, with all the consequences that point of view entails. ... The actor, once placed in the position of the conjuror, must use his skills to the fullest extent. Through every movement in his body, every change in vocal intonation, he will try to communicate innumerable aspects of humanity to the spectator, and the vast world which lies hidden in stock types and their expressions. It is not surprising that the world which is being passed to us from this new movement is: 'Back to the booth and the *commedia dell'arte'*. One cannot imagine a greater coincidence of views. But how do we go about *getting* back?[1]

Unlike Meyerhold, Copeau was immediately aware that the re-empowering of the actor would entail the disempowering of the director:

> Introduction of the characters in the new comedy by their ancestors from the Italian comedy and the French farce. They evict from the theatre: the poet who comes offering his written play, the pretentious actor, the prompter from his box, etc. Finally the director appears, looking sad, constantly searching for a good literary play. ... They tear off his wig and his beard ... rid him of his director's clothes and he appears in the costume of a jester.

And the improvisation begins.[2]

He realised that the key lay not with the individual actor but with the ensemble:

> To create a brotherhood of actors. I had really felt from the
> outset that this was the problem. People living together, working
> together, playing together; but I had forgotten that other phrase,
> the one which inevitably remained: creating together, inventing
> games together, extracting their games from within themselves
> and from one another. . . . Many social games (charades etc.) come
> out of primitive comedy. It is amusements such as these, improvi-
> sation after improvisation, that led Maurice Sand and his friends
> towards a fleeting renovation of the *commedia dell'arte* in their little
> theatre in Nohant around 1848.[3]

Elsewhere, in a special notebook devoted to the idea of developing a new genre of improvised comedy, based on the re-creation of the principles of Commedia without the shackles of historical reconstruction, he wrote:

> From the start we have to beware of the greatest danger: behaving
> like sight-seers or dilettantes in love with a lost art-form. There is
> no question of making historical reconstructions, or of exhuming
> the old scenarios of the Italian farce or the French medieval
> mansions in the name of historical curiosity. We shall study the
> *commedia dell'arte* and the fairground theatre. We shall learn the
> history and development of improvisation, the manners, the
> methods and peculiarities of the actors who practised it. But our
> goal is to create a new improvised comedy using contemporary
> types and subjects. . . . Not morality characters symbolising an
> aspect of the soul, a human passion or a certain social class. But
> the grand-nephews of Pierrot, Arlecchino, Doctor Bolonais, etc.,
> whole characters in their being as in physical appearance. . . .
> Three characters have already come to mind. I do not yet know
> their names, only their generic ones: the Intellectual, the
> Bureaucrat, the Adolescent.[4]

But how were such characters to evolve other than as literary fictions, authored characters who would then end up in search of an audience? One idea was to watch children at play, because 'when they observe life, they have a tendency to ridicule everything that smacks of awkwardness, gratu-itous refinement, affectation and fashion, everything that is not natural and personal'. Another suggestion was to attempt character composition through 'the accumulation of traits':

During the winter of 1915, in the War Ministry, Sergeant Lavarde: blond, ungainly, who spoke oddly through his nose, commenting on all aspects of war with intense pessimism. With these two traits, *a nasal voice* and *pessimism*, Ghéon and I composed a ludicrous character whom we acted out in turn and whom we made fun of, attributing to him the most preposterously pessimistic opinions concerning military operations.[5]

Other characters that Copeau invented on paper during the wartime period of enforced separation from his company included a type of French Zanni:

a certain *Bonhomme*, not so much, in fact not at all because of, Jacques Bonhomme [typical French rustic, akin to the English medieval Hodge]: he just happens to resemble him. The idea came to me one day because, during the war, one spoke of the 'bon-hommes'. They were the typical Frenchmen. Nothing more than that for the present, just everything that the name implies, especially the manner of the Frenchman and his way of speaking.[6]

He also conceived of a Pedrolino/Pierrot derivant,

an *adolescent boy* whose name I have not come up with yet and whom I imagine with the traits of Suzanne [Bing – Copeau's leading actress and principal collaborator in the Vieux Colombier School] because we have often spoken of it together and she has given it some thought. This character is often very quiet. I have one scenario in which he does not utter a word: it is called 'The Comedy of Resemblances'.[7]

And in the mind's eye there was also a character with the pervasive personality and roving brief of a Capitano: 'a *Monsieur Paul*, who is the travelling salesman – in everything: politics, religion, Bordeaux wines and several manufactured products'.[8]

Also one character who was arguably not new, but renovated:

Jean Boche (or Caboche). He once existed in a small part, in the old Franco-Italian comedy. He was not a German, but I make him one because the German is part of our comedy, together with his accent and his mentality, his qualities and his faults. I don't know what he will do, but I know that I shall create a faithful portrait of him.[9]

Copeau described these characters in letters to the novelist and playwright Roger Martin du Gard. The latter seized on the notion of a revivified

Commedia and in 1917 he made twenty-five pages of notes on the 'comédie des tréteaux' which he saw as a potentially restorative influence in post-war culture. Whereas a return to 'théâtre à thèse' would 'rub salt in our wounds', the comic vein, particularly that of Aristophanes and Beaumarchais, would in Martin du Gard's opinion,

> spread around those invaluable seeds of good sense, whose germination is never fruitless, disseminating the clear-sighted and benevolent vision of those who have not forgotten how to smile amidst the social perturbations of our time. It is on simple trestle stages, in the spontaneous fantasy of some farce, that I can already hear this simple, young, clear voice, railing without being in the least aggressive, laughing for laughter's sake and without partiality. On a modern mountebank's platform, with no scenery, in the motley costumes of fictional characters, as grossly unreal as fabulous beasts, I can already see a capering saraband of contemporary ideas and sentiments, without ulterior motive, hurtful intention, taking of sides or deliberate destructiveness, with no purpose other than to amuse, or any other intention than to reduce everything down to its proper size and to make evident certain truths about common sense, which have been generally forgotten during the years of upheaval. . . .
>
> Let's try to approach this scarcely formulated dream; let me try to be exact about what could be attempted . . . and even at this stage give some outward appearance to the characters that should one day compose the joyous troupe of the 'comédie des tréteaux'.
>
> I think in principle their number should be limited to a few essential types, brought constantly in front of the audience. Let's remember that between Pierrot, Arlequin, Colombine and Polichinelle timeless dramas could be written.[10]

Martin du Gard then offered a few imagined silhouettes, 'marginal drawings' as he called them. Unfortunately these merely illustrate how far the idea could get out of kilter when extended (during the cultural desert of a 'war to end all wars') into the world of fiction without recourse to the living performer and spectator. Much précised, he proposed:

> The bourgeois class being represented by a *M. & Mme Punais*: *Hector Punais*, or *Toto*, a rich businessman . . . making show of his own honesty, conscientiousness and patriotism, but only interested in feathering his own nest. His wife, *Carmen*, the great lady, a former dancing girl, now powdered and gross, giving herself all the airs acquired through her marriage to Punais. Their son *Jean*, known as *Jeannot*, their heir in every way, a faded cherub

who fails all his exams; *Disert*, a lawyer, politician or diplomat; *Monsieur Tiède*, a learned professor involved in everything and useless at anything; the insidious *Oui-dire*, everyone's friend and dinner guest; *Falempin*, a Parisian mechanic, a born revolutionary who can turn his hand to anything; at his side *Miteux*, a disillusioned bandit, made bilious by reading too many anarchist hand-books; in his shadow, *Chemineau*, the joyous criminal, drunk on freedom; a woman as well, *Midinette*, a little Parisian elfin, a typist or a model, even a prostitute, forever dying of consumption, who loves life and love and remains friends with her old lovers.[11]

Although he envisaged the Vieux Colombier company playing these roles, there is no evidence that he ever communicated them to Copeau. As a set, they now read like a writer's notes on the characters for a soap opera. Indeed, after his demobilisation in 1919, Martin du Gard's thoughts turned more towards the *roman fleuve* that was to become *Les Thibaults*. In Copeau's judgement he

> began to dislike this too human instrument, this medium which is too much exposed to weakness and accident, which sooner or later escapes from the strict control of the artist, whose work it deforms and betrays. He wanted to keep everything in his own hands and let nothing slip from them.[12]

While the novelist was making sketches, Copeau the theatre practitioner was taking such practical steps as were open to him. With another author, André Gide, he went to the Cirque Medrano in Paris several times and concluded that the clowns had some of the qualities he was looking for:

> Ceratto, the stutterer (from the tradition of one of the mummers in the *commedia dell'arte*: Tartaglia, the stammerer), is a 'fantastical clown', the most accomplished actor of them all. Everything about him has a personality: his costumes, his wigs, his whole mimicry, his facial expressions, his walk.[13]

The Fratellini Brothers, in particular, appealed to him and he later had them teach at the Vieux Colombier School and wrote in his preface to their autobiography:

> Stay together always, the three of you. It is your supreme trinity. Three great actors knowing how to play together can represent the entire drama of the universe. Do not hesitate to remain simply *clowns*, the heirs to the divine *commedia dell'arte*.[14]

After meeting Edward Gordon Craig in Florence, Copeau's sense of the divine, or rather the Dionysian, in Commedia intensified and he began planning a production of Molière's *Les Fourberies de Scapin* which would connect him to it. In the last two years of the Great War he was able to reassemble some of his company in New York and it was this production which opened their first season, followed by a *reprise* in the Vieux Colombier on their return to Paris in 1920.

It was in the attached Vieux Colombier School, however, that he was able to make the first concrete experiments in working with student actors on the development of new stock types. He had them first develop the externals of a character, finding its silhouette and characteristic outline, then gradually develop its movements and mannerisms by working, almost puppet-like, with different bodily isolations. They created, for example, a timid hairdresser, a rich bourgeois lady (who may or may not have resembled Mme Punais) and a myopic Polish woman. Hardly yet the distillations of their epoch, but an exciting enough glimpse of what he was after for Copeau to abandon his theatre in 1924 and take his school to Burgundy in the quest for more time and a different kind of space to pursue the experiment. As well as the apprentice group from the school, he was joined by some of the actors, including Léon Chancerel and Jean Villard, as well as his right-hand woman, Suzanne Bing. Also in the group was his nephew, Michel Saint-Denis, destined to take over the directorship of the acting company Les Copiaus when Copeau himself stood down after the failure of the school project in 1925.

Some of the Copiaus developed versions of the original characters with a view to playing short Molière farces: Copeau himself as Pantalone, Léon Chancerel as Il Dottore and Jean Villard as Gilles, the eighteenth-century French Pierrot actor much drawn and painted by Watteau. For the new plays written and devised by Copeau and the company, new Masks began to emerge. None of Copeau's earlier written embryos were to see the light of the sun on the outdoor *tréteau* that the Copiaus put up in towns and villages throughout Burgundy. Saint-Denis describes the actors' work process, as opposed to an author's: he started with an old late nineteenth-century coat purloined from the wardrobe together with a pair of mouldy, black-green, baggy trousers 'which were so pliable they took on the shape of every move I made'. To these he added two props, a stick and an old piece of carpet which the character was to use as a sort of rod of office combined with security blanket.

> These four inanimate objects, the coat, the trousers, carpet and stick, started my imagination working and began to give shape to my early intuitions of Oscar. This was not happening at an intellectual level: I had no 'idea' about Oscar; it was something I could feel in my bones.[15]

Chaplin's accidental discovery of the little tramp's baggy trousers and stick comes to mind, as does Beryl Reid's developing a character by first getting the right pair of shoes. Working from externals, the process is then one of trial and error, doodling and leaving in only the lines which intuitively 'feel' right. This process can also be informed by other outside influences: Saint-Denis states he went through a period of observation – of a politician and a night porter – as well as examining some memories of his father and looking at some literary sources – Dostoevsky and Dickens. He then made his own mask and,

> from the feel of the clothes on my body, from my observation of the politician and the porter and from the mask came my inspiration. With the last minute addition of a hat, I had equipped my character from head to foot.[16]

After all this preparation the work could begin: 'Oscar was not actually born yet; the birth of a character is a very slow process. All that existed was an embryo, a silhouette.'[17] To begin with, for example, Oscar could only mumble: since the character was not fully articulated, how could his speech be? Finally, 'Oscar Knie was born: naïve, sentimental, weak (but imperious when successful), carried to extremes, quick to anger and despair, often drunk, a great talker, full-blooded and, sometimes, obscene.'[18]

In similar ways, Jean Dasté, one of the former pupils of the school, developed a M. César ('a kind of dry fish, a sort of Don Quixote, but with much more common sense and much more pessimism') and Chancerel a Sebastien Congre ('archivist, timid palaeographer, molly-coddled and ridiculous'). Saint-Denis also had a local character-cum-mascot, Jean Bourgignon, but he was much more deliberately constructed to suit a dramaturgical purpose, that of leading *parades* and delivering prologues at local fairs and festivities. Oscar Knie, on the other hand, had to have a drama devised around him. It was eventually entitled *La Danse de la ville et des champs* and told the complementary stories of a country boy going to the big city and a Knie, a 'townie', being lost in the country. The piece was a patchwork of styles, song, dance, group mime and chorale, with the Knie sub-plot being treated as a farce embedded within the rest. The première in 1928 was a resounding success – for everyone except Copeau. In his view the mask was being exploited, the context was not that of the new improvised comedy of which he, Gide, Martin du Gard and others had dreamed. He withdrew from active participation and a year later the company disbanded, to regroup as La Compagnie des Quinze. Although continuing to work as an ensemble with the styles first developed in the Vieux Colombier School, the artistic coherence of the company came not from actors improvising in masks, but from a writer recommended to them by Copeau – André Obey. The laboratory had had to close before its experiments were complete without, even, a product to test.

Copeau's preliminary work on Commedia, both old and new, was, however, further developed by Jean Dasté and Léon Chancerel in their separate enterprises (Dasté with his Comédiens de Grenoble (founded in 1945) and as director (1947–71) of the first regional Centre Dramatique, the Comédie de Saint-Etienne, Chancerel with his youth work, in particular the Théâtre de l'Oncle Sebastien (founded 1935) and in his writing for the *Revue d'Histoire du Théâtre*, which he began in 1948.

Charles Dullin: letters from the front

Charles Dullin first earned his living as an actor playing melodramas on the outskirts of Paris. The first troupe he started of his own was a Théâtre de Foire in 1908 in Neuilly, with Saturnin Fabre, based on texts by Alexandre Arnoux. 'The unique goal of this artistic decentralisation? Making some cash. The booth? Had been lent to us by a flea circus proprietor who had fallen on hard times.'[1]

At the dress rehearsal they were full to bursting. At the first performance there was an audience of three: the author, his wife and an army corporal who bought a concessionary ticket at one-quarter price. At the second performance there was one spectator (probably drunk, recalls Fabre). The next day they closed.

In 1910 Dullin 'created the role of Pierrot in Saint-Georges de Bouhélier's *Carnaval des Enfants* at the Théâtre des Arts which Jacques Rouché was managing'.[2] (The character was that of a petit-bourgeois disguised as Pierrot, a timid, well-meaning man.) The next Commedia figure he was to play was Arlequin in Jean-François Regnard's *Divorce* (1921), when he wore the traditional mask for the first time in public. This was for the opening season of his theatre, the Atelier, in Montmartre: influenced by Copeau's vision it was to be a school integrated with a theatre, a laboratory for the regeneration of the actor. In it he gave primary importance to the study of improvisation in developing the actor's instinct: this was the first *practical* research into Commedia, but we have little evidence of what was done. *Parades* were also performed at the Atelier, again reminiscent of Copeau's curtain-raisers for his Molière productions.

During his time in the trenches, Dullin corresponded with Copeau on the possibility of starting a new *commedia dell'arte* troupe after the war, but (perhaps significantly) his letters to 'le Patron' do not give as full an account of his discoveries there as those he wrote to his mistress, Elise Toulemon:

I have discovered a genuine actor and three improvisers, two of whom must descend in a direct line from fairground performers. I give them a scenario and they improvise anything I like. They sing, clown, do Japanese, Spanish, and Italian dances, speak gibberish that sounds just like foreign languages! Evoke for them one word in some foreign civilisation about which they know nothing and it's enough to trigger the most unforeseen and droll fantasies. The eighteenth-century and fairground theatre survives in these blokes intact! One is a jack-of-all-trades from the Faubourg Saint-Antoine. Galvani is a woodcarver from the Faubourg Saint-Antoine, and another a carpenter, also from the Faubourg. . . . It comes from instinct, all this, from the *génie de la race*. I have always had a predilection for the common people, but now more than ever I am determined to move in its direction. No one but the *peuple* possesses the secret of great revolutions in every sphere.[3]

Together they put on a show in three acts: *Monsieur Badin* and *Théodore cherche des allumettes*, two pantomimed *parades*; *La Dernière Parade de l'illustre Tom Jeary, clown*, in two tableaux, by Messieurs Dullin and Levinson, and *Aux Frais de la princesse*, a farce in one act by a certain Pierre Louis Duchartre, who later wrote in his book, *The Italian Comedy*:

Marcel Levinçon, a cabinet-maker in civil life, was a small, wizened fellow with a profile like the plaster-cast head of Dante so often seen in schools. He and his two friends, 'Tuture' and Bonnat, had always made themselves conspicuous by their incredible adventures, their original pranks, and their ability to keep themselves supplied with all the necessities of life – wine in particular. Levinçon was endowed with unusual manual dexterity, as well as exceptional wit, and during the War he had plenty of opportunity to employ both to good advantage . . . a master of cold and penetrating irony; his movements and expressions were rather deliberate and measured, but were none the less irresistibly droll, and he spoke vividly and picturesquely without ever becoming vulgar. Generally he displayed good humour and was ready for any kind of nonsense; no-one could play the 'silly ass' better than he whenever he was in the mood for it. To this day I am convulsed with laughter whenever I think of his absurd remarks and clowning every time we came out of the trenches. He was a natural acrobat, and seemingly had no joint or bone in his body. He could walk with the whole upper part of his body bent back, as though his spine were broken, forming a right angle with his legs, and he also had a trick whereby he could increase his

height by several inches. He was the constant despair of discipli-
narians and representatives of law and order. . . .

It was while they were at the front that Dullin undertook to
make a pantomimist and improvisator of Levinçon. Dullin
persuaded his friend to play in 'skits' to amuse the soldiers during
rest periods, and it goes without saying that their entertainments
never failed to be tremendously successful. At many of their
performances a soldier would sing from the wings of the
makeshift stage some popular air . . . while Levinçon would stand
in front of the audience and interpret the words of the song
entirely by means of his facial expression. It was the most impres-
sive bit of acting I have ever seen. He could tell the complete story
without speaking, in the same manner as the great Scaramouche.
Dullin also persuaded him and two of his friends to enact improvised comedies, and their performances were witty and subtle,
and truly amazing. If Dullin ever succeeds in organising a real
company of finished improvisators I shall be willing to mount the
heights of Montmartre on my knees, just to be allowed the privi-
lege of seeing them perform.

Once after an attack Levinçon raised his canteen, saying, 'They
didn't get me that time.' The next instant he crumpled up with a
bullet through his brain.[4]

Duchartre's conclusion was that,

Were it ever possible to create such a troupe of engaging souls as
Levinçon, we might at last envisage a new form of theatre, the
product of the *commedia dell'arte*, yet by no means a copy of it. The
original group of characters would be replaced by modern types,
speaking their everyday language and exhibiting all the idiosyn-
crasies, vices, customs, and characteristics of their various callings
and stations in society. Nor would it be long before appropriate
masks were devised for them.[5]

When he did get round to writing to Copeau, Dullin enthused:

I organised a show which had a great effect on the Brigade! What
is even more interesting is that I discovered three *marvellous
comedians*! Possibly four, but certainly *three*. I knew that they were
no ordinary lads, but I had no idea that their drollery and gift for
inventiveness was capable of adapting to the demands of the
stage. . . .

Listening to the three jokers who made my scenery, I had the
idea of getting them to improvise a little interlude. I gave them a

scenario and these three buggers immediately went off into the most comical contrivances . . . I was afraid that on the evening of the performance they would be intimidated by the occasion (we had the General and all the top brass of the Brigade) but they were dazzling in their tomfoolery. So much so they were asked for an encore. At this point I had a little shudder. How would they manage it. Would they repeat the same jokes, make them stale? You can see the danger . . . In no way! They only kept my scenario and found a thousand new bits of business, with irresistible comic dialogue. One of them is practically double-jointed. He mimes everything he wants. The other dances every kind of dance and speaks every known language . . . all made up, of course. He'll sing you a song which he has made up from two or three words . . . of Japanese! . . .

I will send you their photograph and you will get some idea of our three *farceurs* that I am very proud to have discovered. They themselves are very astonished at the talents they have discovered in themselves and which they had never previously exploited except in horseplay amongst themselves.[6]

And in a second letter he continued:

They improvised a real *parade* for me. One of them dressed up as a woman and appeared at her window and Galvani and Levinson were Italian singers who came to serenade her. Galvani sang an Italian romantic song whilst Levinson danced and, at the moment when he knelt in front of her, he received a bowl of flour right in the face. Galvani made fun of him, Levinson broke his guitar over his head. Galvani fell on his backside and Levinson tumbled over him with a magnificently dangerous back-flip. . . .

The worrying thing will be how to hang on to them . . . They are types who have never and will never follow any particular path. But Levinson seems very taken with the theatre and Galvani will do what Levinson tells him to do . . . Andry is another sort, more sentimental and more honest. I think he will ask nothing better than to join us, even though he is thirty. . . .

There's someone else who is absolutely one of us and who could do a thousand useful things for our work and would make just the sort of secretarial assistant that you are looking for, his name's Duchartre, an altogether superior type.[7]

He was also in correspondence with Louis Jouvet, as was Copeau. To him he proposed the following outline characters for the new Commedia, part circus-, part *commedia dell'arte*-based:

The clown, a cosmopolitan businessman, good at anything – sales representative, ambassador, MP, Minister or Police Commissioner. Pilot, Cavalry Officer, etc. A musician, changes and varies as do his clothes.

Auguste, the average elector, the common man, a good lad, a little naïve, modified from Sganarelle by Primary School teaching and national service. Private, second class – a small-time grocer, or a bourgeois from a good district, a man of good sense and good manners.

The eccentric American, who I will call 'Tom Jeary' for example, will be the man who makes extraordinary finds, discoveries and revelations – an inventor, illusionist, scene-shifter, surgeon, charlatan, dancer, etc. One would have to find a way of clearly differentiating him from the clown.

The female braggart, a pronouncer of delicate stupidities – gross thighs, gross appetite.

Until Copeau managed to work their release to join the Vieux Colombier in New York, there was little the two actors could do during the war but dream. Not only about such characters, but also who would play them: 'I attach a great importance to the choice of my young farceurs, to their physical appearance, to their way of life', wrote Dullin,

> I would like them to be as near to the people as possible – simple folk – artisans – this genre is incompatible with aestheticism and rhythmical and other chinoiseries. Our farceurs would have to be dancers, acrobats, jugglers, musicians, but with the natural ability of clowns and fairground acrobats. They would have to be *alive*, good drinkers, tellers of jokes and tall stories, good to be with. . . . In order to effect such an education, we must first forget that we are actors, forget there ever were such things as actors or plays. Wipe any concern for the farceurs of the Middle Ages from our minds, forget Molière lock stock and barrel. . . . Start from nothing in order to arrive at everything. One of the essential conditions, I think, would be great camaraderie and, if possible, living a virtually communal life.[8]

Many years later, when director of his own theatre, the Atelier in Montmartre with its own 'feeder' school, he did engage Georgius, a popular circus clown whom he considered a natural descendant of Arlecchino, to play the lead in Roger Vitrac's comedy *Le Camelot* ('The Hawker'). He explained his intentions in an article entitled 'De la comédie italienne aux grands comiques de café-concert':

> It is in the *café-concert* and the circus that one may find *commedia dell'arte*'s true descendants. It is there . . . that the true masks of Harlequin and Scaramouche, Pantalone and the Doctor, Brighella and all the others are re-embodied.[9]

Despite the experiments in animal mimicry and improvisation at his Atelier school, no-one he had trained for the company had Georgius's comedic ability; fortunately, 'From the very first rehearsals, Georgius seemed to me to have always belonged to the Atelier. The reason is that the Atelier also has many points in common with the *commedia dell'arte*.'[10]

And, as we have seen, that compatibility between comic artiste and ensemble players was one that Copeau had also fervently desired after his visits to the Cirque Medrano. For Dullin, however, it now became an end-stopping observation as far as legitimate theatre was concerned. Vitrac's play was a writer's revival of Commedia, not a scenario for a clown to improvise with actors, and the experiment with Georgius did not pass into the repertoire. Between 1922 and 1939 at the Atelier that was Dullin's only excursion into Commedia proper: his repertoire otherwise included French classics and Aristophanes, Shakespeare, Jonson and Pirandello in translation, and the occasional new French play.

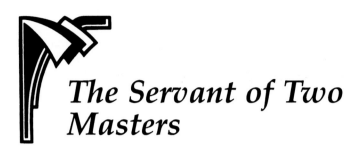

The Servant of Two Masters

The Piccolo Teatro di Milano was founded by Paolo Grassi and Giorgio Strehler in 1947. Their intention was to assist Italian theatre to catch up with the rest of European culture after the bourgeois, even petit-bourgeois, domination of the fascist years: 'From 1903 to 1943, what triumphed on the stages of Italy was not even a neo-classical theatre, it was theatre of adultery, cuckoldry, the worst kind of boulevard theatre, French theatre at its worst.'[1]

They sought and welcomed the influence of Copeau because they found themselves in a similar position vis-à-vis a prevailing decadence of the medium, albeit some forty years on. What they aspired to was a new convergence of theatre with life, with the whole spectrum of Milanese and eventually Italian society, initially through the reintroduction of a Vieux Colombier-style eclectic repertoire which was to include classical Italian authors (Goldoni, Gozzi), foreign masterpieces (Sophocles, Shakespeare, Molière, Büchner), late nineteenth-century realists (Ostrovsky, Becque, Gorky), contemporary classics (Chekhov, Pirandello), present-day writers (Salacrou, Camus, Sartre) and a few new Italian writers.

Goldoni's *The Servant of Two Masters* was the fourth and last play to join the repertoire of the Piccolo Teatro in its first season. The other three productions were Gorky's *The Lower Depths*, *Les Nuits de la colère* by Armand Salacrou and *El magico prodigioso* by Calderon – a humanist but somewhat intellectual rereading of non-Italian classics. *The Servant of Two Masters* balanced the programme with a quest for house-style roots in popular Italian culture, providing 'a joyous and carefree note among the other more absorbing texts'.[2] Grassi considered that

> *The Servant of Two Masters* was the beginning of what could be called our Goldoni cycle. This Goldoni play has an interesting singularity: it is both the crowning and the demise of the *commedia dell'arte*. Goldoni originally wrote only a scenario in the traditional

Commedia fashion. One day, in Pisa, he attended a performance and was extremely unhappy with it: the improvisations of the actors seemed flat etc. Returning home he wrote out the entire text. *The Servant of Two Masters* is thus a written Commedia play – which is itself a paradox; Strehler directed it as representative of the age of decadence of the *commedia dell'arte*.[3]

With Jacques Lecoq, Dario Fo and Marisa Flach, Strehler spent long nights working the mask to see how the chin and neck should be interposed, how the head should be inclined, and how voice, intonation, speech rhythms might emerge. At the same time the Piccolo actors began physical exercises designed not only to enable them to do acrobatics, but also to be able to put themselves in a state of internal justification for doing them.

They did not realise that they were preparing for arguably the most successful production in twentieth-century theatre. The first performance was given in May 1947. The 1,559th performance was on 22 July 1984 at the Olympic Games in Los Angeles. Not only was the production constantly reprised in Milan, but it also undertook numerous national and international tours. Up to the end of 1977, for example, when the company found themselves at the Odéon in Paris, 349 performances had been given in Italy, 402 in Milan, 502 abroad, in 159 Italian towns and 160 foreign ones. There have been continual changes of cast, *mise en scène* and scenography in the course of which the following versions can be distinguished:

1 24 July 1947
2 17 April 1952
3 27 August 1956
3a 10 July 1963
4 24 June 1973
5 4 October 1977[4]
(and a sixth, created for the fortieth anniversary of the Piccolo in 1987).

Version (1) was performed in a rather academic style allusive to the theatre of marionettes, a graphical semi-caricature in two dimensions, based on the *commedia dell'arte* rather than making an attempt to embody it. In taking this approach, Strehler was influenced by Max Reinhardt's 1924 production at the Komedie de Berlin which was highly elegant and stylised. Reinhardt had not taken his own counsel:

> The theatre owes the actor his right to show himself from all sides, to be active in many directions, to display his joy in playfulness, in the magic of transformation. I know the playful, creative powers of the actor and I am often sorely tempted to save something of the old *commedia dell'arte* in our over-disciplined age, in order to

give the actor, from time to time, an opportunity to improvise and let himself go.[5]

At this stage in his quest, Strehler had neither actors nor techniques ready to be 'let go'. He used, for example, naïve costuming which increased the sense of looking into a toy theatre. The décor consisted of a painted back-cloth with two periaktoi (revolving triangles) at the sides with doors drawn on to them. There are four locales in the play: (i) room in Pantalone's house; (ii) a courtyard, ditto; (iii) the saloon of Brighella's inn with two doors at the back and sides; and (iv) the street with a view of the inn. Strehler elided (i) and (ii). The scene was changed by pivoting the periaktoi and having Brighella change the cloth by drawing another one across (hung on a parallel wire). The acting space was a wooden dais placed on stage, 7 metres long by less than 4 metres deep and reduced at the sides by the size of the periaktoi.

Version (2) saw a decisive change to a 'sense of a realism which, on the one hand, recreated the universe of the "Company of Comedians" and on the other evoked an atmosphere which is typically Italian'.[6] The allusion to puppets and toys was abandoned in favour of the re-creation of the world of a company of *comici dell'arte*, brought to play *The Servant of Two Masters* in a public place on a festival day. The costumes were now historically accurate and the leather masks of Sartori made their first appearance. The action was embellished with authentic *lazzi*. In rehearsal the 'marionette' style of acting had been found less and less satisfying, and the plasticity of the action changed from within, from the discoveries of the actors them-selves. It was no longer the characters or their intrigues, but actors playing the actors playing Goldoni's play which interested Strehler. The show became a realistic representation of the everyday life of an itinerant eighteenth-century Italian troupe.

Since 1947 Strehler had mounted three other plays by Goldoni: *The Honest Young Woman*, *The Lovers* and *The Military Lover*. The first two of these are from Goldoni's later psychological realism period: Strehler had become drawn to his idea of theatre as a transcription of reality.

New designs, by Gianni Ratto were, however, still based on a scenic structure identical to the 1947 production. The lines remained abstract, but were now more curved and elegant. Pantalone's house became Regency, the interior decorated with medallions depicting exotic subjects. It was visibly the house of an eighteenth-century well-to-do bourgeois. The inn was now more up-market – still an antechamber surrounded by six doors (numbered in the original version), but more realistic, with *trompe l'oeil* painting giving a greater sense of space. The travelling trunks of Florinda and Beatrice, previously simple and neutral, now became ornate, showing the class of their owners. The platform stage was now set further back, creating the beginnings of a sense of a theatre within a theatre.

Version (3) was the first of what might be called the definitive versions. Strehler's developing regard for Brecht manifested itself. His first Brecht production, *The Decision*, had been in May 1954 with the Piccolo Teatro School. In May 1956 he mounted *Threepenny Opera*, and in 1958 *The Good Person of Szechuan*; the reprise of *The Servant of Two Masters* was thus sandwiched between two Brecht productions. As a result Strehler became more concerned with setting the classics in historical perspective than in a historical setting *per se*. The new *mise en scène* also had a Pirandellian influence, developing a complex theatrical world with an 'ambiguous rapport between stage and wings'.[7] What was created was theatre-outside-the-theatre rather than a play-within-a-play. The dialectic between playing and social conditions was sharpened by the décors becoming more neo-realistic. The dais was reduced to 4 metres square, not unlike what Copeau would have called a *tréteau*, and the three painted cloths could now be pulled in both directions. The designer (Ezio Frigerio who had designed several of the costumes for the 1947 production) limited the vertical space by dropping in three sets of cloths above, like a ship in full sail. They perhaps indicated a sunshield for actors, an image of Mediterranean washing hanging from upper windows or the décor of an eighteenth-century *salon*.

Indications of the ruins of a seventeenth-century *palazzo* were placed in the background, cracked walls, rubble and the remains of doors and windows, forming a sad, sombre context for the frivolities in front, isolating the stage both from its own period and from our own. In the offstage foreground were remnants of an even more distant past – Roman, Corinthian, perhaps indicating the immutability of the seemingly ephemeral form of *commedia dell'arte*. The farce on stage remained lively, irrepressible, but its history lay in ruins around it.

Offstage the actors were still onstage: masks pulled up after their exits, they would pause a while to watch the continuation of the action, check out the reaction of the audience, then, leaning on the ruins, chat among themselves, take a swig of wine and begin preparing for their next entrance. After so many performances Goldoni's dramatic narrative became less important than the way of presenting the Commedia characters, the techniques employed, the way the *lazzi* were played. Equally the interaction between the characters became of less interest than the interaction between the actors. 'There was no longer a preoccupation with history but above all with the theatrical convention within which history realised itself.'[8] Pantalone's house was now positively opulent, with painted columns, portals, etc.; grandiose, truly 'magnificent' with a Louis XIII chair which only he, the successful capitalist, was permitted to sit on. The street, also, was no longer a *campiello* but a large avenue, more realistically painted than in 1952 with neo-classical architecture and traditional Venetian wrought-iron balconies in the distance. A contrast was thus implied between the poor players' trestle stage and the monumental wealth indicated by their two-dimensional backdrop. The inn scene moved into the kitchen itself. Its backcloth became a realistic representation of a period *batterie de cuisine*, more like that of a Renaissance palace than a humble inn.

Theatrical illusion was consequently reduced to a minimum by repeated framing devices – periods within periods, settings within settings. Wings were no longer appropriate as the painting onstage and the architectural remnants off it became more realistic in order to point up the decadence of the the epoch being presented when viewed from a contemporary perspective.

In 1963 Strehler again reworked the production. He retained the critical and historical perspective, but went further in establishing the parallel action before, during and after the play. It was performed in the gardens of the Villa Litta in Attori in the outskirts of Milan, and might be numbered (3a), but Strehler denies that this was a new version. Marcello Moretti, the actor who created the central role of Arlecchino, had died on 18 January 1961 and for some time neither Strehler nor Grassi could bear to hear the text or look at the costumes and masks so closely associated with their lost colleague. Strehler wrote:

> I would like it if, through the memory of one of its children, the theatre could find help in loving and understanding the collective distraction with which we are surrounded. What is more definitive than the death of a theatrical performer? What the actor Marcello Moretti was is now fixed for ever only in the memory of those who saw and heard him one evening, one among many, in an ensemble of scenic movement, actions and feelings and in the interior extension which his presence, in that moment, created in those who witnessed him. Photographs, tape recordings and writings can only be the means of bringing back memories, not the material for an evocation.[9]

Meanwhile Strehler directed Brecht's *Schweik, The Exception and the Rule* and *Galileo*.

Playing outdoors in front of a perfectly preserved palatial villa, the fake ruins would have had no meaning. The 'sails' had to be abandoned for fear of them filling with real wind. The stage was set in a pool of light with nine floats in front which were lit by the prompter before he gave the ritual three knocks to announce the beginning of the show. In fact most of the actors were already to be seen. On the steps up to one of the wagons, the Lover could be seen flirting gallantly with the actress playing Smeraldina. . . . A young actor smacked the cheeks of a stage manager who had given him a broken sword, the prompter was practically deafened by a bang on the tambourine 6 inches from his ear. Each actor invented a personal, private role as an eighteenth-century player. The villa was used as a background with a cloth stretched across the ground floor like a Brechtian half-curtain. The arcades became real wings. The upper floors were lit with chandeliers in each window in order to make it seem as if the whole building were involved in some important festive occasion. However, the wings were too far from the stage to exit into, so two wagons of indeterminate period were placed either side of the platform for actors to disappear behind. Rather than ruination, the production was accordingly now framed by well-preserved, politically self-important architecture. The decadence, therefore, had to be cultural, in the players themselves, as the cabotins of a moribund theatre.

Version (4) was prepared for two open-air runs, first in the Villa Communale in 1973, then at the Villa Litta again the following year. There had been further progress in the reconstruction of *all'improvvisata* playing and the craft of the actor was made more and more visible.

The wooden frame for the curtains now had eight lanterns hanging from it, complementing the nine floodlights. Pantalone's house developed a Renaissance grandiloquence, painted stucco with a real golden rococo arm-chair. Red carpets and flamboyant damasks were still betrayed as mere painting each time the curtain moved to the rhythm of the actors entering, brushing against it behind or lifting it up from the bottom. Its surface sumptuousness was thus undermined by its mobility. The street was also reworked into a sort of postcard view that could have been titled 'View of a canal: eighteenth century'. Venice, more Moorish than baroque, curved in perspective into the distance. But the realism of the scene was again undermined by ever more frenzied playing. The inn scenes were played in the kitchen again, but now with a real fire, pheasants, a log pile, caged birds, a buffet, disordered cooking stoves, flickering flames, all serving to abolish the rather formal historical reconstruction of the previous version. But again the backdrop was played with by the performers, thus undermining the sanctity of its images – for example, at one point Arlecchino lifted up the chimney breast in order to enter.

Version (5), created for the Odéon in 1977, seemed no longer to hold to the so far carefully underlined distinction between life and convention, epic realism and *commedia dell'arte*. 'Symbolic lassitude seemed to take hold of both the troupe and the story they represented, as if the theatre itself, in the image of decadent *commedia dell'arte*, was nothing but a moribund epic à la Beckett.'[10] Strehler decided

> to abolish the little raised platform, to replace the most obvious aspects of the continuous playing with interior exteriors from the first versions, with a mysterious line separating the theatre from the rest. A circle of light inside which the story unravelled is all that separates Arlecchino from the auditorium.[11]

The 1956 ruins reappeared, differently worked, representing the *salon* or entrance hall of an abandoned château: grey walls, debris of the statue of a horse; décor gloomier, heavier.

> The years had passed . . . and the troupe had lost a little of its lightness, it seemed to have aged; that which had changed it most was the climate in which the show seemed to take place: off the platform – on which, naturally, the gestures and rhythms remained the same – the space was limited and an atmosphere of melancholy, almost of decadence, hung in the air. The proprietors of the palace had never manifested themselves, but now their absence was significant, the sign that something was changing or was about to do so. It certainly affected the anecdotal elements which surrounded the actual play, which were perfectly capable of substitution with others, according to the whim of the individual performer. But over and above these gratuitous details, there remained something concrete and essential: this was the fact that by virtue of this splendid intuition – both poetical and method-ological at the same time – this *Servant of Two Masters* . . . made the event of a performance of *commedia dell'arte* live again as its interpreters first matured and then aged.[12]

Above all what Strehler had wanted was to rediscover *form* as a source of vital acting. In this quest the most crucial role was, obviously, that of Arlecchino (actually called Truffaldino in Goldoni's original). The rapport between Moretti and Arlecchino was, according to Strehler, a complex one, loving but full of contradictions, stemming from an understandable reluc-tance that all actors (who live in the moment) feel in embracing a mask (which lives outside temporal considerations):

> At first sight one would say that Moretti did not like Arlecchino. He underwent him, as a sort of tyranny by one stock *commedia dell'arte* character over an interpreter. The actor Moretti resented Arlecchino as a cruel limitation on his expressive possibilities in other scenic dimensions. The actor, up to a certain point, both for the audience and for other theatre workers, became identified with his mask.
>
> For Marcello this was almost a condemnation. I remember his sadness on certain nights after a fantastic success, his anguish about the future. 'What when I am old and can't play Arlecchino any more?' he would say.[13]

Yet Moretti himself had limitations as an actor in his own right. Strehler notes that he was perhaps intellectually a little inflexible, diffident and pernickety, physically limited and vocally heavy and unclear. But in the painstaking reconstruction of Arlecchino he revealed 'an absolutely exceptional interior richness'. It was a labour of love, a model for those around him. Not the sort of passion that declares itself only in intimate diaries and in theatrical declarations, but in the hard, monotonous continuity of every-day exercise. 'Marcello was one of the most disciplined actors there could be, disciplined not only in my respect or in his own regard, but disciplined for his *métier*, for the theatre.'[14]

And that discipline became nowhere more apparent than in the passing on of the role of Arlecchino. After a cartilage operation on his knee (necessitated by injuries sustained during the trunk scene) Moretti's performance, although maturing (as Kenneth Tynan noticed when the company played the Edinburgh Festival), slowed. With a tour to the States in prospect the company was obliged to have an understudy, and Strehler and Moretti spent many hours training a young actor, Ferruccio Soleri, in the role. During these rehearsals Moretti preferred to be left alone. The old and the new Arlecchino worked together mysteriously, *sotto voce*. Little by little a shy new Arlecchino emerged, at times the double of his parent, but also showing signs of individual life. When, later, he performed in technical rehearsals, Moretti would watch from the wings, nodding approval or making notes for later private discussion. In developing his successor, he was as meticulous and as demanding as he had been on himself. And as unselfish.

Let's turn back to the production itself. Dario Fo:

> The objection that I hear offered most frequently to this production is that it did not contain so much of the spirit of improvised performance, rather that it presented itself as an extraordinary comedic machine, with pre-programmed rhythms, not much imaginative freedom and great precision – in short, it worked like a clock. . . .
>
> I would first reply that finding any comedic mechanism which is capable of functioning like a clock is quite an extraordinary thing, certainly not an everyday occurrence. Specifically, however, it should be said that the *commedia dell'arte* with which Strehler was occupying himself was that of the end of the seventeenth century, that of Goldoni.[15]

In Fo's opinion, Goldoni was trying to re-Italianise the *commedia dell'arte* after a century of comings and goings of the major companies to Paris and elsewhere. Reform of theatre for him was a reform of culture which would lead to a more ordered Italian society. Seen in this way, Goldoni is essentially a political writer who did not want to give carte blanche to actors to improvise his meanings away in search of cheap laughs. Thus Truffaldino, although a mischievous fast-moving imp, is not the Arlecchino of Martinelli

(1595) or of Biancolelli (1627 on), because he was refined of his brutishness, offensiveness and obscenity. Fo prefers the earlier figure but sympathises with Strehler's sense of stylistic appropriateness. And, Fo points out, through all the versions and reworkings, the actors, especially Moretti, were allowed creative space and were not subjected to a directorial straitjacket. The production, in the manner of the Berliner Ensemble, was a workers' collaboration. Fo quotes his brother Fulvio:

> The *mise en scène* remained constant, as a matter of fact, and any developments were due to things the company brought to it, the additions made by those exceptional performers, the experience which people like Franco Parenti brought directly to bear during the rehearsal period . . . and again the contribution of Marcello Moretti, of Battistella, etc. In this way the production was created in an atmosphere of great collaboration and generosity: the famous scene of the crumb of bread played by Moretti, for example, came from Franco Parenti; it was typical of Franco to invent something, and then make a present of it to the company.[16]

The production did in fact become a clockwork mechanism, but it was not directorially preconceived as such. It was created in a manner appropriate to the spirit of the *commedia dell'arte* and from improvised discoveries made by the actors and refined by Strehler's direction into something brilliant and almost magical. I understand that it is today back in the repertoire, the *batocchio* of Arlecchino having been ceremonially handed on by Soleri to a new actor.

The Lecoq school

Jacques Lecoq was a fencer before he became an actor. In 1945 he worked with Jean Dasté's Comédiens de Grenoble. There he assimilated Copeau's ideas from Dasté and Léon Chancerel, returning to Paris two years later to teach. In 1948 he went to Italy, where he was to remain for eight years during which time he founded the Teatro dell'Università di Padova and began mask work with Amleto Sartori. As a movement director he worked on some sixty productions in Syracuse, Rome, Venice and finally at the Piccolo Teatro di Milano where he collaborated with Strehler and with Dario Fo. That work has already been described in Part I of this book and the resulting production of *The Servant of Two Masters* in the previous chapter.

The roots of Lecoq's teaching, inherited via Dasté from Copeau, lay jointly in *commedia dell'arte* and in Greek tragedy. In 1957 he returned to Paris to set up his school, in the brochure for which he lists *commedia dell'arte* as 'one of the boundary lines of theatre', along with Greek tragedy, classical Japanese theatre and *pantomime blanche*. Through the study of what he calls these 'finalised' forms, he considers

> the student might gain an understanding of the extremes of acting which would employ his entire being. It serves him as a point of reference.
>
> Thus Commedia, where the play is action, and Greek Tragedy, where the word is flesh, are the form of theatre where the actor is entirely engaged; pelvis, solar plexus, and head.

This trilogy is one which Lecoq inherited from François Delsarte, the nineteenth-century singing teacher. The vocal dimension is significant because, although his school is often thought of as a mime school, Lecoq never trained as a mime and, like Copeau, he does not like 'pure' mime. The mime he teaches is 'open to the theatre much more than a mime for solo

200

performers, or a mime which would be completely silent. I made mimes speak.'[1] More specifically he considers that:

> In the history of the theatre, mime as a separate art has no permanence. It is an *art de passage*, a transition, a channel for nourishing drama and dance. It appears at certain times, at the end of one theatre and the beginning of another. It retains action and conserves gesture in that interim in which theatre, having lost the force of words, renews its forms.[2]

Thus Marcel Marceau-style mime is only learned as a historical discipline, not as a performance form in its own right. The school is dedicated to the study of all forms of movement: 'Movement is the basis of everything. We call the art of acting *le jeu* – it's a physical act.'[3] And it is the disciplined control of this physical act which can reauthorise the performer: 'Mine is a school of creativity. I remind the actors that they are auteurs.'[4]

Like mime, then, Commedia is not studied at the school for its own sake as a curio form:

> I don't bury myself in historical references. I try to rediscover the spirit of these forms. Commedia has nothing to do with those little Italian troupes who export precious entertainments. It's about misery, a world where life's a luxury.[5]

Lecoq teaches that it is not the easiest but the hardest option for the actor to use stereotypes: the internal emotional validation of external movement has to be extreme and the interplay between the two equally extreme in its intensity:

> Lecoq progresses towards use of Commedia masks both through work on breathing and through exercises which raise the level of intensity of expressing emotion: each feeling, for instance, can be progressively 'scaled up' by every new character entering a scene.[6]

A line drawing of Arlecchino figures prominently on the school's letter-heading and

> Lecoq considers Arlecchino a key personage to what goes on in the school. He has a tragic element on the one hand and a comic element on the other. He really unites the two elements of what I love in theatre.[7]

I believe, however, that he has recently dropped the teaching of Commedia from the school's programme, perhaps due to a reluctance to continue to have women playing in male masks, especially that of Arlecchino. If so, it is interesting to contrast the gender manipulations of a supposedly traditional troupe such as the Carrara family who clearly consider the challenging of sexual stereotypes as a means by which the Masks can continue to 'modernise' themselves.

The Lecoq school has had a profound effect on the development of non-text-based theatre in the last three decades of the century, not only inspiring revivals of *commedia dell'arte*, but also the interconnection of mask, mime, vocalisation and, ultimately, text – a fusion which can be seen in the English-speaking theatre in the work of such Lecoq-trained troupes as The Moving Picture Mime Show and Théâtre de Complicité, as well as in a host of new troupes working at the international margins. The school has provided a crucible in which much contemporary work with a Commedia stylistic component, or attitude to performance at least, has been forged.

Le Théâtre du Soleil

The Théâtre du Soleil can perhaps best be said to have formed around Ariane Mnouchkine in 1964: it consisted of a group of actors and technicians from the Association Théâtrale des Etudiants de Paris, which had been founded by Mnouchkine while she was a student of psychology, but from the outset the working principles which were sought were ensemble-, not director-dominated. A spirit of amateur enquiry informed much of their early work, which had an almost deliberate naïvety of approach to a magpie collection of forms and styles. There were to be no ready-made answers to the question they were asking themselves through her as mediator. Echoing Copeau, she formulated this as 'Are we the agents of a past that is beyond repair? Or are we rather the harbingers of a future which can barely be discerned at the extreme limits of a dying epoch?' In her view these questions were ones that all contemporary theatre practitioners were trying to answer,

> frantically, pathetically, even, in the confusion which engulfs us, and which at the same time both unites us and sets us against each other. Those among us who accept the terrible sentence implied by the first question, find recompense for their renouncement in the manifold delights and marvels that the old world confected, so many subtleties to worry and agonise over, so many majestic processes, so much Order in fact, that they understand (if they have the talent for it) how to uncover for us the route to nostalgia, and to help us fall in love with Death.
>
> Those among us who, without even knowing if anyone is listening, decide to respond to the second question have, through this choice, taken only the first step on a long journey which will take them from despair to despair across deserts, toward mirages, into quagmires and down false tracks and dead-ends.[1]

She tried taking the company on rural retreat, Copeau style, to L'Ardèche, but two months later they returned to Paris without seeing the light of bucolic serenity and rehearsed *Les Petits-Bourgeois* (by Gorky adapted by Adamov). After this claustrophobic and depressing play came a more light-hearted project: an adaptation (1965–6) of Gautier's *Le Capitaine Fracasse*. The novel was taken apart chapter by chapter, discussed, its situations improvised, recorded and written down by Mnouchkine and Philippe Léotard; the results were then rehearsed, rewritten and re-rehearsed. It was the company's first encounter with *commedia dell'arte* and the beginning of the Théâtre du Soleil's preoccupation with theatre within theatre. A critic wrote:

> What gave me the most vivid enjoyment in this show was the appropriateness of accent found by a fervent young company in rendering homage to the theatre and to its fabulous universe: an appropriateness and fervour which are also those of Corneille in *L'Illusion comique*, or of Renoir each time he declares his love of spectacle (the *commedia dell'arte* in *Le Carrosse d'or*, or the music-hall in *French Cancan*).[2]

During 1966–7 Mnouchkine attended the Lecoq school in order to develop a more fundamental basis for the company's work methods: in the evenings she taught the other members of the company (who all had daytime jobs) what she had learned during the day.

The Stanislavskian realism of the Gorky play and the Commedia physicality of the Gautier experiment were then combined by the Théâtre du Soleil in the production of Wesker's *The Kitchen* (1967), the company's first big success. This was followed in 1968 by *A Midsummer Night's Dream*, created under the direct influence of Jan Kott, with Puck played not as a legendary sprite, but as an Arlecchino with devilish origins. Nevertheless, despite what she had been learning at Lecoq, Mnouchkine's production had no further aspirations towards Commedia. It was very successful for three months but was then abandoned because of the May 68 upheavals out of which, not surprisingly for a company with avowedly collectivist principles, a new political perspective emerged.

The members of the company again left Paris for a commune-type existence in the country, this time at Arc-et-Senans. There they read Shakespeare, Elizabethan tragedy, Chinese and Japanese classical theatre, but nothing excited. Disillusionment set in. None the less they remained faithful to visions of a new life, a new approach to theatre, and began to work on non-textual sources including *commedia dell'arte*, masks and improvisation. The performance which emerged, *Les Clowns*, was given its first performance at the Théâtre de la Commune d'Aubervilliers in 1969.

This is not the place to recount the story of the two history plays which followed and which for most people are synonymous with the company's identity: *1789* (1970–1, filmed 1974), followed by the less successful *1793* (1972–3). These were followed by an attempt to move from past into present-day history: *L'Age d'or, première ébauche* (1975). The intention of the latter, on which I will now concentrate, was to recount the history of our times, by showing the complex social mosaic of contemporary life as a farce, creating, as they said in their programme, 'a celebration that was both violent and serene, through the reinvention of the principles of popular traditional theatre'.

The company began by interviewing workers in mines, factories and hospitals, as well as pupils and students, in an attempt to find a measure of everyday hopes, fears and ambitions, as well as accumulating newspaper cuttings about contemporary events. They then turned to what had by now become an established working method of creating character types and improvising sketches which portrayed them in essential situations. Next they developed a loose storyline round the misfortunes of an immigrant worker called Abdallah (played by Philippe Caubère), who eventually became the subject of one of the news clippings – 'Death of worker in building site accident'. To this was added another layer of largely improvised scenes delineating social problems and injustices, such as property scandals, drug abuse and inadequate communication between generations of families. The structure remained loose and depended on nightly improvisation in performance. They called it a *première ébauche* (first draft) in order to emphasise that it was work-in-progress; their idea was that in non-scripted performance there can never be a definitive version. Constant changes reflected the company's overall objective: 'a theatre in direct contact with social reality: not just a representation of reality but an incitement to change the conditions in which we live'.[3] The actors imagined characters through individual inspiration from those of the *commedia dell'arte*, but not as reconstructions:

> In their human and social definition, Arlecchino, Matamoros, Pantalone, Pulcinella, Zerbinetta, Isabella or Brighella only exist through and for the theatre. We are not resuscitating past theatrical forms, be it Commedia or traditional popular Chinese theatre.[4]

They took the view that a

> 'Worker' with a capital W has no existence in reality, it is an archetype, even (who knows?) a false political concept. If I select Pulcinella to show one of these workers, then I am making use of a character that has desires, passions, ideas, contradictions, and through the enjoyment that I will have in playing them, through the enjoyment to be had from watching them, will come understanding; one will see the road he takes before becoming aware of his condition, which will incite him to go on strike, at which

25 Abdallah/Arlecchino, the immigrant worker in Théâtre du Soleil's *L'Age d'or*.

moment he will stop accepting his lot and begin to fight. And in
doing that I will have made a work which is both theatrical and
political.[5]

Philippe Caubère was at first wary of mask work as a means to such
concretisation, but 'the more the work progressed, the more I realised the
freedom and power that the mask could offer me if I managed to discover
the rules implicit in the wearing of it'.[6] Gradually he learned to wear the
mask and to inhabit the character, mostly through watching other actors'
efforts. Mario Gonzales's Pantalone was the first to emerge. Then a difference developed between Caubère's Abdallah and the traditional
Arlecchino:

> Arlecchino inhabits a relatively simple world whose workings he
> generally grasps and within which he can perform. He knows
> Pantalone, the merchant, like the back of his own hand, and is
> therefore in conflict with someone whose vices, habits and
> schemings he knows and which he can oppose with his own. He
> knows more or less who his allies are and who are his enemies.

As for Abdallah, at the beginning he knows nothing. He arrives in Marseille not knowing a word of French, with nowhere to live, in eastern dress, and his mind full of delusions: he disembarks on the quay like 'a desert prince'. Then he discovers that he is alone and penniless in the face of a society which is unbelievably rigid in its hierarchies and brutally hostile towards him. His only allies are his own kind, the other immigrants and, perhaps, Demosthenes, who wants to teach him to read. . . . His adventures will be as amusing as those of Arlecchino, but undoubtedly more crude, more cruel and sometimes more dramatic.[7]

Other Masks in *L'Age d'or* did not have a Commedia parentage, but were intended by their maker (Erhard Stiefel from the Lecoq school) to be as universal. Given the lack of masked roles for women in traditional Commedia, not surprisingly it was the women in the company who in the main took advantage of the 'new' Masks. Lucia Bensasson developed a character called Salouha:

One day, Stiefel brought in new masks for the modern comedy, something which he was doing more and more regularly. Among them, one mask appealed to me greatly. I found it had a Semitic feel to it, I tried it and it seemed to adapt perfectly to my features. I looked at it and had a great desire to do something with it. I showed it to Ariane, it seemed to inspire her as much as me. It had a downcast feel, the weight of history behind it.

The first time I used it I entered into a state that was psychologically complete: I felt the mask only from the inside, without managing to exteriorise it, to show it, to find a physicalisation for it. Then Ariane reminded me simply that one must never forget that one is in a fairground; I started again and suddenly it clicked: I find externals to show what I am feeling internally, that is to say that I see my character at the same time as showing it, I delineate it: Mademoiselle Lanzberg was born.[8]

Then there was Lou, 'The fat, positive character', performed by Dominique Valentin who describes how she 'found' her:

Through the mask. I put on a mask with round contours, rather by chance. There was no option for me but to develop a round body to go with this round mask. I became 'the Fat Lady'. For me, the actress, it was important that she stay that way. It is, for example, a way of fighting back against the conditioning of women by advertising.

And the internal image which she used: 'Before improvising this woman for the first time, the image came to me of the casinos of Las Vegas with halls full of fat women playing one-armed bandits.' And her two main characteristics:

> If my 'Fat Lady' found herself in a situation where she had to tackle a specific subject, she never came straight to the point, but could not prevent herself telling anecdotes and recounting memories of past experiences. She thinks herself a liberated woman and fights for women's rights (such as abortion).

And the function of the character she describes as

> a teacher of English, or perhaps a doctor or a lawyer. I have improvised the character at the Lycée d'Ales in front of pupils who asked us to act a disciplinary tribunal. 'The Fat Lady' defended the rights of children who were supposed to be going to be expelled from the school.
>
> This character was created with the help of a modern mask in an actual situation. I have, however, transposed her into the past, where I have noticed a similarity with certain servants in Molière who are very emancipated, such as Toinette in *Le Malade Imaginaire*.[9]

In many ways the production was a dialectic between creative actor disciplines drawn from Commedia and the use of the alienation techniques posited by Brecht for the performance of his scripted works: 'We wanted to reinvent the rules of acting which expose everyday reality by showing it not as familiar and immutable, but surprising and transformable.'[10]

Every gesture, word, intonation even was to be 'a sign immediately perceptible by the spectator' - in Brechtian terminology a *gestus*. The work of Brecht's to which they had most reference seems to have been his essay 'Alienation Effects in Chinese Acting'. There is a problem here: why did not Brecht himself turn to Commedia, given his interest in 'finalised' forms from other cultures? Could it be argued that *commedia dell'arte* and Marxism are incompatible, that Commedia, being essentially a comic, occasional, celebratory form, tends to be a safety-valve for the status quo, not a critique of it, capable of satirising the owner class, but not of leading the social revolution which would abolish it?

This inconsistency inherent in the Théâtre du Soleil's thinking (they were perhaps working with an incompatibility when they thought they were having a dialectical approach) was compounded by the existence of a third influence in their work, Mnouchkine's use of 'states' or 'humours' which, although 'A'-effectual in the sense of recognition of the spectator and of the theatrical act, related to an internal psychological process for the actor which had nothing to do with either epic acting or the *commedia dell'arte*. She recorded that

> Every time in rehearsal that the actors found themselves talking among themselves, it did not work. I said to them 'Tell the audience'. . . .
> When the state, the emotion that the actor must express through the character, is not sufficiently clear, there is always a tendency to 'take refuge in a psychological rapport with a stage partner'.[11]

The idea of direct relating to the spectator is used both by Brecht and the *comici dell'arte*, but what was the state (*état*) that Mnouchkine was asking her actor to relate? The theory stemmed from her early interest as a psychology student in Stanislavsky's teachings about affective memory which she applied in particular to the production of Shakespeare. She developed it as a colour theory:

> The actor cannot and must not play more than one state at a time, even if he only plays it for a quarter of a second for it then to be replaced in the next quarter of a second by another, something which happens in Shakespeare all the time. Shakespeare uses an extreme versatility of emotions: in one line of verse he can give you a green rage; in the next a blue euphoria.[12]

Before the actors come to build up their succession of differing states, they must first discover their particular 'état de base'. Philippe Hottier (who played three parts, eventually six):

> There are two things: the basic state of the character and the successive states which it undergoes. I would say that the basic state is that of the attitude to life. Arlecchino does not have the same basic state as Pantalone. . . .
> Once he has found this basic state, he goes on to live it through moods of joy, anger, aggression, etc. The basic state is modified through secondary states.[13]

It starts with the body, i.e. is a basis for movement, and culminates with the voice. Thus, although inspired by Stanislavsky, the theory owed more in practice to the work of Lecoq. A basic state for Arlecchino, for example, could be happy, unhappy, feeling cold, hungry, over-full, etc. Secondary contradictions were then added: perhaps 'pretending he is someone who never feels the cold going for a walk in a thin shirt on a freezing cold day in December'.

It was considered particularly important for a character to establish such a basic state on entry:

> Each character must make an entrance which is its own by show-
> ing through the general disposition of the body, a certain state.
> This state creates a parallel situation which, whether in the form of
> a shock, or whether through harmonisation, will explicate the
> general state of progress of the play.[14]

I did not see the production and do not wish to comment further on the success or otherwise of this trilogy of influences; David Whitton considers

> *L'Age d'or* was the last in the Théâtre du Soleil's cycle of historical
> chronicles and perhaps the least successful. Although audience
> figures were good it was sensed that on this occasion the
> company's theatrical brilliance was not matched by their material.
> Its weakness was noted by critics who were generally supportive
> of the company. Alfred Simon found its politics superficial and
> naïve. Raymonde Temkine criticised the weakness of the text
> which on the level of expression was prosaic and overall gave the
> impression of an arbitrary collocation of scenes. On the technical
> side, however, with its rigorous exploration of acting styles and
> use of environmental staging techniques, *L'Age d'or* confirmed the
> Théâtre du Soleil as having a distinctive theatrical language as
> innovative and as accomplished as any to be seen.[15]

The San Francisco Mime Troupe

The San Francisco Mime Troupe began operation in 1959, temporarily named the R.G. Davis Mime Troupe, after its founder. It did not mime in the sense of silent *pantomime blanche*, but based its work on the *mime corporel* which Davis had studied in Paris for six months in 1957 under Etienne Decroux:

> In the Frenchman's studio the ability to exercise an isolation or a weight change was based both on internal and external expertise. The quasi-ideological explanation for a stance or a gesture by Decroux gave the work a seriousness that few Americans could abide, yet Decroux's dictum, a pre-Cartesian concept, 'Nothing in the hands, nothing in the pockets', cleaned the stage for the new concept of Mime Corporal.[1]

On returning to the USA, he joined the Los Angeles Actors' Workshop, hoping it would provide a radical alternative to bourgeois-dominated culture, but left disillusioned when a grant from the Ford Foundation was accepted – a move which he considered implied a sell-out to corporate sponsorship and attendant artistic censorship.

The troupe's early work might best be described as eclectic performance art, including experiments in mixed media, but the style the performers sought was a political one: 'The Mime Troupe was a cultural coalition of disaffected people.... Politically the Bay area was the happening area. Between 1962 and 1972, there was a real, almost cultural, revolution.'[2]

A production of *Ubu Roi* helped them develop the scale of their social and artistic revolt, but still they felt circumscribed by the elitism of indoor performance in 'art' theatres. They decided to go public, into the parks. But clearly corporeal mime would not provide a stylistic base for popular work. *Commedia dell'arte*, like *Ubu*, they discovered, 'pleased its audience by farting and belching at the stuffier stuffed classes'.

211

Their first Commedia, sourced mainly from Molière and entitled *The Dowry*, was assembled in 1962. During the early rehearsals,

> we were fortunate in meeting Carlo Mazzone, a mime from the Lecoq School. He had played Brighella under Giorgio Strehler at the Piccolo and possessed eight leather masks made by Amleto Sartori. . . . Mazzone left us with a sense of some impossible magic about the masks. In the seven years of playing commedia, we found only one artist . . . who could make a few usable masks. In 1968 I realised there was a simpler method and sent a letter with a cheque to Sartori.[3]

They went to work on *commedia dell'arte*

> by jumping in and splashing round. We ploughed through all the books, Italian, French and English. We improvised from old scenarios and plays by Molière and Goldoni; wrote our own scenes; tried different characters. We discovered that the stereotypical characters operated both as an escape valve for irritation and as an integrating force. To the liberal, they often appeared to show prejudice. However, if you dig the people and the contradictions, the stereotypes are more accurate in describing social conditions than bland generalities.[4]

Eventually they learned, through trial and error, 'researching, stealing, gleaning and improvising', how to 'make stereotypes carry the burden of social satire'. The focus was, however, still historical, based on a perception of the spirit and style of the 1600s.

> *The Dowry* opened at the Encore but when that theatre dried up as a source of 'new work', we went off to perform at the Spaghetti Factory, a cabaret in North Beach, on Thursday evenings. We worked through the winter rains polishing and learning the show so well that real honest-to-goodness improvisation actually took place. After a few months inside, we finally got our chance to perform in the open air as commedia had done three hundred years before.[5]

The first outdoor performance was in Golden Gate Park in May 1962. An actress who had so far been struggling with her character came offstage and yelled at Davis, 'The reason for the large movements and gestures is that they performed outside.'

> That's what it said in the books; that's what we based our exaggerated movements on; yet, inside the beer hall and the small

theatre it was not always evident. Once outside, theory and reality crashed together into a screaming joyous perception.[6]

In a programme note, Davis stated:

'Adaptation' may be a misleading term for the relation of our commedia shows to their originals. We do not usually set our-selves the task of translating an author's intentions; rather we exploit his work to suit our own; using what we can and discard-ing the rest, writing in new scenes and characters, to say nothing of new emphasis. . . .

Our interest in this 16th century form is not antiquarian: we use it because it is popular, free, engaging, and adaptable.[7]

To create a bridge for themselves and for the spectator into the world of Commedia, they would rush around the park in a sort of parade before the show, and then perform an elaborate company prologue, designed to intro-duce the characters and conventions (as well as to get the company onstage together and establish themselves as performers before being exposed as Masks).

The outdoor Commedia experiments continued for several years: in 1963 a show called *Ruzzante's Maneuvers* was a self-confessed fiasco at the San Francisco Art Museum. This setback was recovered the following year by the insurance of working more closely from an established text – *Tartuffe* adapted from Molière by Richard Sassoon. Again they worked their 'asses off', and the company began to settle:

We had, with the vibrance of Commedia, attracted people to the company but more often the excited overworked themselves and left. Fortunately the cast was composed of four old-timers (those with some experience) and three new, highly talented actors. We had promised to perform the first preview of *Tartuffe* for the San Francisco New School. We were only able to finish the first half; nevertheless, our first performance was a night of magic![8]

In 1964 followed *Chorizos*, adapted from a scenario by Saul Landau, directed by Tom Purvis; in 1965 *Il Candelaio* by Giordano Bruno, adapted by Steve Berg, was the subject of the famous bust-in-the-park which won the troupe many sympathisers and lost the San Francisco Police Department a lot of credibility; the 1966 show was *Olive Pits*, a *commedia dell'arte* adaptation by Peter Berg, Peter Cohon and the company of a play by Lope de Rueda; in 1966 they returned to Molière – *The Miser* adapted by Frank Bardacke, directed by Joe Bellan.

Peter Coyote played Il Dottore and remembers 'the most amazing thing about Commedia was how liberating it was. No work I've done since has been as free.' Now secure as free-speakers on their platform in the park, he spoke the prologue – which can be seen on the company's video *Troupers*, and offers a strong glimpse of the company's ability to synthesise traditional form with their contemporary political stance, particularly in relation to artistic sponsorship based on war-machine profits:

> Allow me to introduce myself: Dottore. Chairman of the Board of Business Unlimited. We buy, we sell, we spend – having made millions we give away thousands. But we're not appreciated. (*To the audience*) You're the real patrons of the arts. (*Hands out dollar bills*) Have some money – after all money must be spent. If there were no money there'd be no rich, if there were no rich there'd be no poor. If there were no poor there'd be no debt, if there were no debt there'd be no colour tv, no washing machines. If there were no money there'd be no church, no church there'd be no God, no God there'd be no godless enemy, no godless enemy there'd be no wars, no wars there'd be no war economy, no war economy – without that what would we do with ourselves. Spend some money . . .

And children clustered round the front of the stage, clamoured for it. Dottore then introduces Pantalone, the Miser, as being out of date: modern capitalism depends on spending, not on hoarding. Coyote's physical performance retains little of Mazzone's passing on of the form, but the Sartori mask and the sheer energy of the performance create their own authenticity.

By 1967 the Mime Troupe were ready to bring their work wholly into the twentieth century and deal with contemporary issues with a minimum of historical pretext: an adaptation by Joan Holden of Goldoni's *L'amante militare*, entitled *L'Amant militaire*, was their first full anti-Vietnam War play. This was followed in 1968 by *Ruzzante or The Veteran* from a play by Beolco, again adapted by Joan Holden.

In these Commedia-based shows, Davis (who directed them all except those specified) encouraged his actors to use three performance levels: 1) playing themselves; 2) playing the mask; and 3) playing a 'golden age' Italian playing the mask, for example, Francesco Andreini as Capitano Spavento, Guiseppe Biancolelli as Dottore, Isabella Andreini as first *innamorata*, Tommaso Fortunati as Brighella, Domenico Biancolelli as Arlecchino.

> These levels of reality, one concrete (self) and the other two assumed (mask and Italian actor), allowed for constant shifting of characterisation and play. When the actor lost the character's

believability or failed to make the audience laugh, he could change to the Italian role and say, 'Well, I tried thata one, no?' Or when a dog walked across the stage, the performer could break character as the Italian actor and comment from his own vantage point or if he was skilled enough he might stay inside the mask (role) and deal with the intrusion as the character. The ad-lib (improvisational wisecrack) was the oil of transition.[9]

Thus a sort of comedic safety-net was provided for experienced and inexperienced alike.

Why go through this elaborate structure? In the twentieth century all three levels made up only an approximation of the sixteenth century form called commedia dell'arte. There was no way of deluding the audience or creating an illusion that we were really commedia dell'arte performers just in from the Duke of Mantua's palace.[10]

Holden saw the three-level structure more as a Brechtian device. In *L'Amant militaire* she created a narrator, Punch, who commented on the action, working from a loose script according to spectator reaction at different performances, like 'the Singer in *The Caucasian Chalk Circle* [who] highlights the specific parallels with the audience's contemporary situation'.[11]

But Davis admits the rationale and the dramaturgical handling of the Punch role was actually pragmatic in its development:

The addition of this outside voice, or puppet, with [*sic*] a commedia play was an extension of the political intensity we were beginning to require of our shows. Punch was supposed to give the audience direct actional information, i.e., come out and precisely say what the stage action only implied. Our first Punch in *L'Amant* was played by Bill Lyndon, who was given the role and asked to write his own lines. Eventually we thought it more appropriate if the actors, in turn, played the puppet, everyone getting a chance to make his or her own political point. The whole thing was cumbersome. Finally the job fell to Arthur Holden and Darryle Henriques, who not only had the time to get the puppet box in hand, but were also good at executing the part. They eventually re-worked the lines to suit audience response.[12]

In *L'Amant militaire*, the Spanish army is fighting in Italy and Pantalone, a big city mayor, connives with the Spanish general to make a profit from the conflict, which is not difficult since the general is determined 'to pursue peace with every available weapon'. As Italy's largest arms manufacturer,

Pantalone obviously stands to lose out if Spanish forces were to withdraw from their occupation:

> I got a lot in this war. I own 51 per cent of the shares, I got muni-
> tion plants in Milano, I got weapon labs in Turino, I got banks and
> pawnshops outside of every base – when you end the war you
> end the war industry. You murder my markets – you assassinate
> my economy – you expose me to recession – to depression – to
> suicide.

The metaphor for Vietnam was thus extremely thinly veiled with clear references elsewhere to bombing and the use of Agent Orange.

To secure his interest, Pantalone wants to marry his daughter Rosalinde to the old Generale, but she is secretly in love with his young lieutenant, Alonso. Arlecchino, meanwhile, disguises himself as a woman in order to avoid military service.

Each of the Masks was assigned an accent coming from an American ethnic minority:

> The play also reflects the role of minorities in the army since to
> them it represents a step up the social ladder. In truth they are
> 'partly responsible for . . . American Imperialism'. By doing this
> the play shows an aspect of Mime Troupe productions that still
> endures today. It is not just the leaders and 'the Right' who
> mislead the public, but the public's inactivity and malleability that
> allows conflicts to arise.

This is a criticism of the Left that the troupe still maintains today. One possible resolution of the play was in favour of Flower Power, but in fact the ending tells a different story. The story had gone from conflicts of youth versus age, through political conflict and class conflict to such a state that it could not be resolved within the play itself. By the end, Arlecchino's disguise had been penetrated and Alonso was also to be executed, for dereliction of duty. What was needed was an outside force like Brecht's messenger with a Royal Pardon at the end of *The Threepenny Opera*, and it came in the form of one of the characters, Corallina (Colombina), dressed as the Pope. As the Generale shouted 'Ready! Aim!' to the firing squad, she appeared to a trumpet blast above the backdrop and everybody froze. After singing a 'little song' ('When the moon hits your eye like a big pizza pie, dat's amore'), she declared peace and ordered that arms factories be turned into olive oil factories. The 'Pope' then explained to characters and audience alike: 'You can't fight yourselves by destroying other people . . . the real enemy, mi bambini, is ignorance.'

Corallina then stepped out of her role before the end of the play and

26 Da Pope's appearance in *L'Amant militaire*, San Francisco Mime Troupe, 1967.

explained directly to the audience that the play would not end the Vietnam War, nor would apathy – that was something that only direct action could achieve. Thus Commedia, for the Mime Troupe, provided the vehicle for satire which provoked the will to change by revealing truths, but not purging them:

> Commedia requires a happy ending, much like epic Drama. The commedian [*sic*] attacks or runs from fate. The epic character may even stand still, but the audience learns that fate or environmental conditions are changeable. . . . We had avoided an inevitable end by using a traditional theatrical device, deus ex machina, but the war continued. The play intended to expose a pacifist's impotence, it did not intend or pretend to stop the war.[13]

It would have been inconceivable for a seventeenth-century company to have used Il Papa in this way. And Davis did in fact get busted, not, however, for irreligion, but for using 'bad' language when performing in the parks without a permit.

Eventually the work on *commedia dell'arte* was seen to have served a purpose as an actor's apprenticeship, but not as a permanent stylistic solution to the popular presentation of political issues. According to Holden although 'we liked commedia because the characters were so clear, it had a broad comic style, it was funny, it was highly stylised and it was really good for us to work in',[14] by 1970 they had become dissatisfied with using the metaphor of another time and culture, and were seeking to make direct statements about the American present. The company turned instead to melodrama and found through it American stereotypes that could be used in a similar way – the capitalist, the naïve young man, the strong woman. What the troupe now calls 'the style' is in fact composed of three styles, Commedia, melodrama and Brechtian epic acting. And other forms have been used such as the minstrel show, the detective genre, Broadway musical and rap music.

The summer seasons in the parks continue at the time of writing and, in addition to the permanent company, use volunteers who

> in return for their work are taught the basics of either *commedia dell'arte* or American melodrama in two four-hour mid-week workshops which run for the duration of the Summer Parks season. This year [1990], Dan Chumley taught us commedia skills, working on physical characterisations of a range of commedia characters which developed into basic improvisational scenarios or lazzi.
>
> To emphasise the dexterity of the form and athleticism needed, we were also taught to walk a low-wire, juggle with clubs, and

balance poles on ourselves. We also studied *The Italian Comedy* by Pierre Louis Duchartre, to develop a sense of history about *commedia dell'arte.*

Dan Chumley is an actor/director within the collective and was taught *commedia dell'arte* by R.G. Davis and now runs the workshops. The effect of the workshops is to give the volunteers a feeling of being *in* the Troupe during the summer season.[15]

TNT (The New Theatre)

The New Theatre (TNT) is one of many lesser-known companies that I could examine at this point to show the proliferation of contemporary interest in *commedia dell'arte* technique by those performers seeking a physical theatrical style as an alternative to the pervasiveness of text-based realism. The group has an English origin, but has developed an international perspective which is reflected both in personnel and in repertoire. In 1980 they created a manifesto production entitled *Harlequin*, which began from the premise: 'if Meyerhold were to construct a theatrical autobiography what would it be like?' coupled with a 1905 statement of his that 'every serious dramatist should be forced to write a pantomime'. The starting point of TNT's play was Meyerhold's production of Blok's *Fairground Booth*. *Harlequin* remained in their repertoire, touring Great Britain, Sicily, Switzerland and Germany, until 1984. In 1989 the company reworked the play, adding a German dancer, Inge Kammerer, as Columbine, using an Italian actor, Enzo Scala as Meyerhold/Harlequin and changing the title to *Glasnost Harlequin*. They toured West Germany, Poland, the USSR (twice), East Germany, and Great Britain:

> Spanning 1897–1940 it centres on the struggle of actor/director
> Meyerhold to resist firstly the stage realism of Stanislavsky,
> later the icy grip of Socialist Realism from Stalin, his eventual
> murderer.
> The underlying question is how art relates to politics, the form
> is *commedia dell'arte*, a simplification of great political issues and
> times which risks the short-comings of agit-prop, but also stops us
> falling asleep.[1]

This version is still in the TNT repertoire at the time of writing. The original play, devised by Paul Stebbings and Phil Smith, was based on a rule which the company assumed to be the *commedia dell'arte* method, that all material had to be either documentary or spontaneously improvised. The script was thus made up of blocks of research material arranged chronologically, interspersed with historical scenarios about theatre or politics, initially left open to improvisation in performance but later becoming more or less fixed.

The set consisted simply of a large triangle made by ladders and covered in *Pravda* newspapers, a chair, a star and a moon hanging. The action is as follows.

Introduction: Columbine polishes the moon. Harlequin observes her with a mixture of lust and love. She sweeps the stage, he pursues her, she fends him off and his heart breaks. Harlequin takes off his mask. He is Meyerhold, he introduces himself saying 'this is the *commedia dell'arte* of my life'.

Pierrot enters. He is Stanislavsky. He introduces the première of Chekhov's *The Seagull*. He commands Harlequin to play Constantin and Columbine to play Nature. He insists on absolute realism, ignoring the Commedia costumes and symbolic set. They perform the dialogue between Constantin and Sorin prior to the play within the play. Columbine provides bird noises behind a bush.

Harlequin/Meyerhold breaks free from the constraints of realism and rebels. Stanislavsky ties him to the chair and continues with the play, forcing Columbine to make ever more excessively 'naturalistic' sound effects. Harlequin interrupts verbally and the scene collapses.

Pierrot saves the play by performing the final words and the curtain call. He then announces the triumph of *The Seagull* and invites the audience to the cast party, where he improvises and flirts with the public. Harlequin remains tied to the chair and Columbine is treated as a servant while Pierrot bombastically expounds the ideas of Stanislavsky. Harlequin breaks up the party by offending bourgeois convention. Pierrot is dismissed. A poem by Akhmatova suggests the end of old Russia.

Harlequin/Meyerhold now has the stage, he has won the heart of Columbine and liberated her from her role as servant (though she remains a non-speaking figure who expresses herself through movement only). Harlequin expounds the theatrical ideas of Meyerhold, using acrobatics, juggling and stilt-walking while teaching tricks to Columbine. He forces Pierrot to play Rasputin (using beer-crates as stilts) and when Pierrot rebels he humiliates him and turns their fight into a parody of the First World War including dancing bears and a kazoo parody version of Tchaikovsky's *1812 Overture*.

The revolution. The Tsar/Bear is beheaded and a red flag 'bleeds' from him. Harlequin and Columbine dance a left foot ballet across the stage. The star in the sky turns red and an angular dance culminates in a hammer and sickle pose. Columbine speaks for the first time: a revolutionary poem by Mayakovsky.

Pierrot has been defeated, he mourns and offers a sad poem by Esenin. Harlequin mocks him with balloons. They fight – a wooden sword against the hammer and sickle. Pierrot loses. Harlequin and Columbine wrap him in a rope and throw him round the stage quoting Meyerhold's manifestos of the 1920s. They then offer him a chance to produce a radical performance of *The Seagull* and Constantin/Pierrot is whirled around on the rope to mirror the imagery of the Chekhov text. Harlequin is in complete control, although Columbine has also been transformed by the revolution into an active and heroic figure.

Columbine offers to marry Harlequin but he rejects her, always wanting new forms. Columbine becomes sad and works herself into a frenzy of repeated labour. Stalin bursts through the *Pravda* screen. He is the Commedia Doctor, masked, carrying a medical bag and wearing a Russian fur hat. He addresses Columbine as Russia, prescribes rest and, throwing a sheet over her head begins to terrorise the audience, biting the heads off the jelly-babies that represent his enemies while pretending to cure them of headaches and other disorders. At first Harlequin welcomes the Doctor and declares that he is not sick, he is a healthy revolutionary. The Doctor asks Harlequin to find Pierrot – impossible because the role is doubled by the same actor as the Doctor himself. Harlequin instead produces a letter from Pierrot which is a political and theatrical manifesto – but it turns out to be blank. To Harlequin's surprise the Doctor is impressed and offers it to the (blindfolded) Columbine to read. The Doctor then turns on Harlequin and makes a comic diagnosis, pronouncing him a very sick man. He then tests his blood to see if he is a revolutionary. He sucks a syringe of blood from him and squirts it on to *Pravda* in the form of a hammer and sickle. He cheats and bullies the audience into saying the blood is not red, but fascist black. But Harlequin fights back and with the help of the audience drives the Doctor from the stage. Harlequin then shouts for Pierrot to come and defend himself.

Pierrot tries to be Constantin enjoying nature but Harlequin confronts him with his blank manifesto on politics and art. But Pierrot retaliates, confronting Harlequin with the beheaded jelly-babies. A poem by Akhmatova on the purges and terror is spoken. Harlequin is cowed. He tries to ally with Pierrot against the terror but Pierrot retreats into literature, leaving the stage. Harlequin wakes Columbine and together they collect the beheaded sweets and burn them as if they were dead.

The Doctor/Stalin returns as a fireman and blows out the fire. Colombine hides. The Doctor sees Columbine is out of 'bed' and tricks Harlequin into revealing her hiding place. Columbine is tied up with chains for her own good as if she were being given jewels. He then announces his diagnosis of Harlequin: he is sick, art should only depict real life (Socialist Realism) and only a serious operation will save the patient and his art. In a clown-style operation the Doctor cuts out Harlequin's heart, which involves first drawing strings of sausages out of his chest. As the operation proceeds, the Doctor reads out the damning editorial from *Pravda* that preceded Meyerhold's arrest. As each 'organ' is removed, Harlequin shouts out a theatrical or political belief as if they were being cut out of him. At last his red balloon heart is removed.

At first it seems as if the operation is a success and Harlequin praises Stalin and Socialist Realism. But at the last moment he throws away the book given to him to read from (the same book as Stanislavsky/Pierrot used in the Chekhov scenes) and restates his love for Columbine. He speaks a poem about art and honesty by Pasternak. The Doctor reacts with fury, announcing that the patient is very sick. He handcuffs him and forces him to his knees, drawing a gun. Columbine – chained and blindfolded – strains towards Harlequin and speaks Mayakovsky's poem on the suicide of Esenin: 'Dying in this life is not so hard, building a life is harder.' The Doctor shoots Harlequin with his (realistic) gun.

The resulting performance is exciting, if not always 'readable' at a first view-ing. It is, however, stronger on its perception of Meyerhold (Stebbings and Smith trained under Edward Braun at Bristol University) than of Commedia. An immediate misapprehension on both counts is that, as we have seen, whoever plays Meyerhold should also play Pierrot. The role given to Pierrot is too active and manipulative for the mask, being, curiously enough, more suited to the earlier Pedrolino. Also, in terms of *commedia dell'arte* proper, Columbine should not become a victim (although this nineteenth-century misapprehension is one that Meyerhold also inherited) and the Doctor should not have the role of oppressor – which might prop-erly have been given to Pantalone.

Such insistence on propriety in terms of role-assignment might seem academic if it did not reveal an underlying difficulty in TNT's approach to their work. In the escape from the authority of authorship, they willingly sacrifice anything (even the form on which they claim to be basing their performance) to immediacy of theatrical effect. These effects are designed to be vivid to a wide range of audiences who often do not speak the language(s) the company is working in, and when strung together they do create a style which is arguably popular in the widest international sense. However, their 'new' language is not a truly universal one like its Commedia ancestor, because it relies for its types not on the demanding absolutes of the mask forms, but on the stereotypical casting of the actors within the company itself: Stebbings always plays the organiser/interlocutor, Kammerer a victimised woman/child given to obsessive behaviour, Scala a chameleon, dancing round the symbiosis of the other two – and other actors joining the company soon find themselves similarly limited in terms of the expectations made of them. Such limitations can be a strength in terms of intensity of playing within a narrow confine, particularly when actors are asked to find emotional reactions for fictional stereotypes encountering real situations, but it is also consumptive of the company's raw material – its own personalities. Without the novelty of international touring and its attendant necessities in terms of travel and accommodation, it is doubtful whether such mutual self-sacrifice could be sustained.

In their latest piece, *Europa! Eureka!*, after excursions (*à la* San Francisco Mime Troupe) into other popular forms such as music-hall and melodrama, Commedia was once more intended to provide the working base. Again, however, the Masks were required to inhabit the world of a predetermined Stebbings/Smith scenario: on the Day of Judgement the whole of Europe is condemned out of hand. Shakespeare, Freud and Michelangelo protest and are allowed two hours by God to show that Europe (portrayed by Kammerer as confused, romantic, over-subtle and suicidal) should be saved. This they choose to do via a Commedia version of *Romeo and Juliet*, but with a happy ending where Juliet is saved from suicide by Freudian analysis.

> *Freud*: We must set this play somewhere essentially European.
> *Michelangelo*: The Club Méditerranée?
> *Freud*: Maastricht in 1991?
> *Shakespeare*: I thought of sixteenth-century Italy.
> *Angel*: 1914.
> *Devil* La Guerre Mondiale.
> *Angel*: The Great Suicide! 1914 – set your *Romeo and Juliet* then if you dare.
> *Shakespeare*: We accept: we are not frightened of blood in *Romeo and Juliet*! Two households both alike in dignity, in fair Verona where we set our scene, . . . One of the households, our modern Capulets, are the Stockhaus family from Vienna . . . you Juliet play Julia a dutiful if romantic daughter.
> *Juliet*: Viennese, *danke sehr*, William.
> *Shakespeare*: And you, Freud, play her mother, the psychologically curious Frau Stockhaus.
> *Freud*: Vot, a woman! Brilliant, one in the eye for the feministen!
> *Michelangelo*: And me, Willi?
> *Shakespeare*: Improvise a new Romeo.
> *Michelangelo*: How?
> *Shakespeare*: Commedia. The Italian *commedia dell'arte*.
> *Michelangelo*: *Molte grazie*, genius.
> *Shakespeare*: To your positions, my characters! Dear deceased. (*To public*) So this is now the two hours traffic of our stage that which if you with patient ears attend, What here shall we miss our toil shall strive to mend!
> Act One, scene one, Vienna 1914.

It was decided to make the Devil into Arlecchino and the Angel into Brighella, immediately travestying one of the *comici dell'arte*'s golden rules, never to mess with religion. But then, assuming Julia to be an *innamorata*, what Mask could Michelangelo adopt? Since the script demanded him to be a Professor of Fine Art – the obvious solution was Il Dottore, but then what is an *innamorata* doing in love with the Doctor? Scala tried changing him from the fat Bolognese to the more dashing French academic type, but the relationship still did not gell. Poor Freud (played by a French actor) discovered that he was obliged by circumstance to play Frau Stockhaus as Pantalone in drag, and Stebbings/Shakespeare briefly flirted with playing a Capitano, before adopting a potentially 'new Commedia' type of Ron, a Texan complete with stetson and Zorro mask. The result was described in French (one of the four languages used in rehearsal) as 'un bordel' and, not surprisingly, the use of Commedia masks was dropped after the show's première. However, many of the performance structures discovered while rehearsing in the masks remained and others were subsequently reinstated. With hindsight, the formal demands of the masks had provided a rehearsal discipline: the mistaken assumption was that they could provide performance pegs on which to hang a predetermined scenario written without the practice of *commedia dell'arte* in mind.

Dario Fo

In 1940 Dario Fo went to Milan to study painting and later enrolled in the Architecture School of the Polytechnic Institute, stopping some way short of completing his degree. He already had an amateur interest in theatre, but did not begin professional consideration of its possibilities until he was 25. Although scathing of academicism, as indeed he still is, he was aware of the need to construct for himself a research base, a footing in the past on which to raise the walls of a contemporary performance. He felt the same standards ought to exist in popular theatre as in the popular architecture he had been studying. Simple churches, built by their congregation from locally quarried stone, did not need the intervention of architects to achieve an expressive functionality, especially in creating levels and acoustic chambers appropriate to the rituals and dramatic enactments of the Mass. His quest started in the same era as those pre-Renaissance churches:

> I started with medieval theatre because it has always been regarded as a second-rate art form, whilst at the same time being plundered for ideas. On the one hand there was great poetry, and on the other there was minor, second-rate literature which was treated as second-rate theatre. But without the influence of the street poets, Dante could not have had such worthwhile material to work on. In *De vulgari eloquentia*, his research into popular speech, he shows that without this investigation, without knowing what was happening at street level, Dante couldn't have achieved such great poetry.[1]

This predisposition to research the vernacular, he came to realise, was something that he had unconsciously inherited:

> I come from the people. I was born [1926] on San Giano on Lake Maggiore. [A small town in the province of Varese, Lombardy, near

the Swiss border. His father was a railway worker, his mother came from a peasant family.] Then as a boy I moved to another village. A funny place where all sorts of jobs were on the edge of the law. For example there were poachers, smugglers and glass-blowers. These jobs kept the village up all night. The inns were full of people, there was talking, singing, storytelling. . . . When I was at University I realised it was a rich, dense culture. Not a sub-culture. I realised that it was a link back to the whole tradition of the *commedia dell'arte* . . . and further back to the medieval jester. When I began to work in the theatre, I naturally went back to my roots. I saw right away that such a theatre was disrespectful of the people in power because it attacked and cut down the importance, the presumptions and affectations that power claims as its own.[2]

Especially, one might add, the political and economic power of a certain church which, in Fo's opinion, is more concerned with behavioural strictures than religious scripture.

Until 1967 he was satisfied with the role of agent provocateur within the theatrical system (and indeed on television, subverting the popular variety show *Canzonissima*). Then he decided

we could not remain the paid jokers of the bourgeoisie. We'd become a bit like Alka-Seltzer. We provoked the bourgeoisie. They enjoyed being slapped around the face – they'd laugh at us and say 'he's got it in for us. He stimulates us like a masseur.' So in 68 we left the traditional circuit and devised an alternative one.[3]

He performed (with Franca Rame and a co-operative called Nuova Scena) in factories, football stadia, forging links with radical student movements and striking workers. When this company split in 1970 (largely through internal political dissension) Fo's own predilection for solo performing *sul piazza* came to the fore. His one-man show, *Mistero Buffo*, a cycle of anti Mysteries laced with insights into medieval counter-culture, including viciously satirical attacks on the papacy, confirmed his sense of the superior political courage of the *giullare* over the self-preservationist instincts of the Commedia troupes:

The *giullare* was born from the people, and from the people he took their anger in order to be able to give it back to them, mediated via the grotesque, through 'reason', in order that the people should gain greater awareness of their own condition. And it is for this reason that in the Middle Ages, *giullare* were killed with such abandon; they flayed them alive, they cut out their tongues, not to mention other niceties of the time.[4]

Giullare is a difficult word to translate: from the Latin *iocus*, it has the same roots as the French *jongleur*, but the English word juggler (which has the same origin) now has a much more specific sense. Fo is fond of noting that in the heyday of *commedia dell'arte*, the very name *giullare* had become a term of abuse:

> Francesco Andreini had tried to train his company in new acting techniques, and to familiarise them with a new kind of relationship with the audience. He experienced exactly the difficulties which Goldoni, at the other end of the tradition, would encounter. The actors simply could not adapt to a type of theatre for which they had not been trained, so that when Andreini fell ill, they reverted to their old ways. A letter from Andreini roundly abusing them for their failings is still extant, and Andreini resorted to the worst of the insults within his vocabulary. He called them 'giullari', and this because they had returned to the tradition of 'lazzi, of anecdotes, of direct asides'. Finally he told them: 'You must forget that the audience are in a public square: imagine you are in a theatre and not a market place.'[5]

Mistero Buffo is all anecdote coupled with a licence to drop the story whenever an improvised aside *in propria persona* is more telling.

Since the immense success of *Mistero Buffo*, Fo's performance work has become more and more singular, less and less ensemble, with the result that, although he himself is a personal working example of what he intends, his relations with other performers, even Franca Rame, have become strained or even non-existent. His interest in Commedia has developed, but still from the perspective of the solo performer. From the pantheon of Masks he has picked out Arlecchino as most germane to his purposes. In his own estimation he had always been unable to escape the persona of Arlecchino, the ever-hungry underling:

> I have always played Arlecchino whether I wanted to or no. Every time they skip or turn round my characters are stuck in his mould. What fascinates me about Arlecchino is his characteristic ability to destroy any and every convention.[6]

Here is my own transcription of an early performance by Fo of Zanni/Arlecchino:

> I am consumed with hunger. I could eat my eye. Tear off my ear and eat it. Pull out my innards, clean them out and scoff them up . . . Such a hunger I could eat my foot, knee and my hips, my willy and my stomach. My mouth could eat itself. I could eat a whole

donkey . . . *(Looks at the audience)* Eat you all, one by one. I could
eat mountains, the birds in the sky! A good job, God, that you are
so far away! I'd eat you too, with a few cherubs. How my hunger
burns. *(Change of attitude)* I'm dreaming. I see a huge pot. Fire
underneath. *(Makes crackling sounds)* I take a few vegetables . . .
(Puts in an armful) Polenta flour . . . *(Puts in a whole sackful)* I take
my big spoon . . . *(It needs two hands. String noises. Sniffs.)* The lid.
(Puts it on, forcing it down until the pot boils over) Another pan.
(Establishes it to the right of the other one) Fat, onion, garlic, a little
salt. A sprig of rosemary. The wooden spoon! *(Stirs, then goes back
to the other pot)* Pepper! *(Adds some and mixes it in)* Tomato!
(Squashes it one-handed and drops it in) An egg! *(Same treatment as
the tomato! Licks fingers and hand.)* Salami. Some meat. *(Stirs other
pot, while giving the first one a kick)* A little salt. Rosemary. A little
cinnamon. *(Produces a squawking chicken and wrings its neck. The
head comes off in his hand and, after a moment's surprise, he eats it.
Opens up the chicken and discovers an egg. Eats it whole. Stuffs the
chicken with other birds.)* A thrush. A sparrow. Rosemary. Sew it
up. *(Huge stitches. There is a little thread left. Eats it together with the
needle. Sings as he stirs. Changes pots again, indicating to the one he's
leaving to be patient.)* It's hot! *(Drops lid)* Wine. *(Pours some in and
the dish flames in his face. Tips the contents into the second pot and
scrapes the pan and licks the spoon.)* Chop! Chop! Chop! Chop! *(The
last chop takes off his finger which he throws in for good measure. Stirs)*
Cheese! The grated cheese! *(Final stir, then he picks up the whole
huge pot above his head and pours the contents down his mouth. Brings
the pot down and scrapes it, licking the spoon avidly. Suddenly realises.)*
I've eaten the spoon! *(Tries the effect on his hunger, but realises that
nothing is really going down)* It's all a dream. It's not true. What a
pain! *(Sees a fly)* Go away or I'll eat you![7]

Needless to say the fly does not go away and suffers the traditional fatal
lazzo. Fo performs without a mask (except the considerable one of his own
bulging eyes, large squashy nose and huge, elastic mouth) and much of the
above is delivered in dialect and *grammelot*, accompanied by onomatopoeic
sounds of cooking and eating.

Pulcinella would have provided a more powerful solo working base, but
Fo seems wary of his cynicism. In 1985 he created a new one-man show
based, not on an imaginary *giullare*, but on Arlecchino himself. It has not met
with such universal popular and critical approval as *Mistero Buffo*:

> The brief – and somewhat superficial – introduction to this show,
> tracing the significance of the *commedia dell'arte*, in no way
> enriched the pieces of clowning which illustrated the tradition.

The lazzi . . . and sketches that attempted to recreate Commedia material were entirely dwarfed by Fo's own stand-up contemporary material. These parodies and satires of modern Italian life did show the influence of Commedia, yet by shedding the pseudo-academic trappings employed elsewhere they showed Fo's independence of them and correspondingly gained in seriousness and weight.[8]

But at least one section of the show, *Arlecchino Fallotroppo*, where Arlecchino/Fo drinks an entire bottle of potion intended for the afflicted prostate gland of Pantalone, with priapic consequences of gargantuan proportions, is now played separately with convulsive effect. The truth is, perhaps, that Fo has become a modern satirical clown in his own right and no longer needs (for the spectator) the pretext of a popular historical role. But he does seem to require one for himself: the conservatism with which he researches such figures seems to provide him with the obverse, a licence to be offensive, subversive and still Marxist, even.

> Now, as regards the *commedia dell'arte*, I should say that there are great misunderstandings, particularly on the part of foreign actors, about the Commedia. I have noticed it also among teachers who teach in universities all over Europe . . . and in Italy too. Why? Because they always treat the *commedia dell'arte* as a unified whole. When one thinks of the *commedia dell'arte* one thinks of the Carissimi and the Geloso [sic], and that's it. Just the big families of the *commedia dell'arte* . . . the Andrini [sic] etc. Now these were theatre companies that worked in the most important courts of Europe. For example they worked for the Dukes of Ferrara, and for the Sun King, Roi Soleil (and for his father before him and his father before him). They were so important in their time . . . in fact there's a story that precisely indicates their importance:
>
> The Geloso family, or rather theatre group, were working for the Duke of Ferrara. They were a bit like those football teams nowadays that are owned by big industrialists. Just like Juventus is run by FIAT . . . ! Anyway, at a certain point the King of France asked the company to be present to perform at his daughter's wedding. This was King Francis I, who was fighting against the Huguenots in that period. This king had captured, ten days previously, some 1,000 Huguenots, and had thrown them into prison. Now, when the Gelosi were passing on their way through Lyon, a group of Huguenots captured them and promptly sent a letter to the king. The letter said: 'If you want the Gelosi back, you'll have to release all the 1,000 prisoners you captured.' And sure enough, the king released all the Huguenots, all 1,000 of

them! Because it would have been a terrible disgrace for him to have gone ahead with the wedding without the Gelosi performing. This demonstrates the tremendous importance of *some* of the Commedia performers, at a cultural and political level.

The point is that, given that these families existed, they were performing a certain *kind* of Commedia which was generally conservative, and often downright reactionary in content (you should look at these pieces, see for yourselves) . . . There was, however, quite another tradition of comic actors within the *commedia dell'arte*, also professionals, who didn't frequent the courts and nobility, but worked in taverns, worked in town squares, worked in far lowlier circumstances. And it is no accident that *their* work has never been collected and published. They've never been catalogued, they've never been studied.

So, when you study the *commedia dell'arte*, you have to decide which political line, which cultural direction you are going to take as the basis for your work.[9]

Carlo Boso and
Antonio Fava

The intentions of these two contemporary Italian practitioners in seeking a vital role for Commedia in the repertoire of modern theatre have considerable similarities, but their personal style and actual practice are quite distinct. Boso, although formerly an actor, now seems to see his contribution as that of a director of contemporary works of art with Commedia as an inspiration and an influence, Fava as a practitioner of Commedia itself, whether as actor, director, teacher or dramaturge.

Carlo Boso attended the Piccolo Teatro school in 1964: there he worked with Giovanni Poli, Peppino de Filippo and Giorgio Strehler (on whom he seems to have modelled himself in later years). On joining the company, he acted various roles in *The Servant of Two Masters* between 1967 and 1978. When Ferruccio Soleri took over from Marcello Moretti as Arlecchino, Boso joined him in another Commedia work, a pastiche entitled *Arlequin, l'amour et la faim*, which they toured from 1971 to 1978 with Soleri doubling Pantalone with Arlecchino and Boso playing Zanni. Meanwhile, in 1972, he began to branch out as a director with a production of *Turandot* for the Teatro Stabile, followed in 1977 by *Maschere*, a *commedia dell'arte* show for a company called Il Carro dei Comici. By the late 1970s and early 1980s, he was also gaining a reputation as a teacher, taking a number of *stages* (workshops) in Paris, as well as others in London, Cardiff and elsewhere. Unlike Lecoq or Fava, however, Boso has no desire for a permanent school of his own, considering that the original *comici dell'arte* learned their business through doing it in theatres, in market places and at festivals, and that the only worthwhile technique is that learned through performance. In his view the real problem for the contemporary actor is to find enough time and the right place for the exchange of experiences and for a dialogue to develop between actors from diverse backgrounds. His present company, Teatro Tag, which convenes irregularly in Venice whenever time and funds permit, and does an international round of festivals, conferences, etc., is thus deliberately internationalist and temporally pluralistic in its composition:

For Tag, Commedia is pop theatre. . . . It is also articulate, using not one but several languages at once. Tag are a truly European company who play in Italian, French, Spanish and English. Peter Jordan plays the lecherous English Barone, who regularly refers to 'my friend Will'. Shakespeare is plainly Tag Teatro's comic contemporary, yet they are not presenting a museum piece. A modern popular song is as relevant a reference as a medieval dance.[1]

An earlier company, the Scalzacani ('the ragamuffins'), was born from the meeting of a few Italians resident in Paris (including Alberto Nason, Michele Patruno, Tommaso Simonini and Dimma Vezzani) with a convergent aim: the common research of an artistic and cultural form of expression which, while still having its roots in Italy, would be able to have an international dimension, representing in particular the historico-cultural link between Italy and France.

After attending Boso's Parisian *stages*, *commedia dell'arte* became the obvious choice of a form through which to express such expatriate ambitions. Some of the performers had also worked previously with Dario Fo and Giovanna Marini. They considered that with, and since, Goldoni, the role of the playwright had become separated from that of the actor and that with the written text replacing improvisation, the virtuosity of star performers had pushed out ensemble acting. Furthermore the development of Mime as a separate form had destroyed the organic link between gesture and speech. For the Scalzacani, rediscovering the *commedia dell'arte* today signified recovering its roots in a double sense:

> in its globality, that is to say in the synthesis of gesture, dance, mimicry, etc. which makes the whole man the protagonist, and in its role of primordial mediator between actor and spectator, with an exchange of psychological intentions, comedic complicities and choral play.[2]

Thus to propose the 'rediscovery of the *commedia dell'arte* was at the same time to propose or repropose to the audience a prestigious theatrical genre and to recover the very sources of playing in public, that is to say improvisation and mask'.

Three characteristics of Commedia took their attention:

> 1. The force of its communication is *immediate*: the masks and the 'lazzi' which are the base of the technique reawaken the spirit and verve of the actors and of the audience who become an active element in the game-cum-show of the Commedia.
> 2. Its finality is *concrete*: not being entirely at ease in institutional theatres it requires a real ambience and performing context. . . .

3. Its language is *popular*: that is to say that coming from the deepest, most anonymous strata of collective creativity, it needs to encounter an audience which is sociologically differentiated and culturally heterogenous.[3]

Their first show, *Commedia in Commedia*, was based on three moments. First was *Piazza*: the reconstruction, from contemporary documents, of a sixteenth-century Venetian piazza on a festival day, was a pretext for the reconstruction of the birth of the *comici dell'arte*, from the jongleur, the mountebank and the acrobat. Zanni and his interlocutor-master Pantalone emerged. Next *The Madness of Isabella* was set in the baroque golden age of the *commedia dell'arte* when the great companies were going all over Europe,

imposing, with the excessiveness of adventurers, their taste on an enthusiastic public and on reticent writers. Zanni has become Arlequin, the Magnifico has aged into Pantalone the Venetian merchant, the great actresses like Isabella Andreini, fascinating and cultivated, announce the modern phenomenon of the star.[4]

The madness scene not only reconstructed a typical Commedia of this period, but also permitted the actors to attempt to play the Masks with virtuosity with *lazzi*, dances and songs and playlets stylised into a saraband. Finally came the ceremony of the passing on of Arlequin's bat:

the Italian Comedy has become Franco-Italian; the Italian players survive above all in France: an old Arlequin leaves the company: the audience are invited to witness the ceremony of the transmission of the tradition to a new Arlequin. The Commedia is dead. Long live Commedia.

This first production can hardly be said to have lived up to the company's manifesto: taking out the toys and playing with them is enjoyable for those involved, but it is one thing to hand out the famous roles, another to achieve the *maîtrise* of the originals. The historical and documentary aspects of the performance were of interest to performers and spectators alike, what they did not provide was a basis for that sense of comedic collusion between actor and spectator which is the only true basis for improvisation. As the company moved from set-piece to set-piece there was something a little chilling in their cleverness.

The next production was *The Life and Death of Arlecchino*, based on a 'Commedia on Commedia' written by Basilio Locatelli in 1620. In the Scalzacani version, a troupe of Commedia players tackled other theatrical genres: parodies of opera – Bizet's *L'Arlésienne*, Shakespeare's *Hamlet*, even Japanese Noh theatre. They were now aiming to emphasise the contrast between actor and character; between the historical tradition of Commedia and the contemporary re-creation of the tradition. The play is built upon double takes: comedians play Commedia characters who, in turn, play and parody other theatrical personae within other theatrical conventions. Theatre within theatre within theatre.

The game of mirrors serves to reflect the numerous facets of the Commedia tradition: its adaptability, its cyclical progress through the centuries yielding ever new guises and ever old insights, its genius for revolving the same old human nature until its shape strikes us anew.[5]

Rather than accepting the need for a greater directness of approach after the over-embellished and introspective pattern of their first essay, this new production merely added a level of illusionism to the quest for a framework which would accord the company virtuoso status. The assumption and, where necessary, self-awarding of such an accolade runs through Boso's work and, to my Anglo-Saxon temperament at least, renders much of it unappealing and concomitantly unfunny. The 'puff' for their next production, *Don Juan in the Underworld*, drawn from Dostoevsky's *The House of the Dead*, continued to reflect this tendency: 'Alternating hilarity and profundity the production combines Commedia masks, popular song and dance, and musical quotes from Mozart's *Don Giovanni*, marking Carlo Boso as one of the great directorial originals of today.'[6]

The narrative was set in a Siberian prison camp with inmates seeking to lighten their gloom by rehearsing Molière's *Don Juan*:

The all-conquering lover appears here, thoroughly recognisable, as an army captain enjoying a well-earned damnation. With his servant Arlecchino he serves under the likely commander Pantalone. . . . One ordeal follows another to reveal Don Juan not just as a soldier or lover or *bon viveur*, or even as Mr Machismo Numero Uno, but as more than the sum of his parts: a man of spirit with a redeeming sense of humour. Storm upon storm of comic duels rage, to be interspersed with the sunny intervals of love scenes until this unsettled weather becomes the climate of hell itself; Arlecchino appears as the devil and a legion of wronged women appear to torment the Don. However hot it gets for him, both Don Juan and we the audience are spared the pains of morality and Arlecchino breaks the illusion and sums up life and death and heaven and hell as a joke.[7]

In choosing Don Juan as a theme, the company were again trying to place their work in the realms of high art, attempting to inherit more of the baroque Commedia of the seventeenth century than the rude immediacy of the sixteenth.

> There is no doubt that the origin of Don Juan is in the baroque . . . in the taste for death which predominated between the sixteenth and seventeenth centuries. It is a violent protestation against this taste and this culture as well as an affirmation of independence from morality and religion. The sentiment of the void so typical of the seventeenth century (momento mori) is thus positively transformed into a vital obsession, into an exultation of woman, not in the medieval and Petrarchan sense, but as the source of inexhaustible earthly delight.[8]

Yet, in principle, Boso claims he is interested only in the

> simple direct analysis of social contrasts . . . texts developed 'on the go' on the basis of other extant texts or through analysis of the life which surrounds us. As Peter Brook says, and I personally believe it, theatre divides into two: that which is deadly to its audience and that which is vital. The goal of the *commedia dell'arte* is to be vital, never boring, to make theatre with important analysis of social contrasts.[9]

This goal is no more developed in the work of the Teatro Tag than it was in that of the Scalzacani: in their much-heralded, but seemingly little-enjoyed production of *Scaramuccia*, for example, the actors seemed to have little confidence in the technical basis of their roles – and the audience shared some of their unease. A kind of artistic *bravura* was offered in place of genuine virtuosity of the performers, and basic confidence in each other's ability to hold the stage also seemed lacking. Nor did directorial devices such as a circle dance in which the actors almost entirely ignored the audience help establish comedic rapport. The set was overdesigned and failed the actors where they needed it most – on their entrances and exits. There is an arbitrary effectualness in Boso's work (the use of a blue mask for Mezzetino for example) which leaves even the uninformed spectator with a suspicion that Commedia has been misappropriated.

   Tag's latest offering, *The Gypsy Woman*, was performed at the fifteenth London Festival of Mime. It regrettably offered a verbosity quite at odds with its host environment and with the published intentions of its director; lest my own view of the company seem jaundiced, I quote the *Observer* review:

> Carlo Boso's company work very vocally to a script . . . Tag has been well received on previous visits and the Purcell Room on the

South Bank was packed. Rather it was packed to begin with.

During the first 45 minutes in which we had been shrieked at in Italian (and occasionally in French and English too) in pursuit of a plot that though incomprehensible clearly bore no relation to the typed synopsis we had been handed, the first coats were being collected from the cloakroom. Three-quarters of an hour later, the cast misguidedly announced that it intended to take a two-minute break. Once the two minutes had extended into three or four the festival director went backstage and told the Venetians to get on with it. But by then a good quarter of the audience had taken its chances while it could and disappeared into the night.[10]

Antonio Fava was born in Calabria in the south of Italy in 1949. The same year his family moved north to Reggio Emilia, between Bologna and Milan, but he retains strong affinities with the south, including a supply of olive oil from his grandmother's trees. He plays the flute and his father, mother, five sisters and two brothers are musical – singers and instrumentalists. In America he would presumably, therefore, have been under considerable pressure not to leave the family barber's shop, but that is what he did in 1968 in order to join Dario Fo in Nuova Scena. His flute playing ensured him a variety of work in the succeeding years, including a move to France to work with the Théâtre National de Strasbourg as an actor-musician. In 1976 he moved to Paris to study with Jacques Lecoq until 1978, when he became a teaching assistant at the school at the same time as working as actor, director and writer with the Parisian Théâtre de la Jacquerie.

In 1979, back in Reggio, he founded the Teatro del Vicolo with actress Dina Buccino. As well as mounting touring productions, the company runs an international summer school in Commedia and an autumn semester dedicated to research into the past, present and future of the comic actor. At times the students' work can become a Babel – when I studied there, there were fourteen different nationalities present, speaking eight different languages. Fava himself speaks several Italian dialects, as well as perfect French, Catalan and Spanish. Although he considers himself a Mediterranean man, he has gradually come to terms with the right of access of northern temperaments to Commedia, though it is doubtful whether he will ever find our climate fully acceptable. Much of what I have said in the Introduction of this book about the potential of Commedia as a lingua franca of performance is attributable to him as well as a lot of the *savoir-faire* expounded in later chapters.

For him, he says, being an actor, playwright, director, musician, mask-maker and teacher of theatrical disciplines are all one and the same. Unlike Boso's preoccupation with the baroque, both Fava's teaching and his performance work are based on the first century of *commedia dell'arte*'s existence.

Fava practises *commedia dell'arte* not only as a theatrical poetic, but also as a philosophy of existence based on the cyclical in nature as well as in social events and their dramatic transposition into sad themes: hunger, poverty, crossed love, death, etc., which tend otherwise to become tragic. For Fava, comedy is transcendental: 'All our shows are *comical* and each one corresponds to a gradation of comicality, using a criterion of the "hierarchy of laughter" which I follow punctiliously.'[11] Therefore, Teatro del Vicolo's productions use a variety of comic genres as well as Commedia. For example *La Santa Luna degli scampati* (1983) was a cartoon-style attempt to play a tragedy in comic form. On the other hand *Morti di fame, d'amore e di paura* (1981) he considers was 'pure' Commedia, including demonstrations of *lazzi*, and as such toured Italy, France, Switzerland, Senegal, Mauritius and New Guinea.

Bisticcio grazioso e sciocco (1987); (untranslatable; French title was *Paté de cuir*) toured Italy, Spain, France and Switzerland. Fava describes it as an imbroglio of situations, characters, rogues, villains, *lazzi*, masks and floured faces. But the title is also an allusion to a certain fundamental cruelty which he perceives as characteristic of the Commedia from its origins around the middle of the sixteenth century onwards. It is certain that in this period, from which Fava draws his inspiration, the Commedia was 'sordid' and 'mercenary', not least according to its numerous calumniators. His most recent research has been into the lesser-known southern Masks – Pasquariello, Coviello, Cola, etc.

In Fava's opinion there is nothing progressive about Commedia – he contends that progress is constructive, and that the comedy of these early troupes, and of the partisan southern tradition which endured while all the big northern companies were drawn towards bigger prizes in the rest of Europe, was furiously destructive. Comedy, like maneating, is bloody, at least until it becomes approved of. Left to itself it retains its cruel charm, but it becomes accessible, even acceptable, only when tamed, as Fo would also say, by the bourgeoisie.

Fava sees *commedia dell'arte* in Italy today as a confused memory – worse, a confusion of memories – left over from the nineteenth-century centralisation on Venetian tourism and puerilisation. He is thus in favour of rigorous scientific reconstruction:

> We worked up *canovacci* and constructed scenes, trying to keep ourselves 'fresh' (if the masks have been able to traverse the centuries it is because new actors were always coming to them).
>
> We avoided the use of original scenarios and 'little fragments of the period, entirely written'.[12]

The first because he didn't want to repeat overused *lazzi*, the second because it smacks of intelligibility and a somewhat intellectual gratification. So for

Bisticcio they took situations which they considered universal and therefore always fresh, played them in the ancient masks and allowed rather than forced modern rhythms and significances to emerge.

Some of the scenes in the *Bisticcio* repertoire (which was constantly changing and evolving) were: Graziano's tirade (the A to Z of Lasagne); The crumb; The trunk; The stepladder; The well; Tartaglia saying hello; The serenade; *Contrasto* between lovers; The meeting of Titans; The gold coin; Pantalone's ghost; Water in the mouth; etc.

Unlike Boso or the Carrara family, Fava does not have the resources (and anyway would not be tempted) to play full-length works, preferring instead to play almost a kind of variety show within the stylistic framework of Commedia. He also has his own 'one-man show' as a Pulcinella, inherited from his father, the most recent of which (1992) is entitled *Frittata di luna*, described by Fava as a 'Pulcinellata vera'. And, like Fo, he also takes something of an academic interest in performing complete archaeological finds, the latest of which is *Le Tremende Bravure del Capitano Bellerofonte Scarabombardone da Rocca di Ferro*, a text from 1596 by Giulio Cesare Croce discovered by Roberto Bruni of the University of Exeter and Diego Zancani of the University of Canterbury.

27 Antonio Fava as Capitano Bellerofonte Scarabombardone with Pietro Mossa as Zanni.

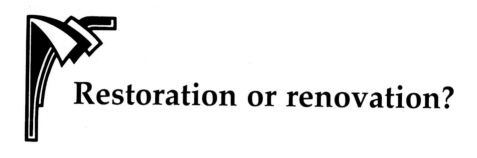

Restoration or renovation?

Any twentieth-century practitioner concerned with popular theatre, its past forms and potential for new social significances, is bound to feel impelled to investigate the phenomenon of *commedia dell'arte*. Like many other actors, directors and drama teachers of my generation, my enthusiasm for Commedia, kindled by the writings of Meyerhold and Copeau, became a blaze in the late 1960s after seeing the production of Goldoni's *Servant of Two Masters* directed by Giorgio Strehler for the Piccolo Teatro of Milan; the resulting flames were for a while obscured by smoke from the work of Carlo Boso, but the fire has recently been stoked again by the teaching of Antonio Fava. After more than two decades of experimentation (for which I thank those students and young actors who have been so brave as to perform publicly work which was, strictly speaking, 'in progress'), I am still, however, only able to offer an interim report rather than a conclusion to the investigation. The abiding question is in fact a composite one: to reconstruct from first principles or to repair a decayed tradition? Or to follow the initiative of Copeau, Mnouchkine and others and attempt a new form of popular masked comedy on a *commedia dell'arte* base, either 'translating' the original Masks into contemporary equivalents or inventing entirely new stock types? Or to join Fava in asserting that Commedia is an absolute form which can still be learned and which is able, through its empowerment of the actor as improviser, to be as contentious and satirical, scurrilous and rude, up-to-the-minute and unashamedly celebratory as it ever was? Or is it now best to think of Commedia techniques as a training form to place alongside other immutable disciplines (mainly from the east) as in the work of Eugenio Barba's International School of Theatre Anthropology?

By way of response please permit me some anecdotes from my own experience, on which I will try to be at least as severe a critic as on the work of others.

The scene of the first one is the Cornish fishing village of St Ives. It is spring, the occasion is the South West Festival of New Art, 1968. The

240

intrinsically Wesleyan resident community are understandably suspicious of an event which seems to be happening *to* rather than *for* them. Within living memory, fishwives have thrown canvases into the harbour if the artist painted on a Sunday. There is an uneasy, volatile mix of locals, early tourists, invading artists and hippies sleeping on the beach. Neo-primitive paintings by Monica Sjöo, of black men and white women copulating, which are hanging in the Town Hall, are causing a stir and will soon be censored. Into this somewhat steamy atmosphere arrive drama students from Exeter University: they erect a platform in the street in order to perform historical, even rather academic, reconstructions of sixteenth-century *commedia dell'arte*, improvising from scenarios they have devised themselves – *Il Dottore's Miraculous Medicinal Magic*, *The Fantastic Fable of Franceschina's Foibles* and, less extravagantly entitled, *The Prodigal Daughter*. They are not quite sure why they are there since this is hardly 'new art', more a respectful attempt at an old one. Unfortunately, however, one of the things which has been authentically reconstructed is Pantalone's phallus.

After the second performance I find myself standing in the street next to a member of the constabulary, who is in turn standing next to Pantalone and holding his helmet, streaker style, over the offending padding, while intimating that subsequent performances cannot take place without detumescence. It would be presumptuous to claim that our little contretemps had the reverberations of the San Francisco Mime Troupe's asking their audience to stand up for free speech as they were hauled away, but the next day, questions were asked in the House, where, I am glad to say, the then Minister for the Arts, Jenny Lee, wittily defended the right of both the neo-primitive and the Aristophanic to have public exposure. In retrospect, what transpired offstage had a great deal more of the makings of Commedia than what had happened on it prior to the 'bust'. I mention this because I now think such reconstructive attempts to play full-length scenarios as if they had never gone out of fashion lead up a blind alley. There is no evidence that anyone attempted to do so in English *then* and to try to do so *now* creates a hybrid form which quickly wilts. There is one company, and one only, that can manage three-act scenario-based improvisation with *sprezzatura*, and that is based on the Carrara family from Vicenza, led in the present generation by Titino Carrara who plays both a young, French-style Dottore and Arlecchino. And of course they play in Italian, not in 'Speaka-de-Eenglish'.

The Pantalone of the troupe is Argia Laurini who married Tommaso Carrara in 1948, playing the role for the first time in 1977 – the first woman to do so. The tradition of professional playing of *commedia dell'arte* has been continuous in the family for 350 years, over ten generations. Like the Rame family, they used to erect a wooden travelling theatre, moving on each month from town to town. They are now based in Vicenza and play seasons in Italy's oldest theatre, the Olympio Palladio, but also travel to festivals (Munich, Nantes, Rome, Stuttgart, Cologne, Hamburg, Paris, Copenhagen, Vienna,

28 Titino Carrara as Arlecchino in *Pantalone sulla luna*.

London, Bath, etc.). Their two London appearances have been with Anthony Rooley and the Consorte of Musicke, *The Marriage of Pantalone* (1985) and *The Revels of Sienna* (1986), both at the Queen Elizabeth Hall. Additional actors from outside the family form with them a co-operative called the Piccionaia, which includes Pierluigi Cecchin who joined in 1982 and now plays Franceschina, probably the first male to do so (he also plays Zanni and Brighella). Thus the company clearly feels gender-based casting to be irrelevant to mask work, unlike Copeau and Dasté, for example, who argued atavistically that the semi trance-like state required for improvisation in the mask might be too demanding for women. *Autre temps, autre moeurs . . .* Antonio Fava makes no such discrimination in his school, although he does not have men playing Colombina: while the female students work on her, the men study his version of Pedrolino (whom he calls Zerbinotta).

I digress. Even such a company as the Carrara/Piccionaia, with superb individual and ensemble skills, today feels a need for textual underpinning when undertaking full-length works: for example their *Il Pantalone sulla luna* (1984) was a re-elaboration from Goldoni's *Il mondo della luna* (itself based on the plot of *Arlequin empereur dans la lune*, written by Roland de Fatourville in 1686 and quoted from earlier in this book, p. 81). In the first part of the Carrara version, Arlecchino tries to fool Pantalone into betrothing his daughter to his master, Ottavio. Taking advantage of Pantalone's fondness for astrology, he leads him to believe in the existence of fantastical life on the moon, where all senses can be gratified – gratis. The second half of the play takes place on what Pantalone believes to be the moon, a fantasy which all the other Masks support except Arlecchino, who moves in and out of different roles as a sort of Arcadian magician. He both wanders and wonders about the theatre as he 'stands up for comedians, claims a dignity for them because theatre, same as life, is just an illusion and honours go to those who labour to give it birth'.[1]

In my view, then, to try to undertake such full-scale works in English sells *commedia dell'arte* short. That was the conclusion from the St Ives experience and it has been reinforced by what I have seen of the work of the English troupe, the Unfortunati. Led by mask-maker Ninian Kinnier-Wilson, they originally based their work on extant scenarios, trying to make them relevant to today. Acrobatics were used but in a signalled way that was often intrusive to the action rather than arising from it. There were some well-worked *lazzi*, but again laboriously introduced rather than pinging off the wall. Only two members of the company were *commedia dell'arte*-trained, as opposed to picking it up as they went, and it is very difficult to remain in spatial and rhythmical control for long when the basics are not coming as a matter of habit. A sense of more being bitten off than can be chewed means that spectators are rarely transported on to the moon, though they often remain pleasantly intrigued by the strangeness of the form. Without the political drive which rendered the technical inadequacies of the San Francisco Mime Troupe irrelevant, the focus fell on skill and as a result one felt at best that one was getting a privileged glimpse of work-in-progress. That such development is long and hard in the achieving was poorly understood by funding bodies, and it had to be more or less abandoned. The company later developed into the *Fortunati* after appearing at the EEC-funded Harlekin Art Theatre Project at Bayreuth. The new troupe offered in its publicity to 'give an original and contemporary edge to Commedia whilst retaining its energy, wit and timeless characters and masks'. *Beyond the Mirror*, a 'hilarious tale of a young man's attempts to prove his manhood (or lose his inheritance)', was directed by Didier Doumergue from the Lecoq school. The company is now in abeyance.

As we discovered in St Ives, if you are not part of a living tradition, are simultaneously translating and reconstructing an alien cultural form, it takes you all your time onstage to get the plot over plus a few set-pieces: one becomes trapped into trying to make the story funny rather than diverging from it *ad libendum* whenever the audience/actor relationship stimulates a possibility for appropriate *lazzi*. Such work might just as well be polished into a Goldoni-style mechanism with a permanent text: both actors and spectators will be the happier for it. The danger then is that, like Carlo Boso's productions, it will smack of 'Art' rather than smack home as *arte*.

My next essay, a couple of years later, and with a different group of students, was into the development of new fixed types by grafting on the stock of their Commedia ancestors. One of the pieces which emerged was called *Toby Rodd's Revenge*, with Masks as follows:

Samuel Poke: an ageing entrepreneur arrived at by amalgamating Pantalone and the English impresario Lord Grade
Toby Rodd (his 'minder'): a Pulcinella derivant, based on the English Toby Jug, a traditional florid-faced drinking pot
Doreen (his secretary, not employed for her typing skills): a *servetta*
Alicia (his daughter, a finishing school product, in love with Julian): an *innamorata*
Dr Prickmore
Julian Prickmore (his feckless sibling, engaged to Alicia, in love with Melanie): an *innamorato*
Melanie (Alicia's sensible friend): *seconda donna innamorata*
Happy Jack (a not so latter-day hippie, based on Jack Kerouac and 'into' music): related to Brighella
Mrs Bunnage (a charlady): la Guarassa

In the first scenes, the main plot had Poke sack Toby Rodd for being on the take, and Rodd seeking revenge by persuading Happy Jack to have his band play a free concert outside the hall where Poke intended speaking at the annual dinner of the Noise Abatement Society. Dr Prickmore meanwhile prescribed different medicines for symptoms complained of by Poke and Mrs. Bunnage which, inevitably, got confused. Let's pick up the scenario half-way through Act III:

> *Mrs Bunnage* comes on in a state of sexual arousal and makes a bee-line for TOBY RODD who is at first surprised then runs off with her.
>
> *Samuel Poke* complains to DR PRICKMORE about the laxative effects of his prostate pills.
>
> *Doreen* brings along a companion for Dr Prickmore (a blind date as previously arranged in a sub-plot – it is actually ALICIA in

disguise). PRICKMORE takes a fancy to her but POKE recognises his own daughter and flies into a rage, sacking DOREEN. The two men go in to the dinner.

Happy Jack arrives to set up the gig. TOBY RODD and MRS BUNNAGE return from their offstage encounter. HAPPY JACK offers round a joint. ALICIA gets stoned and decides to become a groupie. MRS BUNNAGE joins the band.

Julian wanders on in a daze. TOBY RODD knocks him over the head again. The band strikes up cacophonously and the two old men rush on. HAPPY JACK reminds Poke that he is his manager and offers him his groupie, as promised. POKE, recognising his own daughter again, flies into an even greater rage but is forced to let her stay with the band under threat of more music being played (he is standing for president of the society). He is also obliged to re-employ Toby Rodd and Mrs Bunnage.

Melanie arrives repenting her treatment of Julian. The DOCTOR revives his son and is forced to agree to his marriage with Melanie. HAPPY JACK has been rolling more joints and all ends 'happily'.

The students involved in this project went on to set up their own company after graduating – Medium Fair, which

> tackled a broad front of community theatre activities, including game-based participation pieces with young children; shows relevant to older children, such as a number of short plays linked by songs about juvenile delinquency and the problems of growing up . . . , programmes for older people – which toured Old People's Homes; short pub entertainments which mixed songs, very broad comedy and characterisation and political satire.[2]

One of their first productions, in July 1972, was *The Fairground Show* which opened at the Piran Round, the medieval theatre-in-the-round near Perranporth, now regrettably overgrown again after a few years of revival. The show took the form of an environmental promenade, with different booths portraying different popular theatre forms animated at different times. Included were examples of both reconstructed *commedia dell'arte* (originally directed by Maria Sentivany) and new Commedia (directed by me). By this time only some of the characters described above had survived: like historical reconstruction, such an approach had been perceived to be a dead-end. A much more difficult process, that of developing new types without basing them on original Masks, had begun. The actors had made their own masks out of latex (a disgusting substance, we soon discovered, to wear next the skin when working hard and sweating profusely) and, as I recall, had had to adjust their characters when a mask gave something powerful but unintended by its maker. One such was Gaston de Pouvoir, who became a rather weedy, know-it-all Frenchman who was fond of claiming he was from Interpol.

Here are some notes from a more recent (1989–90) and more methodical experiment in evolving new Masks: this time, students were asked to feed and fatten their character type by using themselves as a resource: in other words the roots of the persona were to be discovered within their own personality. As one of them noted,

> In this sense our task was to 'classify' our own personality. When selecting a type to work on I found it hard to choose just one element of myself, and it was more valuable to ask friends to label me as a type.[3]

The next stage was to make real-life observations. These were then developed in class through mimicry, with stress laid on not rushing – no forcing, no premature finalising. From the work of Mnouchkine we next took the idea that each type had a basic state of being, a ground emotion which could be described as a colour – or rather two, a primary colour with a secondary tone underlying it which is only occasionally glimpsed. The next question was what drives the character, what does s/he want? For short this was known as the 'gimme' – in Pantalone's case, for example, this would have been 'gimme money' and 'gimme sex'. (This work was informed by the notion of 'hungers' described by Berne in his *Games People Play*.)

In the first practical exercise small groups took it in turn to pester one of the 'Masks' who were only allowed to grunt in response:

> It was very valuable to be restricted to using only sounds, as these expressed what the character felt without the intrusion of cerebral language, and I discovered a real energy which would always inform the character, although the forms it took would change. I also discovered a definite physical trait.[4]

Which was that of picking at things – fluff, buttons, blades of grass, etc.

The second practical class was based on hierarchy and status: 'For this exercise the space was organised with benches facing a blackboard in auditorium format. Initially we were asked to enter the space and sit down where we felt was appropriate to our character's status.'[5] Different inputs, 'the performance is very loud'; 'the show is obscene', etc., were written on the board. After the 'show' was over, characters left the space only to be told that it was on fire and they just had time to rush back and grab one personal object.

The third development was physical: work on the character's centre of gravity, then its leading bodily focus which when moved enabled the discovery of a basic walk.

The fourth stage was vocal: allowing the Mask first sounds, then a single word in among the *grummelot*, then a small vocabulary that was crucial to its feelings and needs.

The fifth process in this preliminary work was to improvise a situation in which the character would become agitated in order to reveal its true self rather than the one which it wanted to present to the world.

The problem with the miscellany of types which emerged was, again, that few of them were funny and, although some had universal traits, none was potentially 'stock'. The process had set up an over-involvement of the performer in the character leading to an unwillingness to be exposed comedically:

> The character was much more free about sex than I was. I was surprised that during the exercise of the escape from the fire, she collected a vibrator from it. My social person, when faced with the prospect of having to admit this even in front of people I had worked with all year, backed down and re-created the object into a purse! I discovered (later) that many people assumed that my character *would* have collected a vibrator (well, maybe that says something about the way people were seeing my character, there were some continuities and obvious characteristics . . .) if only I'd been able to see the humour of the situation![6]

At this stage the characters were not masked; later, in an attempt to achieve such comedic distancing, the students made masks for each other's characters rather than for their own. With hindsight it might have been preferable if each role itself had been passed on together with a mask made by its originator: the process of teaching it would in itself have been clarifying (and the role could have been subsequently reassumed by its creator if necessary). The actual masks were arguably made too soon and, although they fitted physically, they did not do so in every case in terms of image. The most comedically successful character to emerge, for example, bore a strong resemblance to Chico Marx and we could perhaps have saved a lot of time by using him as a model from the outset. Other figures undoubtedly suffered from what I now see as an over-psychological approach to their development and spectators could sympathise with their neuroticism but rarely laugh at their shortcomings.

The other difficulty inherent in this kind of approach (and even though it does not lead to new Commedia there may be a lot to be said for it in terms of dramatic exploration) is that all the characters are attempting to grow up together, to find a form for themselves that will carry them through their nonage. Having to invent scenarios for characters whose limits are not yet set can lead to yet further insecurity in the actor rather than providing the structure which they and their characters need in order to be comedically adventurous.

From more recent work with Antonio Fava I realise that the form does still exist, not perhaps as well-preserved as, say, Japanese Kabuki, but it does not need reinventing. The traditional constituents of Commedia can be learned both as individual practice and, preferably, as a group discipline – the present volume is above all intended as an introduction to such study. For a troupe then wishing to obtain greater contemporaneity in their work, I now suspect the addition of one new character-type at a time would be quite sufficient. That figure would thus be entering an established comedic suit rather than being part of the invention of an entirely new deck. Such a process was, furthermore, as we have seen, the very one by which all the Masks, with the exception of the original ones of Zanni and Pantalone, were added in the sixteenth and seventeenth centuries by actors, as they found they needed them.

As to the often complained of irrelevance of the *commedia dell'arte's* dramatic situations to contemporary life, I can offer you no more than an echo of Dario Fo's conclusion: don't mess with the Masks unless you already have your own present-day political and artistic standpoint worked out. Otherwise they will suck you into their own historicity rather than provide you with sharp comedic tools with which to create modern meanings.

Appendix: Making a leather mask

 The 'living death-mask'

To work up a mask properly you need the feeling of having the actual actor's face in your hands so as to develop appropriate contours on the mask. For this purpose you need to take a 'living death-mask'.

Requirements: a large tub of Vaseline or cream aqueous, a soft toilet roll, packets of plaster bandage and a bag of plaster of Paris; a large jug of water, a washing-up bowl full of sand or sawdust, a round-bottomed mixing-bowl for the plaster; a small paintbrush.

For normal mask-making purposes you only need to model from the top of the forehead to the underside of the chin.

The negative

Vaseline the actor's face, especially the facial hair (with special attention to eyebrows and eyelashes), adding strips of soft toilet roll where the hair will not lie flat. Protect the hairline with a bathing cap or an old stocking. No hair of any kind is to come in contact with the plaster.

The subject can either sit in a chair or lie on a table. Cut the plaster bandage (sold in bulk as 'Modroc') into strips about 10 cm long. Dunk each strip into the water, shake off any excess, and apply immediately to the face and smooth down well. Keep all other strips dry except the one you are working with. The subject must keep absolutely still – you will need a good bedside manner. You can insert large drinking straws or plastic tubes into the nostrils: if not you must obviously be careful not to cover them. At least two layers of bandage are necessary, four on the edges for strength.

The subject must then remain expressionless until the plaster has 'gone off'. When it is quite hard there should be no problem releasing the negative from the face, providing the Vaseline coating has been properly put on. Leave to dry for forty-eight hours before making the positive.

The positive

Brush Vaseline thoroughly into the interior of the mould. Settle the mould into the sand or sawdust, taking care not to get any inside it. In the bowl add plaster to water, not vice versa: do not fill beyond half-way, then sprinkle the plaster on until it has reached the surface of the water. Stir vigorously. Leave until the consistency becomes thick cream. Pour into the mould up to the brim. Leave two days' drying time again. If you use dental plaster, the curing time is considerably less, but it is more expensive.

An alternative method

For this you *must* use dental plaster.

Requirements: galvanised wire, soft pencil, sheet of cardboard, Stanley knife, Vaseline, soft toilet roll, dental plaster, powder paint.

The disadvantage of this system is that the weight of the plaster depresses the facial muscles slightly. The subject lies down and has the wire pressed into the shape of the head from the top of the head down to the ears and under the chin. Lay this shape on the cardboard, mark with pencil and cut out. Offer the resulting collar up to the face, mark misfits in pencil, remove and recut where necessary to get a reasonable seal. Cover hair and Vaseline as above. In this case you must use a bathing cap, and it too will need Vaseline. The nostrils *must* be ventilated. Make up plaster as above and pour gently but consistently over the face watching not to create air bubbles. It can be useful to have an assistant ready with a second mix in case the first is insufficient or becomes unworkable.

Tell the subject not to worry about the warmth given out as the plaster goes off. Shape the outside into a bowl shape for strength.

Create the positive by Vaselining etc. as above, but with this system there is no need to support the mould. Add powder paint to the mix for the positive so that if there is any difficulty in prising positive from negative there is a clear level to chisel down to.

Perfection is not necessary in either of the above methods since it is the volumes of the face which are necessary, not the details of the features. Bad gaps can be filled with Polyfilla.

Modelling the mask

Requirements: a raised board, modelling clay, hands, water, rags, wooden modelling tools.

Seat the positive on to the baseboard with clay and cover it with Vaseline yet again, or, if the clay is to be reused, cling-film or tinfoil. Slap large amounts of clay on the areas where the major additional volumes are to be created, usually eyebrows, cheekbones and nose. Work with both hands simultaneously, firmly and rhythmically. Return shapes back on themselves. Keep the hands wet. Remove excess material. Keep moving the board round in order to work from different angles. Stand back from time to time, otherwise work continuously until you are satisfied, or until you feel a problem is insurmountable, in which case cover the work in wet rags and come back the next day: the solution is usually then obvious; if it is not you may need to start again. Use the modelling tools only for definition of final details. Do not fuss! Where the clay is thin it will crack if you do not keep it moist until you have finished using it as a template for your matrix.

The wooden matrix

The measurements from the clay form now have to be carved in wood. As stated earlier, if you cannot already carve, this is probably not the time to learn.

Requirements: a block of seasoned wood. (Various species are suitable but the easiest to obtain are lime and gelutong: they are both soft and fine-grained, and thus can be carved quickly to a good finish. The harder wood is, the longer and more difficult it is to work: thus timber from fruit-trees (for example walnut, pear or even cherry) gives good results but takes much longer to carve. Do not choose timber which has too broad a grain, even if it is soft – pine and deal are to be avoided. Oak is also out: it is too grainy, very hard and splits after carving, even when seasoned.) A bench with a wood-working vice, 'G' clamps, a base-board big enough for the block to be fastened to it, a ruler, one or two try-squares and a pair of dividers; a saw, a set of wood chisels and gouges, a round mallet. (The difference between a chisel and a gouge is that the former has a straight profile while the latter has a curved one. Both are necessary, though an experienced sculptor can, at a pinch, get by with only chisels.) A fine oilstone for sharpening is also a minimum requirement. Wooden blocks covered in leather can be used like a barber's strop, particularly with the addition of a little valve-grinding paste. A blunt chisel is worse than useless, a blunt gouge even worse. Sharp is sharper than you think. Rifflers, which are a sort of special rasp for wood sculpture are useful, but expensive and not indispensable. Fine sandpaper.

Carving the matrix is the most likely point at which the novice will give up. But if you carve a successful one (probably after several attempts) then you have, essentially, made the mask. The rest is craft, not art.

The clay modelling you have done on the plaster cast of the face of the subject has created a mock-up which now serves to offer transferable dimensions of the features: height of forehead, shape of the eyes, length of nose, volume of the cheeks, etc. In order for the mask to be made to these measurements they must be reduced by 1–2 mm (the thickness of the leather) as they are transferred.

Cutting the block of wood

All three dimensions must be right: length, breadth and thickness. The wood cannot be cut in any direction, the right choice must be made. It is absolutely crucial in wood sculpture to have a sense of one's material: the first care to be taken, then, is in determining which face of the wood to address.

Observe the grain of the wood and work with it. The direction of the wood is that of the sap, which rises upwards in the tree. A blow with a cutting tool in this direction severs the wood neatly and leaves a smooth cut; when it is given in the other direction, across the grain, the tool is harder to control and the cut is rough, or even causes splitting. One should always try to work with the grain, and the wood block needs placing with this in mind. For the carving of a face, therefore, the top of the head should be in the direction of the top of the tree.

Measure the length, breadth and depth of the mock-up and carry them over on to the wood block. There are two methods of doing this: the first consists of taking measurements with dividers, using the points to transfer the extreme measurements on to the wood. The second uses a ruler and two carpenter's squares: a rule on its own would not be precise enough to measure exact distances. Place the squares against the extremities of the mock-up, length, breadth and then depth, measure the gap, then draw the same distances on the wood block. The angles of the rectangle thus drawn must be 90 degrees: use the square to verify this.

Once the measurements have been taken and correctly transferred, the rectangle can be cut out. The block is fixed to the bench with one or two clamps, or held in the vice if the jaws are wide enough. A circular saw can be used if the cut can be kept straight. It is a great deal easier to use a band-saw if one is available.

Carving

The sculpture proper now begins. This type of sculpture is called 'round-boss': the round-boss consists in detaching from a mass of wood a head or some other figure which can be seen from every direction and which reproduces, in the chosen scale, every facet of the object one wishes to represent.

The face of the mock-up to be reproduced is a volume. All volumes are composed of planes butted together in a certain way, and that is something one must constantly remember. In effect, all carving of sculpture consists in detaching from the material the different planes which constitute the volume to be reproduced. This task is effected progressively, beginning with the general planes which will then be broken down little by little. In order to succeed, one needs to have carefully studied the planes of which the volume is composed.

It is important to give particular attention to the lighting of the work-space. You need to choose a light which brings out the contour and movement of the smallest details of the model and place the wood under the same light, so as to obtain the same effects.

Trace the median line in pencil down the entire length of the work; this line is the reference point in the difficult quest for symmetry.

The sculpture takes place in stages: first one must reduce the mass, then carve the shapes and finally give them definition. The first stage is to remove the large amounts of wood which are surplus to the requirements of the shape to be carved. This operation will simplify the work. To begin with one reveals the most elevated planes; with the aid of a saw remove all the wood which is excess either in width or depth. It is preferable to augment the measurements slightly, since it can happen that one wrong blow with the mallet can oblige you to go lower. In this way you determine the general exterior contours.

The second stage involves determining the configuration of all the principal parts of which the work is composed. For this operation use mallet, chisels and gouges. The correct use of the implements requires a minimum of practice in order to acquire good hand technique. The blades of the chisels and gouges serve to slice through the wood, the mallet blow on the handle of the tool gives it penetration into the wood. The chisel or gouge must always be held in the direction of the plane to be revealed. The grip must be in proportion to the force of the mallet blow, otherwise the tool slips and without firm direction may go where it shouldn't! At every stage one should examine the sculpture frequently, from a distance and from all angles, comparing each of its planes with those of the model. The work is progressively reduced as you compose the volume down into more and more precise planes following the same principle as in stage one.

The third stage consists in taking out all the tool cuts, large or small, left

29 A matrix for an Arlecchino mask, probably seventeenth century. Note the number of nail-holes showing the number of 'pulls' that have been taken, resulting in the need for the visible repair.

by the carving, unifying the reliefs and the hollows, defining the details and correcting the contours. Tools must be very sharp in order to make perfect cuts. Use rifflers and knives to reach the parts which are inaccessible to chisels or gouges. Then, and only then, smooth the surface with sandpaper, but do not over-rub, or you will dull the contour lines and the sculpture will become muzzy and lack vitality.

Treatment of the matrix

When the matrix is ready, in order to model masks upon it you will be covering it with wet leather. To prolong its life to the maximum, so that it can be used to fabricate several examples of the same mask, it is best to treat it with water-resistant varnish. Otherwise, if the wood stays wet too long or too often it will end up splitting and deteriorating. Make sure the correct drying time has elapsed before using the matrix to make a mask.

▥ Working with leather

You cannot use any old leather; you need a natural skin which has been tanned by a vegetable process. These days nearly all skins are tanned with chrome, and this chemical process makes the material harder and much less malleable than vegetable tanning. Ask the tanner for the neck piece of a cow hide: this part of the beast is very mobile, so the skin there is more supple; the flank is also usable. The thickness varies according to the kind of mask to be made: the finer the detail, the thinner the leather needs to be, but be careful: 1 mm is the minimum thickness, because the planes of the mask must have enough rigidity to hold it in shape.

Requirements: Evostik, brass or piano wire, a tack hammer, brass upholstery pins, a Stanley knife, a wood gouge. You will also need some special tools which are hard to find in shops, but which you can make yourself: a cow's horn or, failing that, a smooth little ball on a handle, about 4 mm in diameter in metal, hardwood or bone – this is mainly used to push down the leather; little mallets of various sizes and shapes, chisel, curved and conical-ended, also made of a hard material and covered in leather so as not to damage the surface of the mask; finally you will need polishing tools, which are simply little lengths of bones, very rounded and polished, also mounted on handles. Again it is useful to have three or four of different shapes and sizes. In order to make them, buy a marrow bone from the butcher and boil it till all the flesh is completely off, and then cut it into little sticks with a hack saw. These are then rounded and polished with fine sandpaper (a trick to get a perfect finish is to rub the bone on a scrap of leather for a long time).

The preparation of the leather

First cut out the piece which is going to be used; apply it to the matrix, pushing it right into the recesses of the sculpture. This is very important so that the piece is not cut too small. You have to leave sufficient slack, because in order to form it the leather has to be crushed by hammering and not stretched, and if it is pulled on the matrix it will be impossible to make it marry exactly with the facets of the sculpture. Draw out in wax crayon the necessary surface, leaving about 3 cm extra to be able to bend the edge back on itself. Then lay out flat and cut out with a sharp Stanley knife.

Then soak the piece in cold water for an hour or two, leaving it completely immersed. When you take it out of its basin, you will be surprised by how supple it has become. Keep the leather wet throughout the forming process: if you are interrupted for a few hours you must cover the work with a wet cloth.

Forming the leather on the matrix

When the leather is out of the water, drain it a little then place it on the matrix, rough side downwards. Push it down into the recesses as before. Now fasten it to the block with the help of the little brass pins – don't use other metals or they will blacken the leather where they come into contact with it. Fixing the leather like this must be done carefully; don't be in a hurry. Begin with the middle of the top of the mask, taking care to nail into the back of the block, not the surface of the mask. Continue by putting in further pins, alternating to left and right. Obviously, with the leather on the matrix, you will not have a flat surface, so the material goes into folds. The hard part of the work consists in chasing these folds as much as possible to the back of the matrix, and distributing them evenly between the nails. That is why it is better to fix the leather progessively, alternating between left and right. The pins should be spaced about 1.5–2 cm apart. The leather is thus fixed all around the matrix.

The hardest part to fix is the middle of the bottom of the mask in the region of the nose. Leave it till last. If the sculpture has a little nose there won't be too many problems; you'll simply need to reduce the spacing of the nails in order to have more but smaller folds. With a big nose you have to make a joint in the mask and then fix the leather back together underneath it. Fix the leather with pins either side of the join, then squash the fold flat. With a Stanley knife take out the two surplus triangles, leaving a thin tongue in the middle which will later serve to cover the join.

Breaking down the fibres

Leather, like all natural materials, is composed of fibres, and in order to make the skin more malleable, they have to be broken down. Use the horn or little ball tool for this, holding it perpendicular to the surface of the leather and giving little short taps. The material will become covered in little holes; the whole of the surface of the future mask should be treated in this way with particular emphasis on the holes (eyes, nostrils, base of the eyebrows). The general forms of the sculpture begin to appear.

Hammering

Now use the little mallets: this hammering is rather like panel beating in metal work. Little by little the leather becomes crushed under the tapping of the mallets and will gradually reflect the facets of the sculpture. At the same time all the little holes left by the ball tool will disappear. This hammering is a long process; you need to be patient to do it properly. Change mallets according to the surface that you are working on, giving special attention to areas of greatest prominence, especially the nose. If there are still folds in the surface of the mask, you have to hammer in such a manner as to crush them and chase them to the back of the matrix. There is a trick to this: the hand which does not hold the mallet has a very important role to play; it has to hold the leather in place around the area being hammered and constantly ensure that it is matching up with the facets of the matrix. The leather covering the mallets must be perfectly smooth and should be changed as often as necessary to avoid damaging the surface of the mask. The long work of hammering is over when the leather surface of the mask is smooth again and has taken up all the facets of the matrix. At this stage the leather can be left to dry.

The joint of the nose, the nostrils and the eye-holes

Do the join in the nose first if there is one. Chamfer the tongue and flaps with a chisel, fitting the tongue down over the join as flat as possible. Then do the nostrils: these can be done with the help of a hole puncher or with the Stanley knife. Proceed as for the eyes. The contours of the eyes should appear already on the facets of the mask, but even so it is better to trace out the cutting lines with a crayon. To obtain good symmetry proceed as follows: trace one eye in crayon and then cut it out in one single piece, slowly so that the tool does not slip. Turn it upside down and place it on the other eye and cut round the outline. Even so you should take the precaution of measuring the distance from the nose to the beginning of the eye and also the height from the eyebrow. At this point the mask must be left to dry completely – the time of drying will vary according to temperature.

Polishing

When the mask is dry use the leather-covered mallets and the lengths of polished bone. As well as polishing the surface this operation will finally complete the acceptance of the shape of the matrix by the leather.

30 Unfinished Zanni mask by Antonio Fava. The leather is untreated and a line of stitching can be seen.

Gluing the nose join

Use the Evostik instructions as to going-off time, then join the surfaces with the greatest possible pressure – a few good blows with a mallet for example. Be careful not to let glue on to the surface of the mask: if you do it will have to be removed with acetone.

A great moment: now you can remove the fixing pins and detach the mask from the matrix.

The overturn

Put the mask back on to the matrix and using a gouge cut as much thickness from the flaps as possible. You can take the material from the shiny side of the leather, since this is easier and anyway the flap is hidden on the inside of the mask. Now take the piano wire cut to an exact length and glue it under the flaps with contact glue; then replace the mask on the matrix and beat it gently with a mallet round the edges.

Reinforcements

Leather reinforcements may be glued into the back of the more prominent features of the mask with contact glue. Then the entire interior surface of the mask should be treated with a nitro-cellulose-based varnish.

 Colouring

The colouring used should contribute to the mask's three-dimensionality, validate its inherent expression and reveal even further that which was suggested in the sculpture. On the other hand colour can also reduce the expressive force of the mask: two identical masks from the same matrix can function in a completely different way according to coloration. Furthermore, the colour of the mask can sometimes help to hide or rectify inherent defects and imperfections. Don't spoil things at this stage: make a long examination of the mask from every angle and under different lighting conditions in order to find its appropriate colouring. Is it going to be used in stage lighting, outdoors in sunlight or outdoors at night in flood-lighting?

A few general principles: the deeper the tint, the less the contours will emerge – black nullifies them more than beige, for example; if the contours do not really seem to catch the light, this can be remedied by using lighter tints of the same colour along the contour lines; as a general rule the hollows should be darker; if the mask is very expressive, it can be coloured without variation of tint; sometimes even, depending on the effect desired, the leather can be left in its natural state.

Two types of products can be used to colour the leather: dyes or paints. Dyes are more appropriate because they penetrate into the fibres of the skin and change its colour in a definitive way. But it is also a relatively difficult technique and furthermore you cannot obtain such lively colours as with painting since the dye integrates with the existing colour of the leather. Acrylic paint is easier to apply than dye and has greater covering power and opacity. However, it does not penetrate the interior of the fibres of the skin and forms a film on the surface of the material. Since the leather of the mask retains a certain flexibility the paint will, with use, crack and peel.

Dyeing

You need to use aniline dyes. Leather shoe dye in little bottles is no good because it does not penetrate the surface. It is more like paint, and should be used as such.

Requirements: keep acetone handy in case of mistakes, off-cuts of leather in order to do tests, little bowls for mixing, a paintbrush, rubber gloves and rags.

Dyeing should be done in successive layers, leaving drying time in between. It is best done with a cotton rag rolled into a ball: you soak it in dye, then wipe it lightly on newspaper to remove surplus liquid. This is an important precaution because too much liquid will immediately give deep coloration without any nuance. As in writing with a pen, blots are to be avoided. Wipe the dye on with little circular rubbing movements, never going over the same place twice: any patches left uncoloured can be remedied on succeeding coats.

The first layer should be the lightest possible, since one can always deepen a colour, but it is very difficult to lighten it. Repeat the process at intervals of about a quarter of an hour until the desired shade is obtained. You can also obtain interesting effects with a little sponge instead of a rag ball, in which case do not use circular movements but light dabs.

Look at the work often from a distance in order to judge the effect. It is preferable to work under lighting conditions close to those under which the mask will be used. The paintbrush is used to dye the cut edge of the leather at the eyes and nostrils.

Hair

For eyebrows, moustaches, bristles and hair you can use different natural materials: fur, horse hair or even human hair.

Requirements: Evostik, Stanley knife, an awl.

It is better not to stick the accessories straight on to the leather, as this would not be really secure or look right. It is preferable that the hair or bristle emerges from the leather as it would from human skin. The material chosen should contrast with the general tint of the mask – dark on light and vice versa. Cut the chosen material to shape with the Stanley knife. Mark the positioning on the mask in crayon and then make incisions in the leather with the Stanley knife. Slip the hair into the slits and glue it inside the leather. You may need to take it right through the mask, glue it to the back and cover with extra leather (see Reinforcements).

Methods of fastening

There are two possible systems: leather straps or wide flat elastic.
The leather straps are more aesthetic; however, they slip with the movements of the head which can be very off-putting to the actor. Elastic is preferable because it ensures a perfect fit, but is only used for training purposes by Antonio Fava. For a performance mask he fits straps with adjustable buckles, not only across the back of the head, but also down from the crown to join the back-strap with a loop. Others consider that although elastic does not look as good, it will be more or less hidden in the hair or disappear under a hat.

To fix straps, you need to make a hole on each side of the mask at the level of the temples. Thread them in and tie them on the inside of the mask with the smallest possible knot. Or use rivets if you can get ones that blend in with the tone of the mask.

If you are using elastic, it should be black and about 1.5–2 cm wide. There are two ways of fixing it: sewing and riveting. For sewing use shoemaker's thread, the best being waxed thread because it flattens out and does not slip. With the aid of the awl make three holes equivalent to the width of the elastic and sew it on with a back-stitch. If you are using rivets, they should be as short and fat as possible: make a hole with a punch, insert the rivet and flatten it with a hammer. Fit one side, offer up the mask to the actor's face and get him or her to find a comfortable but secure fit by holding the elastic to the mask on the other side.

Notes

 Introduction

1 Edward Braun, *Meyerhold on Theatre*, London, Methuen, 1969, p. 127.
2 Edward Gordon Craig, *The Mask*, Vol. 3, No. 10–12, April 1911, p. 147.
3 Kenneth Richards and Laura Richards, *The Commedia dell'Arte*, Oxford, Blackwell, 1990, p. 6.
4 Augusto Boal, *Méthode Boal de théâtre et de thérapie*, Paris, Ramsay, 1990, pp. 23–4. This division is not, of course, one which Boal wishes to see perpetuated. The passage continues: 'The theatrical profession, which belongs to a few, should not conceal the existence and the permanence of the theatrical vocation, which belongs to everyone. The theatre is a vocation for all human beings.'
5 Barry Grantham, Brighton Festival Programme, 1985, p. 82.
6 Edward Gordon Craig, *The Mask*, Vol. 3, No. 7–9, January 1911, p. 99.
7 Introduction to *The Memoirs of Count Carlo Gozzi*, trans. John Addington Symonds, London, 1890, Vol. I, p. 87.
8 André Maurois, quoted in Debra Linowitz Wentz, *Les Profils du Théâtre de Nohant de George Sand*, Paris, Nizet, 1978, p. 8.
9 Maurice Sand, Introduction, *Masques et Bouffons*, Paris, 1862.
10 *Ibid.*
11 Thelma Niklaus, *Harlequin Phoenix*, London, 1956, p. 87.
12 *La Piazza Universale*, quoted in Richards and Richards, *The Commedia dell'Arte*, p. 70.
13 Miklashevski became an expatriate in Paris where he translated his name to 'Mic' as well as his Russian work on Commedia which was published in 1927 as *La Commedia dell'Arte*.
14 Grantham, Brighton Festival Programme.

▓ Origins

1 *The Labyrinth of Solitude*, Allen Lane, London, 1967, p. 41.
2 Gerald Kahan, *Jacques Callot*, University of Georgia Press, 1976, p. 7.
3 Kenneth Richards and Laura Richards, *The Commedia dell'Arte*, Oxford, Blackwell, 1990, pp. 8–9.
4 *Cahiers du Cinéma*, No. 250, 1974, quoted by David L. Hirst, *Dario Fo and Franca Rame*, London, Macmillan, 1989, p. 118.
5 Extract from E. Coco, 'Una compagnia comica nella prima metà del secolo XIV', *Giornale Storico della Letteratura Italiana*, LXV, 1915, p. 55.
6 Quoted in Dario Fo, *Manuale minimo dell'attore*, Turin, 1987, p. 12.
7 *Ibid.*, p. 14.
8 *Discorsi delli trionfi, Giostre, Apparati, e delle cose più notabile nelle sontuose Nozze, dell'Illustrissimo et Eccellentissimo Signor Duca Guglielmo*, Munich, 1568.
9 Thomas Coryat, *Coryat's Crudities* [1611], London, 1776, II, pp. 50–4.
10 *Ibid.*
11 Carlo Goldoni, *Memoirs*, Vol. I, p. 228.
12 Winifred Smith, *The Commedia dell'Arte*, New York, 1912, p. 50.
13 Allardyce Nicoll, *The World of Harlequin*, Cambridge, 1963, p. 226.
14 Italicised names are of non-Commedia Carnival Masks.
15 Franceso Valentini, *Tratto su la commedia dell'arte, ossia improvvisa*, Berlin, 1826, quoted in Sand, *The History of the Harlequinade*, London, 1915, Vol. II, pp. 276–80.
16 A. Mango and R. Lombardi, *Le origini della commedia dell'arte*, 1971.
17 A. Lumine, *Farse di carnevale*, summarised in Smith, *The Commedia dell'Arte*, pp. 37–8.
18 For a full account of this controversy, see K. M. Lea, *Italian Popular Comedy*, Oxford, 1934, pp. 73–8.
19 Pier Maria Cecchini, *Tutti i trionfi, carri, mascherate o canti canascialeschi*, Vol. II, pp. 499–501, Florence, 1559.
20 Smith, *The Commedia dell'Arte*, p. 43.

▓ The mask

1 Giorgio Strehler, *Un Théâtre pour la vie*, Paris, Fayard, p. 166.
2 *The Young Scholar's Latin–English Dictionary*, London, 1863.
3 'Memoirs of M. Goldoni', trans. Barrett H. Clark, in *European Theories of the Drama*, Crown, 1947, p. 249.
4 'The Fairground Booth', trans. Edward Braun, in Edward Braun, *Meyerhold on Theatre*, London, Methuen, 1969, p. 131.
5 Jacques Copeau, 'Réflexion d'un comédien sur le Paradoxe de Diderot', reprinted in *Registres I*, Paris, Gallimard NRF, 1974, pp. 205–13.
6 See, for example, Evaristo Constantini, *The Life of Scaramouch*, 1695, trans. Cyril Beaumont, London, 1924.
7 Dario Fo, *The Tricks of the Trade*, trans. Joe Farrell, p. 26.
8 *Ibid.*, pp. 18–19.
9 *Ibid.*, p. 19.

10 *Ibid.*, p. 67.
11 *Ibid.*, p. 23.
12 *Ibid.*, p. 27.
13 Alberto Marcia, *The Commedia dell'Arte and the Masks of Amleto and Donato Sartori*, Florence, La Casa Usher, 1980, pages not numbered.
14 Jacques Lecoq, 'La geometria al servizio dell'emozione', *Arte della maschera nella Commedia dell'Arte*, ed. Donato Sartori and Bruno Lanata, Milan, 1983, p. 164.
15 Strehler, *Un Théâtre pour la vie*.
16 Lecoq, 'La geometria'.
17 *Ibid.*
18 Strehler, *Un Théâtre pour la vie*, p. 167.
19 Lecoq, 'La geometria'.
20 Strehler, *Un Théâtre pour la vie*, p. 168.
21 Marcia, *The Commedia dell'Arte and the Masks of Amleto and Donato Sartori*.
22 'Le masque en cuir de la Commedia dell'arte', *Bouffonneries*, hors-série, 1988.
23 Charles Dullin, *Souvenirs et notes de travail d'un comédien*, Paris, 1946, p. 122.

 Playing Commedia

1 Quoted in Edward Braun, *Meyerhold on Theatre*, London, Methuen, 1969, p. 129.
2 Henry F. Salerno (trans.), *Flaminino Scala's Scenarios of the Commedia dell'Arte*, New York and London, 1967.
3 Thomas-Simon Guelette, quoted in Virginia Scott, *The Commedia dell'Arte in Paris, 1644–1697*, University Press of Virginia, 1990, p. 127.
4 *Ibid.*, quoted in Allardyce Nicoll, *Masks, Mimes and Miracles*, London, 1931, p. 221.
5 *On the Art of the Noh Drama, the Major Treatises of Zeami*, trans. J. Thomas Rimer and Yamazaki Masakasu, Princeton, NJ, 1984, p. 20, note.
6 Andrea Perrucci, *Dell'arte rappresentativa, premeditata ed all'improvviso*, Naples, 1699, quoted Kenneth Richards and Laura Richards, *The Commedia dell'Arte*, Oxford, Blackwell, 1990, p. 205.
7 Perrucci, *Dell'arte*, trans. M. Bernstein, in Toby Cole and Helen Krich Chinoy (eds) *Actors on Acting*, New York, 1949, p. 57.
8 Carlo Mazzone-Clementi, 'Commedia and the Actor', *The Drama Review*, Vol. 18, No. 1 (T61), March 1974, p. 64.
9 Introduction to *The Memoirs of Count Carlo Gozzi*, trans. John Addington Symonds, London, 1890, Vol. I, pp. 62–3.
10 Luigi Riccoboni, *Histoire du théâtre italien*, Paris, 1728, p. 65.
11 Unattributed contemporary document, quoted in Thelma Niklaus, *Harlequin Phoenix*, London, 1956, pp. 59–60.
12 Maurice Sand, Introduction to *Masques et Bouffons*, Paris, 1862.
13 Dario Fo, *The Tricks of the Trade (Manuale minimo dell'attore)*, trans. Joe Farrell, London, Methuen, 1991, p. 36.
14 Michel Saint-Denis, *World Theatre*, IV, p. 40.
15 Mazzone-Clementi, 'Commedia and the Actor', pp. 62–3.
16 Evaristo Gherardi, *Le Théâtre italien*, quoted in Richards and Richards, *The Commedia dell'Arte*, p. 204.
17 *The Tragic Events*, in Salerno, *Flaminio Scala's Scenarios*, p. 128.

18 *Flavio Betrayed*, in Salerno, *Flaminio Scala's Scenarios*, p. 40.The
19 Mazzone-Clementi, 'Commedia and the Actor', p. 59.

▥ The *Zanni*

1 Carlo Boso, 'Contre "La mort sucrée"', in *Bouffonneries*, No.3, May 1981, p. 9.
2 Alberto Marcia, *The Commedia dell'Arte and the Masks of Amleto and Donato Sartori*, Florence, 1980.
3 T. Garzoni, *Piazza universale*, 1585, quoted in K. M. Lea, *Italian Popular Comedy*, Oxford, 1934, Vol. I, pp. 55–6.
4 Lea, *Italian Popular Comedy*, p. 66.
5 Published in *Bouffonneries*, No.11, pp. 23–32, no date, no source given.
6 From *Arlequin, empereur dans la lune*, quoted in V. Pandolfi, *La Commedia dell'Arte*, Florence, 1988, Vol. V, pp. 68–9.
7 Boisfranc, *Les Bains de la Porte Saint-Bernard*, 1696, Act III, scene 3, quoted in G. Attinger, *L'Esprit de la Commedia dell'Arte dans le théâtre français*, Paris, 1950, pp. 208–10.
8 Giacomo Oreglia, *The Commedia dell'Arte*, London, Methuen, 1964, p. 71.
9 P. Duchartre, *La Comédie italienne*, Paris, 1924, p. 155.
10 Carlo Goldoni, *Memoirs*, trans. Black, 1814, Vol. II, p. 55.
11 Oreglia, *The Commedia dell'Arte*.
12 Duchartre, *La Comédie italienne*.

▥ The old men

1 Maurice Sand, *The History of the Harlequinade*, London, Martin Secker, 1915, Vol. II, p. 9.
2 Winifred Smith, *The Commedia dell'Arte*, New York, 1912, p. 7.
3 Interview in 'The Theatre of Dario Fo', *Arena*, BBC television documentary by Dennis Marks, first broadcast 28 February 1984.
4 Carlo Goldoni, *Memoirs*, trans. Black, 1814, Vol. II, pp. 55–6.
5 Dario Fo, *Tricks of the Trade*, trans. Joe Farrell, London, Methuen, 1991, p. 67.
6 *Ibid.*, p. 67.
7 A videotape demonstration of his technique is available from the Centro Maschere e Strutture Gestuali.
8 *As You Like It*, Act II, scene vii.
9 Andrea Perrucci, *Dell'arte rappresentativa premeditata ed all'improvviso*, Naples, 1699.
10 Evaristo Gherardi, *Pantalon amoureux*, adapted by P. Pezin, *Bouffonneries*, No. 11, 1984, pp. 81–3.
11 Smith, *The Commedia dell'Arte*, pp. 7–8.
12 R. J. E. Tiddy, *The Mummers' Play*, Oxford, 1923, p. 76.

13 Goldoni, *Memoirs*, Vol. II, pp. 55–6.
14 Pietro Maria Cecchini, *Frutti delle moderne commedie e avvisi a chi le recita*, Padua, 1628, trans. M. Bernstein, quoted in Toby Cole and Helen Krich Chinoy (eds) *Actors on Acting*, New York, 1949, p. 51.
15 From a sixteenth-century manuscript in the Vatican library, published in *Bouffonneries*, No. 3, May 1981, pp. 81–4.

 # The Lovers

1 *A Midsummer Night's Dream*, Act I, scene i, ll. 150–5.
2 Pietro Maria Cecchini, *Frutti delle moderne commedie e avvisi a chi le recita*, Padua, 1628.
3 Andrea Perrucci, *Dell'arte rappresentativa, premeditata ed all'improvviso*, Napoli, 1699.
4 K. M. Lea, *Italian Popular Comedy*, Oxford, Russell & Russell, 1934, Vol. I, p. 108.
5 Andrea Perrucci, quoted in G. Attinger, *L'Esprit de la Commedia dell'Arte dans le théâtre français*, Paris, 1950. pp. 54–6.
6   In the art form of the European nude the painters and spectator-owners were usually men and the persons treated as objects, usually women. This unequal relationship is so deeply embedded in our culture that it still structures the consciousness of many women. They do to themselves what men do to them. They survey, like men, their own femininity.

        (John Berger, *Ways of Seeing*, London, Pelican, 1972, p. 63)

Il Capitano

1 One of the lower Spanish nobility, *hijo dalgo*, son of a 'somebody'.
2 Vernon Lee, *Studies of the Eighteenth Century in Italy*, London, Satchell, 1880, quoted in *The Mask*, Vol. 3, No. 10–12, April 1911, p. 129.
3 From Evaristo Gherardi, *Le Théâtre italien*, quoted by P. Duchartre, *La Comédie italienne*, Paris, 1924, p. 238.
4 Dario Fo, *The Tricks of the Trade*, trans. Joe Farrell, London, Methuen, 1991, p. 22.
5 From *Angelica*, 1585, a play by Fabrizio de Fornaris, creator of the role of Coccodrillo, quoted in *The Mask*, Vol. 3, No. 10–12, April 1911, p. 183.
6 From *Bouffonneries*, No. 11, pp. 43–6; no origin given.

Colombina

1 K. M. Lea, *Italian Popular Comedy*, Oxford, Russell & Russell, 1934, Vol. I, p. 120.
2 Maurice Sand, *The History of the Harlequinade*, London, Martin Secker, 1915, p. 163.
3 *Ibid.*, p. 164.
4 K. Dick, *Pierrot*, London, Hutchinson, 1960, p. 129.
5 Prologue for the *servetta* of the *Comici* by Bruni, published in *Bouffonneries*, No. 3, pp. 47–8.
6 Quoted in Bari Rolfe, *Commedia dell'Arte: a Scene Study Book*, California, Persona Books, 1977, p. 31; no source given.
7 From *Arliquiana, ou Jeux de mots de Dominique* by Domenico Biancolelli, quoted in Vito Pandolfi, *La Commedia dell'Arte*, Florence, 1988, Vol. V, pp. 116–17.

Other Masks

1 From *Arlequin, Empereur dans la lune*, quoted in V. Pandolfi, *La Commedia dell'Arte*, Florence, 1988.
2 K. M. Lea, *Italian Popular Comedy*, Oxford, 1962, p. 89.
3 An article quoted by Maurice Sand, *The History of the Harlequinade*, London, Martin Secker, 1915, pp. 111–12.
4 Lea, *Italian Popular Comedy*, p. 89.
5 *Ibid.*, p. 10.
6 Sand, *History of the Harlequinade*, p. 112.
7 Lea, *Italian Popular Comedy*, p. 102.
8 Sand, *History of the Harlequinade*, p. 107.
9 From Placiso Adriani, *Selva, or the Miscellany of Comic Conceits*, 1739, quoted Giacomo Oreglia, *The Commedia dell'Arte*, London, Methuen, 1968, pp. 14–16.
10 Sand, *History of the Harlequinade.*, p. 118.
11 From Placido Adiani, *La pietra incantata*, in *Bouffonneries*, No. 11, pp. 55–6.
12 From Silvio Fiorillo, *Lucilla constante*, in *Bouffonneries*, No. 11, pp. 49–53.
13 P. Duchartre, *La Comédie italienne*, Paris, 1924, p. 166.
14 *Ibid.*
15 *Ibid.*
16 Molière, *Les Fourberies de Scapin*, adapted by John Rudlin and first performed at Rolle College, Exmouth, 1967.
17 Luigi Riccoboni, *Histoire du théâtre italien*, Paris, 1728, quoted in Sand, *History of the Harlequinade*, p. 207.
18 Cyril Beaumont, *The History of Harlequin*, London, 1926, p. 63.
19 *Ibid.*
20 Preface to Angelo Constantini, *The Life of Scaramouche*, trans. Cyril Beaumont, London, 1924.
21 Beaumont, *The History of Harlequin*, pp. 63–4.
22 Gherardi, quoted in Sand, *History of the Harlequinade*, pp. 214–15.
23 Paul de Musset, quoted in Sand, *History of the Harlequinade*, p. 263.
24 Adapted from Girardin, *Le Collier de Perles*, 1672, quoted in Sand, *History of the Harlequinade*, p. 260.

Craig at the Arena Goldoni

1 Edward Gordon Craig in *The Mask*, Vol. 3, No. 10–12, April 1911, p. 147.
2 *Ibid.*, p. 148.
3 Edward Gordon Craig, 'The Actor and the Über-Marionette', *On the Art of the Theatre*, London, Heinemann, 1911, p. 61.
4 *The Mask*, Vol. 3, No. 10–12, April 1911.
5 Edward Gordon Craig, *The Theatre Advancing*, London, Constable, 1921, p. 31.
6 Letter now in the Museum of the Moscow Arts Theatre, quoted in Denis Bablet, *Edward Gordon Craig*, London, Heinemann, 1966, p. 158.
7 Craig, *The Theatre Advancing*, p. 53.
8 *Ibid.*, pp. 120–21.
9 *Ibid.*, p. 130.
10 *Ibid.*, pp. xxvii–xxviii.

Meyerhold *Dappertutto*

1 *Protiv techeniya*, (L–M 1962), p. 219, quoted in Konstantin Rudnitsky, *Meyerhold the Director*, trans. Sydney Schultze, Ann Arbor, 1981, pp. 146–7.
2 Quoted James M. Symons, *Meyerhold's Theatre of the Grotesque*, Cambridge Rivers Press, 1973, p. 33.
3 *La Baraque de Foire*, 1914, in *Vsevolod Meyerhold, Ecrits sur le théâtre*, Vol. I (1891–1917), Lausanne, La Cité-L'Age d'Homme, 1973, pp. 246–57.
4 Nine irregular issues, 1912–16.
5 Quoted Edward Braun, *Meyerhold on Theatre*, London, Methuen, 1969, p. 122.
6 Alexy Gripich, quoted in Symons, *Meyerhold's Theatre*, p. 64.
7 'Programme d'étude du studio de Meyerhold pour l'année 1914', quoted in *Vsevolod Meyerhold, Ecrits sur le théâtre*, pp. 243–4.
8 Gripich, quoted in Symons, *Meyerhold's Theatre*, p. 65.
9 V. Meyerhold, *Le Théâtre théâtrale*, trans. Nina Gourfinkel, Paris, 1963, p. 104.
10 Yevgeny Znosko-Borovsky, quoted in Braun, *Meyerhold on Theatre*, pp. 113–14.
11 Rudnitsky, *Meyerhold the Director*, p. 168.
12 *Ibid.*
13 *Teatr*, No. 46 (19 September 1907), p. 8, quoted Rudnitsky, *Meyerhold the Director*.
14 *Ibid.*
15 Bolislav Rostotsky, quoted in Symons, *Meyerhold's Theatre*, p. 106.
16 Braun, *Meyerhold on Theatre*, p. 185.
17 Leonid Grossman, *Gogol i Meyerhold*, quoted in Braun, *Meyerhold on Theatre*, p. 213.
18 Quoted Rudnitsky, *Meyerhold the Director*, p. 393.
19 *Ibid.*, p. 389.

Copeau's new improvised comedy

1 Quoted John Rudlin, *Jacques Copeau*, Cambridge, 1986, p. 92.
2 From Copeau's unpublished notebook, 'Comédie improvisée', written in Le Limon, dated January–July 1916, translated in John Rudlin and Norman Paul, *Copeau: Texts on Theatre*, London, Routledge, 1990, pp. 152–6.
3 *Ibid.*
4 *Ibid.*
5 *Ibid.*
6 *Ibid.*, pp. 156–7.
7 *Ibid.*
8 *Ibid.*
9 *Ibid.*
10 *Jacques Copeau, Roger Martin du Gard, Correspondance*, Vol. II., ed. Claude Sicard, Paris, Gallimard, 1972, pp. 820–1.
11 *Ibid.*, pp. 821–3.
12 Quoted in H. C. Rice, *Roger Martin du Gard and the World of the Thibaults*, New York, 1941, p. 16.
13 Rudlin and Paul, *Copeau*, p. 161.
14 *Ibid.*, p. 164.
15 Michel Saint-Denis, *Training for the Theatre*, London, Methuen, 1982, pp. 177–8.
16 *Ibid.*
17 *Ibid.*
18 *Ibid.*

 Charles Dullin: letters from the front

1 Letter from Fabre, quoted in Monique Surel-Tupin, 'Charles Dullin', *Cahiers Théâtre Louvain*, 1985, p. 28.
2 Charles Dullin, *Souvenirs et notes de travail d'un comédien*, Paris, 1946, p. 36.
3 From Elise Jouhandeau, *L'Altesse des hasards*, Paris, 1954, p. 222, quoted in Frederick Brown, *Theater and Revolution*, New York, Viking Press, 1980, p. 180.
4 Pierre Louis Duchartre, *The Italian Comedy*, trans. Randolph T. Weaver, London, Harrap, 1929, pp. 300–1.
5 *Ibid.*, p. 302.
6 Letter from Charles Dullin to Jacques Copeau, 15 February 1916, published in *Registres III*, Paris, Gallimard NRF, pp. 344–5.
7 Dated 6 March, *ibid.*, pp. 345–56.
8 Undated letter to Louis Jouvet, quoted Surel-Tupin, 'Charles Dullin', p. 223.
9 *Le Journal*, 27 September 1936, reprinted in *Le Bulletin de la société d'histoire du théâtre*, January–March 1937.
10 *Ibid.*

The Servant of Two Masters

1 Paolo Grassi and Giorgio Strehler in *Théâtre Populaire*, No. 33, 1959, p. 16.
2 Rémy Minetti, '1947–1977: Arlequin au "Piccolo Teatro" de Milan', *Bouffonneries*, No. 3, May 1981, p. 16.
3 Grassi and Strehler, *op. cit.*, pp. 25–6.
4 Catherine Douël dell'Agnola Strehler, 'Cinq versions d'*Arlequin*. Evolution de la scénographie', *Les Voies de la création théâtrale*, No. 16, Paris, 1989, pp. 141–53.
5 Quoted Martin Esslin, 'Max Reinhardt – High Priest of Theatricality', *The Drama Review*, Vol. 21, No. 2 (T74), p. 9.
6 Strehler, quoted Minetti, '1947–1977', pp. 20–1.
7 Douël, 'Cinq versions d'*Arlequin*', p. 145.
8 Minetti, '1947–1977', p. 22.
9 Giorgio Strehler, *Un Théâtre pour la vie (Per un teatro umano)*, Paris, Fayard, 1980, p. 163.
10 Douël, 'Cinq versions d'*Arlequin*', p. 142.
11 Quoted in *ibid.*, p. 145.
12 Luigi Lunari, quoted in Minetti, '1947–1977', p. 23.
13 Strehler, *Un Théâtre pour la vie*, p. 164.
14 *Ibid.*, p. 165.
15 Dario Fo, *Manuale minimo dell'attore*, Turin, 1987, p. 37.
16 *Ibid.*, p. 39.

 ## The Lecoq school

1 Francis Maclean, unpublished interview with Lecoq, quoted Thomas Leabhardt, *Modern and Post-Modern Mime*, London, Macmillan, 1989, p. 90.
2 School brochure quoted in Bari Rolfe 'The Mime of Jacques Lecoq', *The Drama Review*, Vol. 16, No. 1, March 1972, pp. 34–8.
3 Quoted Jim Hiley, 'Moving Heaven and Earth', *Observer*, 20 March 1988, p. 40.
4 *Ibid.*
5 *Ibid.*
6 Anthony Frost and Ralph Yarrow, *Improvisation in Drama*, London, Methuen, 1990, p. 118.
7 Maclean, quoted in Leabhardt, *Modern and Post-Modern Mime*, p. 93.

 ## Le Théâtre du Soleil

1 Théâtre du Soleil, *L'Age d'or, première ébauche*, Paris, Editions Stock, 1975, pp. 17–18.

2 Gilles Sandier, quoted Denis Bablet, *Le Théâtre du Soleil ou la quête du bonheur*, p. 17.
3 Théâtre du Soleil, *L'Age d'or*, p. 14.
4 *Ibid.*, p. 13.
5 *Ibid.*, p. 44.
6 *Ibid.*, p. 31.
7 *Ibid.*
8 *Ibid.*, p. 57.
9 *Ibid.*, pp. 62–4.
10 *Ibid.*, p. 13.
11 Ariane Mnouchkine and Jean-Claude Penchenat, 'L'aventure du Théâtre du Soleil', *Preuves*, Vol. 7, No. 3, 1971, pp. 119–20.
12 Jean Michel Deprats, 'Le besoin d'une forme: entretien avec Ariane Mnouchkine', *Théâtre/public*, Nos 46–7, July–September 1982, p. 10.
13 'Un texte masqué: entretien avec Georges Bigot et Philippe Hottier', *Théâtre/public*, Nos 46–7, July–September 1982, p. 14.
14 Théâtre du Soleil, *L'Age d'or*, p. 144.
15 David Whitton, *Stage Directors in Modern France*, Manchester, 1987, pp. 270–1.

 # The San Francisco Mime Troupe

1 R. G. Davis, *The San Francisco Mime Troupe: the First Ten Years*, Ramparts Press, 1975, p. 14.
2 Peter Coyote, unpublished interview.
3 Davis, *The San Francisco Mime Troupe*, pp. 31–2.
4 *Ibid.*, p. 32.
5 *Ibid.*
6 *Ibid.*, p. 34.
7 Quoted in Theodore Shank, 'Political Theatre as Popular Entertainment', *The Drama Review*, Vol. 18, No. 1 (T-61), March 1974, p. 112.
8 Davis, *The San Francisco Mime Troupe*, p. 40.
9 *Ibid.*, p. 40.
10 *Ibid.*
11 Eugene van Erwen, *Radical People's Theatre*, 1986.
12 Davis, *The San Francisco Mime Troupe*, p. 82.
13 *Ibid.*, p. 86.
14 Quoted Shank, 'Political Theatre', p. 113.
15 Duncan Mallard, 'The Political, Musical Theatre of the San Francisco Mime Troupe', undergraduate thesis, Department of Drama, University of Exeter, 1990.

TNT (The New Theatre)

1 Peter Mortimer, *Guardian*, 22 March 1990.

 ## Dario Fo

1 Interview in 'The Theatre of Dario Fo', *Arena*, BBC television documentary by Dennis Marks, first broadcast 28 February 1984.
2 Interview in a Channel 4 documentary, n.d.
3 'The Theatre of Dario Fo', *Arena*.
4 Dario Fo, 'The Comic Mysteries', in *Mistero Buffo*, trans. Ed Emery, ed. Stuart Hood, London, Methuen, 1988, pp. 1–2.
5 Joseph Farrell, 'Dario Fo: Zanni and Giullare', in Christopher Cairns and Edwin Mellen (eds) *The Commedia dell'Arte from the Renaissance to Dario Fo*, Lewiston/Queenston, Lampeter, 1989, pp. 320–21.
6 Quoted Mario Verdone, 'Arlecchino e i suoi fratelli', in *Ulisse*, March 1985, p. 35.
7 Channel 4 documentary.
8 David Hirst, *Dario Fo and Franca Rame*, London, Macmillan, 1989, pp. 117–18.
9 Dario Fo and Franca Rame, *Theatre Workshops at Riverside Studios, London*, Red Notes, 1983, p. 8.

Carlo Boso and Antonio Fava

1 Robert Hewison, 'Mime Finds its Voice', *The Sunday Times*, 27 January 1991, p. 6.
2 'Une troupe de Commedia dell'arte: Les Scalzacani', in *Bouffonneries*, No. 3, Paris, May 1981, p. 29.
3 *Ibid.*, p. 30.
4 *Ibid.*, p. 32.
5 Brighton Festival Programme, 1985, p. 85.
6 *Ibid.*, pp. 86–7.
7 *Ibid.*
8 'Un spectacle des Scalzacani: Le mythe baroque et comique retrouvé et adapté à partir d'anciens canevas de la Commedia dell'Arte', in *Bouffonneries*, No. 3, May 1981, p. 38.
9 Carlo Boso, 'Contre la mort "sucrée"', in *Bouffonneries*, No. 3, May 1981, p. 8.
10 Andrew Billen, *Observer*, 24 January 1993.
11 Antonio Fava, unpublished biographical notes.
12 *Ibid.*

Restoration or renovation?

1 Barbieri, quoted in programme note to *Il Pantalone sulla luna*.
2 Naseem Khan, 'The Public-going Theatre: Community and "Ethnic" Theatre', in Sandy Craig (ed.) *Dreams and Deconstructions*, Ambergate, Amber Lane, 1980, p. 65.
3 Exeter University Drama Department, undergraduate portfolio.
4 *Ibid.*
5 *Ibid.*
6 Exeter University Drama Department, undergraduate portfolio.

A selection of works on *commedia dell'arte* in English

General:

Pierre Louis Duchartre, *The Italian Comedy*, London, Harrap, 1929, reprinted London, Dover, 1966.

K. M. Lea, *Italian Popular Comedy*, Oxford, 1934, reprinted Oxford, Russell & Russell, 1962.

Allardyce Nicoll, *Masks, Mimes and Miracles*, London, Harrap, 1931, reprinted Cooper Square, 1963.

Allardyce Nicoll, *The World of Harlequin*, Cambridge, 1963, reprinted 1973.

Giacomo Oreglia, *The Commedia dell'Arte*, London, Methuen, 1968.

Maurice Sand, *The History of the Harlequinade*, London, Martin Secker, 1915, reprinted as *The History of Harlequin*, Oxford, Blom, 1958.

Winifred Smith, *The Commedia dell'Arte*, New York, 1912.

On individual characters:

Cyril Beaumont, *The History of Harlequin*, London, Beaumont, 1926.

Peter Bucknell, *Commedia dell'Arte at the Court of Louis XIV*, London, Stainer & Bell, 1980.

Edward Gordon Craig, 'The Characters of the Commedia dell'Arte', *The Mask*, January 1912.

Kay Dick, *Pierrot*, London, Hutchinson, 1960.

Thelma Niklaus, *Harlequin Phoenix*, Oxford, Bodley Head, 1965.

Robert F. Storey, *Pierrot, a Critical History of a Mask*, Princeton, NJ, 1978.

Scenari and Lazzi:

Mel Gordon (ed.), *Lazzi*, New York, PAJ Publications, 1983.

Bari Rolfe, *Commedia dell'Arte: A Scene Study Book*, California, Persona Books, 1977.

Bari Rolfe, *Farces Italian Style*, California, Persona Books, 1978.

Henry F. Salerno (trans.), *Flaminio Scala's Scenarios of the Commedia dell'Arte*, New York University, 1967.

Masks:

Alberto Marcia, *The Commedia dell'Arte and the Masks of Amleto and Donato Sartori*, Florence, Usher, 1980.

Video:

Masks of the Commedia dell'Arte, Antonio Fava with John Rudlin, Arts Documentation Unit, 6A Devonshire Place, Exeter EX4 6JA (available for research purposes only).

Bibliography:

Thomas F. Heck, *Commedia dell'Arte, a Guide to the Primary and Secondary Literature*, New York, Garland, 1988.

Index

Bold, italicised page numbers indicate references to illustrations.